Differentiated Instruction Made Practi

Need to decide when, why, and how to differentiate instruction in the classroom? *Differentiated Instruction Made Practical* introduces teachers to All Learners Learning Every Day (ALL-ED), an easy-to-use framework that enables tailored instruction for every learner. These unique, self-regulated learning routines were developed by an experienced K–12 teacher and researcher in collaboration with an educational psychology scholar. Filled with useful classroom examples, evaluation procedures, self-reflection activities, and relevant background information, this essential guide will help classroom teachers think on their feet and promote success for all students—not just the middle of the pack.

Rhonda Bondie is Lecturer on Education and Faculty Chair for Programs in Professional Education's online course Differentiated Instruction Made Practical at Harvard Graduate School of Education, USA. She taught for over twenty years in urban public schools as both a special and general educator and an artist-in-residence.

Akane Zusho is Associate Professor in the Division of Psychological and Educational Services of the Graduate School of Education at Fordham University, USA. Her research focuses on examining the intersection of culture, achievement motivation, and self-regulation.

The Self-Regulated Learning Guide:
Teaching Students to Think in the Language of Strategies
Timothy J. Cleary

Differentiated Reading Instruction:
Strategies and Technology Tools to Help All Students Improve
Jules Csillag

Differentiation Is an Expectation:
A School Leader's Guide to Building a Culture of Differentiation
Kimberly Kappler Hewitt and Daniel Weckstein

Five Teaching and Learning Myths—Debunked:
A Guide for Teachers
Adam Brown and Althea Bauernschmidt

The Passion-Driven Classroom:
A Framework for Teaching and Learning, 2nd Edition
Angela Maiers and Amy Sandvold

Universal Design for Learning in the Early Childhood Classroom:
Teaching Children of All Languages, Cultures, and Abilities, Birth – 8 Years
Karen Nemeth and Pamela Brillante

Inquiry and Innovation in the Classroom:
Using 20% Time, Genius Hour, and PBL to Drive Student Success
A.J. Juliani

Sticky Assessment:
Classroom Strategies to Amplify Student Learning
Laura Greenstein

Differentiated Instruction Made Practical

Engaging the Extremes through Classroom Routines

Rhonda Bondie and Akane Zusho

Routledge
Taylor & Francis Group

NEW YORK AND LONDON

First published 2018
by Routledge
711 Third Avenue, New York, NY 10017

and by Routledge
2 Park Square, Milton Park, Abingdon, Oxon, OX14 4RN

Routledge is an imprint of the Taylor & Francis Group, an informa business

Library of Congress Cataloging-in-Publication Data
Names: Bondie, Rhonda, author. | Zusho, Akane, author.
Title: Differentiated instruction made practical: engaging the extremes
through classroom routines / Rhonda Bondie and Akane Zusho.
Description: New York, NY: Routledge, 2018. | Includes bibliographical
references.
Identifiers: LCCN 2017045956 (print) | LCCN 2017059508 (ebook) |
ISBN 9781351248471 (eBook) | ISBN 9780815370802 (hbk) |
ISBN 9780815370819 (pbk) | ISBN 9781351248464 (ebk)
Subjects: LCSH: Individualized instruction. | Effective teaching. |
Classroom management.
Classification: LCC LB1031 (ebook) | LCC LB1031 .B67 2018 (print) |
DDC 371.39/4–dc23
LC record available at https://lccn.loc.gov/2017045956

ISBN: 978-0-8153-7080-2 (hbk)
ISBN: 978-0-8153-7081-9 (pbk)
ISBN: 978-1-351-24847-1 (ebk)

Typeset in Sabon
by Deanta Global Publishing Services, Chennai, India

Visit the eResource: www.routledge.com/9780815370819

This book is dedicated to the extremes of our families who inspire and teach us lessons every day,

Francis Markgraff, Rhonda's 106-year-old grandma, and

Emma Moffitt, Akane's seven-year-old niece.

Contents

List of Figures

List of Tables

Meet the Authors

Rhonda Bondie teaches with endless energy and enthusiasm that inspires learners of all ages. She began her career as a dancer and artist-in-residence, teaching required curricula through the arts to K–12 students with diverse abilities. Rhonda taught in urban public schools for more than two decades in both special and general education classrooms, working with many students who were learning English as a new language. The routines shared in this book were first developed and implemented in the New York City Public Schools and the Arlington Public Schools, Virginia, USA.

Throughout her career, she has been inspired by Harvard Graduate School of Education's Project Zero, specifically creating learning routines informed by Multiple Intelligences and Teaching for Understanding that are used in classrooms around the world and featured in publications, including *Making Thinking Visible* by Ron Richhart, and on websites, such as Teaching History. Rhonda also had the good fortune of spending seven years presenting at Carol Tomlinson's Diversity Institutes at the University of Virginia, which shaped her teaching practices.

Currently, Rhonda is a lecturer in several programs at the Harvard Graduate School of Education and the faculty chair of the online course Differentiated Instruction Made Practical. Rhonda maintains the website All Learners Learning Every Day, sharing free materials and webinars to support educators in inclusive pedagogy. Rhonda launched her research agenda at Fordham University, where she focused on differentiated teacher preparation and personalized learning through digital platforms, modeling through teacher preparation and professional development the practices that teachers need to effectively serve students in inclusive classrooms.

She continuously examines the impact of ALL-ED practices on student learning, specifically inquiring about how classroom routines can be used to build equitable classroom cultures, provide meaningful learning for all students, and close gaps in achievement. Rhonda brings her creative beginnings, decades of classroom teaching, and scholarship to the teacher decision-making framework and routines presented in this book. Rhonda hopes that this book will help teachers ensure that every child is valued, engaged, and stretched every day.

Akane Zusho began her research career at the University of Michigan, where—working with distinguished scholars such as Harold Stevenson and Paul Pintrich—her interest was piqued by the applications of psychology to educational practice. As an undergraduate, she worked on both large-scale cross-cultural studies investigating math instructional practices in Japan, Taiwan, and the United States, as well as smaller-scale studies exploring the nexus of motivation and self-regulated learning among college students. In graduate school (still at the University of Michigan), she noticed that much of the research on achievement motivation and self-regulated learning was focused on a narrow segment of American society. As a result, she decided to further explore how to transform classroom cultures to support the learning of all students.

In addition to this book, Akane has written over 40 articles and book chapters on issues related to culture, race, motivation, and self-regulated learning. In 2012, her work was recognized by the American Psychological Association when she received an early career research award. Her scholarship reflects her passion and lifelong interest in using psychological theory to improve the lives of students and teachers. Indeed, this book was written, in part, to introduce teachers to cutting-edge psychological and educational research on learning in an accessible way.

At Fordham University, where Akane is currently an Associate Professor, her primary teaching responsibilities include teaching statistics to graduate students. Statistics is a topic that often engenders strong feelings among students, including anxiety. Akane also noticed that her students often come to her classroom with varying levels of experience. Like Ms. Ford, the teacher in this book, Akane often wondered about precise, efficient, and effective strategies to differentiate instruction. Through her collaboration with co-author Rhonda Bondie, she has learned specific strategies to engage her students so that they do not leave her class confused. She hopes that this book will be equally effective in ensuring that all learners in your classroom learn every day.

Acknowledgments

Our framework represents years of collaborations with P–12 teachers and their students in urban public schools as well as in private, rural, and suburban school communities across the United States and around the world. We would first like to thank the many students we have had the pleasure of teaching and mentoring over the years, as well as those, like Oscar, who have inspired the ALL-ED framework and provided us the opportunity to think about how we can engage diverse strengths in learning. May Oscar, and students everywhere, never leave class confused again.

We are also deeply indebted to the classroom teachers who have worked and shared their stories with us. In particular, teachers at International Community High School (ICHS)—especially the teachers who participated in our first workshop series: Adjoua, Joel, Kim, Ioana, Alhasan, Didi, and all of the faculty. We thank the leaders of ICHS, Berena and Eva and Laurie Gaughran, who have supported our work and contributed greatly in its development. We thank the teachers at Math for America who have consistently participated in the All Learners Learning Every Day (ALL-ED) workshops for the past six years. Our work on targeted practice emerged in collaboration with the early years teachers—a special thank you to Anne, Andrea, Lousie, Ed, and Siobhan, and all of the dedicated faculty at St. Paul's School. Many thanks to them and to everyone at St. Paul's for their support and insight. We would also like to thank Ben Wilkens for his work on structured choice with the nonfiction book project in Chapter 7.

We would like to acknowledge the many teachers who participated in the free monthly ALL-ED webinars sponsored by the New Jersey Coalition for Inclusive Education, and the teachers from Urban Assembly Schools in New York City—particularly Brittany and Eyal at the School for Law and Justice, and Patti and her faculty at the School for Business and Young Women. We are indebted to the Manhattan Field Support team for trying out our framework every month for an entire year. We would also like to thank the many teachers in New Orleans, Columbus, Georgia, New York, New Jersey, Brazil, Chile, Singapore, China, Switzerland, and Amsterdam who have participated in our ALL-ED workshops and research.

Two extremely dedicated teachers and editors extraordinaire—Marvin Antebi-Gruszka and Elena Rodriguez—provided essential contributions. Marvin read every draft and talked with Rhonda, teacher to teacher, and made many contributions to our book through his thoughtfulness. Elena worked tirelessly organizing and cataloging the routines and ideas. She helped us with essential parts of the book, including the glossary. Joanna Huang brought meaning to our ideas with visual representations and the cover design for this book. Her questions and creativity made our ideas vivid and usable. We thank Eric Shed and the faculty and students in the Harvard Teacher Fellow program. They pushed us to articulate the framework in innovative, clear, and useful ways, specifically Chapter 6. Thanks also go to Sande Dawes and Anne Taffin d'Heursel Baldisseri for careful readings of drafts over the years. Finally, thanks to Kristen and Kelly for fantastic editing for clarity and providing essential support for Rhonda.

Sincere thanks to the many doctoral students at Fordham University who have contributed to our work. We also thank Jane Bolgatz, Fran Blumberg, Karen Brobst, Marshall George, Kristen Treglia, and Kristen Turner—for providing needed laughter and for acting as our critical friends both in life and at work.

Rhonda thanks the students and families of the New York City Public Schools and Arlington Public Schools. She recognizes Howard Gardner for his friendship and belief in human potentials. We are grateful for Carol Tomlinson whose work provided a foundation for our framework. Our routines were shaped by the constant support of Harvard Graduate School of Education's Project Zero and Atlas Learning Communities.

We would like to recognize the various researchers whose work has inspired the ALL-ED framework. To the extent that the research presented in this book was shaped profoundly by their wisdom and support, Akane gratefully acknowledges her mentors—the late Paul Pintrich, Marty Maehr, and Harold Stevenson. She also thanks Avi Kaplan, Stuart Karabenick, Revathy Kumar, Lisa Linnenbrink-Garcia, Mike Middleton, Toni Kempler Rogat, Chris Wolters, and Shirley Yu for their continued friendship and guidance. Akane would also like to thank Phyllis Blumenfeld for always reminding her to remember "the kid" in research, and Bill McKeachie, whose *Teaching Tips* provided the inspiration for many of the ideas presented in this book. A special thanks also goes to Stuart Karabenick for being one of ALL-ED's earliest supporters and for coming up with the name, ALL-ED.

Finally, we would like to thank our families for their constant love and support.

Introduction

Sitting next to us in a 60-year-old school building in a busy south Bronx community, Oscar explained what school is like for students who are learning in a new language. He told us, "It is like this ... I come to school, and I know nothing. The teacher talks, and I still know nothing. The one thing that I do know is that I must complete the paper that was passed out during class or I will be in trouble. So, I go to the cafeteria and find someone who has finished the paper. I copy their work, but I still know nothing." In the short amount of time that Oscar has attended an American school, he has successfully learned conversational English and how school works—so much so that his questions and misunderstandings in class are hidden. For Oscar, school is an endless cycle of lessons where, given his current skills, he cannot yet engage in the learning. Oscar is motivated to learn but needs entry points that enable him to use the abilities he brings to class. Speaking with Oscar drew our attention to a common mismatch between the wide range of student strengths in a classroom and the narrow opportunities to use those strengths in lessons.

Even more disheartening than listening to Oscar was watching his energetic teacher, Ms. Ford, literally sweating as she ran from student to student offering help to Oscar and his peers. When students complained that they needed a calculator to solve the problems, she quickly used her math expertise to adjust the numbers. Ms. Ford repeatedly provided clear explanations, used visual aids, and encouraged peers to support each other. To our surprise, even this excellent teacher was struggling to meet the learning needs of all students on a daily basis. Knowing that neither Oscar nor Ms. Ford could possibly work any harder, we wondered, "How can we ensure that all students like Oscar never leave class confused?"

The purpose of this book is to introduce you to the All Learners Learning Every Day (ALL-ED) teacher decision-making framework to determine when, why, and how to differentiate instruction. This four-step process will help you address dilemmas of student differences in the classroom and understand why, based on research, your efforts will lead to better learning. Most importantly, you will learn to adjust instruction using sustainable classroom routines that provide *all* students with equitable, optimal, and rigorous opportunities to learn within every lesson.

Defining Differentiated Instruction

Take a moment to think about how you might describe differentiated instruction to a parent, student, or new teacher. You might say that it is the way the teacher provides students with experiences that are not too hard or too easy, or how a teacher assigns a project where students pursue their interests. You might say that Ms. Ford could have used differentiated instruction to engage Oscar.

Carol Tomlinson (1999) provides the most well-known definition of differentiated instruction. She defines differentiated instruction as "a teacher's response to learner's needs guided by general principles of differentiation such as respectful tasks, flexible grouping, and ongoing assessment and adjustment. Teachers can differentiate content, process, and product according to students' readiness, interests, and learning profile" (p. 15). This definition is helpful as it provides us with the variables teachers can modify to meet different student needs. However, there are unlimited combinations of possible teacher responses, including those that modify content (what is taught), process (how students learn), product (how students demonstrate learning), as well as those that adjust instruction in terms of student readiness, interests, and learning profiles. There are so many possibilities that it is hard to picture what differentiated instruction actually looks like on a daily basis in the classroom. It is difficult to measure the impact that differentiated instruction may have on student learning because it takes so many forms, and so many different elements can be adjusted.

To understand how to help Oscar, we observed classrooms in seven different countries, and witnessed teachers and students experiencing dilemmas like Oscar's. We realized that books written for teachers about differentiated instruction needed an exploration of the moment *before* teachers respond to student differences. We could not find a clear approach to answering the question, "How do teachers make decisions to differentiate instruction?" Our ALL-ED framework developed out of our interest in supporting the teacher's thought process behind the decision to differentiate. We determined that in order to successfully help students like Oscar, teachers need time to think and learn from students *during* lessons. This insight led us to develop classroom routines that provide teachers with time to look, listen, and think about student learning *as they teach*. The routines are designed to make it much harder for Oscar's confusion to remain hidden. In addition, we made a framework to guide teacher decision-making to adjust instruction in response to the wide variety of learner needs that impact learning. We use this framework to limit the possible solutions based on what we know from research about decision-making and effective learning, and the practical constraints of time and curriculum.

We define differentiated instruction as the outcome of a continuous decision-making process where teachers look and listen for academic diversity that will either strengthen or impede effective and efficient learning. Then teachers adjust instruction to increase Clarity, Access, Rigor, and Relevance (CARR) for all students within a learning community. As is illustrated in Figure I.1, we conceptualize three types of differentiated instruction that each require different amounts of planning time. Broad definitions of differentiated instruction may lead teachers to think of differentiated instruction as personalized or individualized learning, meaning that they have to work all hours of the day and weekends to come up with new and different materials for each student. Tomlinson et al. (2008) would join us in arguing that such an approach to differentiation is not only unsustainable, but unnecessary in many cases.

As you will learn, the ALL-ED model of differentiated instruction relies primarily on *Adjustable Common Instruction*, where students are learning with the same goals, resources, and assessments (see Table I.1). With *Adjustable Common Instruction*, the teaching approach uses classroom routines to tailor instruction to

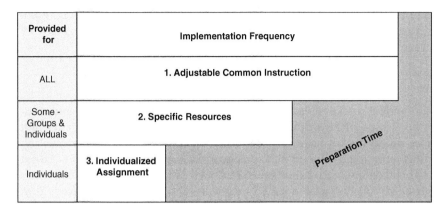

Figure I.1 Types of Differentiated Instruction by Learners, Implementation Frequency, and Preparation Time.

Table I.1 Three Types of Differentiated Instruction

	Objectives	Resources	Assessments
Adjustable Common Instruction	Same	Same	Same
Specific Resources	Same	DIFFERENT	Same
Individualized Assignment	DIFFERENT	DIFFERENT	DIFFERENT

meet learner needs. This approach uses resources that are already present in most classrooms, so the first step is not to make something new.

The second type of differentiated instruction is *Specific Resources*, where the objectives and assessments are the same, but some students (groups or individuals) are using different resources accompanied with a specific teaching approach to achieve the objective. You will learn how to teach students to use help that fosters independence and confidence.

Finally, the third type of differentiated instruction is *Individualized,* like a workout plan. All learners, at times, will need opportunities for individual workouts to review, practice, extend, or pursue an interest. It is important to keep in mind that individualized differentiated instruction should not be confused with specialized instruction for students receiving special education. Because students begin learning with very different backgrounds and experiences and then continue learning at different rates, it makes sense that individuals will need different learning tasks. Using our routines and previous materials, individual workouts can be designed with minimal planning time that does not require constantly creating new materials. Although this type of differentiation is used less frequently, individualized learning can be practical in every unit.

Throughout this book, we offer step-by-step directions for classroom routines that enable you to implement all three types of differentiated instruction in every unit. We hope that our approach builds on what you already know and strengthens your current beliefs and practices related to differentiated instruction, in addition to providing greater clarity and a needed focus on teacher thinking during lessons. We aim to provide specific ways to meet the needs of all learners by helping teachers make instructional decisions that are practical, sustainable, and supported by research in the motivation and cognitive sciences.

Overview of ALL-ED Framework

Along with building on Tomlinson's work, we have been both inspired and challenged by the writing of Howard Gardner. Gardner stated in 1999, "We are not all the same; we do not all have the same kinds of minds (that is, we are not all distinct points on a single bell curve); and education works most effectively if these differences are taken into account rather than denied or ignored" (p. 91). Gardner's words provide a constant reminder that student differences matter every day, not just when teachers have time on the weekend for extra planning. We created *Adjustable Common Instruction* to provide immediately usable classroom routines designed to aid you in responding to student differences on a daily basis. This book will guide you to learn how to implement the three different types of differentiated instruction through our four-step ALL-ED framework:

- Step One: Identify OSCAR,
- Step Two: Look and Listen,
- Step Three: CARR Check, and
- Step Four: SHOp Adjustments.

First, you will learn about how you can identify OSCAR (Objective, Starting Position, Criteria, Action Pattern, and Reflections) to determine the part of a lesson or activity where adjustments to instruction are needed. Then you will learn how to implement individual and group learning routines where the teacher's role is to look and listen to students as they are learning. After gathering student responses, teachers are ready for a CARR Check to determine if all, some, or individual students need greater Clarity, Access, Rigor, or Relevance for effective learning. This CARR Check helps teachers decide how to adjust structures for tasks, help, and options (SHOp) to ensure all learners are learning. Throughout the book, we have summarized this decision-making process using this mnemonic device: At OSCAR, if (all, some, or individual) students need CARR, then adjust SHOp to guide quick teacher decision making. This routine takes the guess work out of differentiation and aligns instructional adjustments to measurable outcomes for students.

Throughout our book, you will learn classroom routines that further student learning and provide teachers time during lessons. These routines fall into three different categories based on their purpose:

- Plan—routines used to plan instruction for diverse learners,
- Teach—individual and group learning routines used during lessons with students, and
- Adjust—teacher habits used during daily lessons to promote and practice agile thinking needed to adjust instruction to better fit student needs.

Each chapter includes Plan, Teach, and Adjust instruction routines to support your implementation of these ideas from the chapter with students. In addition, we use a

Table I.2 Chapter Objectives, Research Roots, and Three Purposes for Classroom Routines

Chapter Objectives	Roots in Research
1 Why do classroom routines promote learning?	Motivation and Cognitive Science
2 Why do we need to adjust or differentiate instruction?	Student Diversity and Teacher Expectations
3 What are the adjustable parts of every lesson?	Self-Regulated Learning
4 When do we differentiate or adjust instruction?	Engagement, Formative Assessment, and Decision-Making
5 What can adjustments to instruction accomplish?	Teacher Behavior and Clarity, Access, Rigor, and Relevance of Learning Tasks
6 How do teachers adjust instruction to meet the needs of all learners?	Autonomy, Choice, and Help Seeking
7 What does the four-step teacher thinking decision making framework look like in practice?	Problem-Solving
8 How can we examine the impact of adjustments to instruction on student learning?	ALL-ED preliminary impact on teaching and learning
Classroom Routines for Precise, *Effective, and Efficient Learning for All* Plan, Teach, Adjust	

Starting Position and Reflection routine to support your reading of each chapter—a routine that you, too, could use with students to support their learning.

The ALL-ED approach to differentiated instruction is deeply rooted in the scientific literature on motivation and cognition. One of the goals of this book is to introduce you to the most recent educational and psychological research by embedding discussions of research in our descriptions of ALL-ED, so that we can demonstrate how the ALL-ED routines align with specific research recommendations. Table I.2, *Chapter Objectives and Research Roots*, shows the connections between the chapter objectives outlining the steps of the ALL-ED Framework and the supporting research summaries. ALL-ED classroom routines were developed by working extensively with teachers and students to address common dilemmas of student differences that challenge effective learning in the classroom. ALL-ED is empirically and theoretically driven, *as well as* realistic. It is our hope that you will find this book to be both practical and scholarly.

Organization of This Book

You can read this book from beginning to end or in the order that seems most useful for you. Throughout the school year, it may be helpful to read chapters with a teacher team or colleagues, discussing your responses to the routines in each chapter, trying the routines with students, and offering feedback to each other chapter by chapter. The first chapter explains how we developed and rooted our framework in research. This is important because we rarely see practical books written for teachers that also explain why the practices lead to better learning. The second chapter invites you to reflect on your own perceptions. This is also critical because you can only respond to the things you perceive while teaching. The following chapters explain in detail with practical examples our four-step decision making framework. It may be most useful to read all four steps and then work on putting one step into your daily practice at a time. In this way, the routines in each chapter will support you to make small but impactful changes to your daily teaching practices. An index of Classroom Routines and additional resources to support your implementation of the routines can be found online at https://www.routledge.com/9780815370819.

Regardless of how you use the book, we recommend implementing one classroom routine at a time. Give yourself time to practice perceiving student differences, thinking, and making adjustments to instruction using one routine at one part of a lesson before going on to the next routine. For example, implementing a *Domino Discover* routine to gather student responses is a great start (see Chapters 1 and 2). You might spend a week or a month implementing just that one classroom routine. This will also enable you to space out your learning over time and return to reflect on key ideas. This approach is both practical and follows the advice for effective learning from cognitive scientists.

By trying out the classroom routines with learners, you will be able to engage, value, stretch, and inspire each member of the learning community in every lesson. The classroom routines are used to teach the established curriculum within given time constraints. The structure of the routines will help you build a daily classroom culture that values thinking and fosters self-regulated learning as a habit. This book is intended for instruction in general education classrooms, sometimes called Tier I in a Response to Intervention model. The routines make it possible to engage *every* learner in *every* lesson *every* day within the given time constraints, curriculum demands, and widespread academic diversity among students. We want to ensure that the Oscars in your classroom never leave class confused.

When considering the organization of this book, we have tried to practice what we preach by organizing the structure of each chapter with cognitive science principles in mind. Turn to the *Before You Read—How to Get the Most Out of Reading this Book* section to see an example of a *Learning Journal* and find out how you can learn more effectively while reading this book.

Before You Start—How to Get the Most Out of Reading This Book

Before you begin, look at the headings of each chapter. The chapters are designed to model the structure we know supports both learning and adjusting instruction. Each chapter begins with the **Objective**, stated as a question, that you can answer to guide and test your understanding of the chapter. **Criteria** are details from the chapter that you should be able to explain and describe in your answer to the chapter question. The **Objective** and **Criteria** will help you assess your understanding as you read. Following the **Objective** and **Criteria**, you will see a **Starting Position**, which is a short routine designed to activate your background knowledge and to record your initial thoughts on the topic of the chapter. The **Objective, Starting Position**, and **Criteria** (the **OSC** of **OSCAR**) enable you to measure the impact of your reading on your understanding of differentiated instruction.

Throughout each chapter we take **Actions** (the **A** in OSCAR) to answer the chapter question by considering a story from the classroom, the relevant research related to the classroom story, and the classroom routines associated with the step of our thinking framework. We end each chapter with **Reflections** (the **R** in OSCAR), inviting you to maintain a *Learning Journal* to record and measure how reading this book may both confirm and change your thinking and teaching. We encourage you to return to your **Starting Position** to reflect on the ideas you take away from each chapter and to make your reading more meaningful. We believe that these elements, **Objective, Starting Position, Criteria, Action Pattern**, and **Reflections** (OSCAR), are essential to both differentiated instruction and effective learning, so we modeled these elements in every chapter. There are five sections in each chapter:

1 **Overview** introduces the topic and activates your background knowledge. The objective, criteria, and starting position will help you establish a goal for your reading and monitor your learning from the chapter.

- **Objective** sets a focus for your learning from the chapter and asks you to think about the Objective from your own experiences.
- **Criteria** provides a means for you to gauge the quality of your understanding of the chapter's information.
- **Starting Position** invites you to complete a short activity designed to activate your background knowledge and to provide a record of your initial thoughts so that you can better reflect after reading how your thinking has been both confirmed and changed. The *Starting Positions* also help you avoid "illusions of knowing" (see Chapter 1) that can make learning more difficult, and enable you to review information from previous chapters to

help you better remember what you have read. We have implemented these routines with students in Pre-K through 12th grade. Starting Position routines can be modified with a topic that you are teaching and used with your students. Save your starting positions! We will ask you to return to your starting positions from earlier chapters as you move through the book. You may want to record your starting positions in your *Learning Journal* so that your reflections are easy to find.

2   **From the Classroom** presents a short story based on our experiences working in schools that provides a realistic context for the ALL-ED step presented in the chapter.

3   **Rooted in Research** summarizes and applies what we know about how people learn to further your understanding of the ALL-ED framework. The summary points from our research roots also establish criteria for effective learning that we aim to apply in our classroom routines.

4   **Try Classroom Routines** provides three classroom routines to implement the ALL-ED framework step described in each chapter. The routines have different purposes: Plan, Teach, and Adjust instruction. The planning routines are to help you anticipate student differences that impact learning and incorporate thinking time for you to make decisions during lessons. During instruction, individual and group learning routines provide teachers with time to listen and look while students are learning. Adjust instruction are habits that you can write into daily lesson plans to make split-second decisions to respond to student differences that are observed in ways that lead to more effective learning.

• **Quality Criteria to Implement Classroom Routines** furthers your efforts to try out classroom routines with students. These include *Must Haves* and *Amazing* criteria, enabling you to monitor your implementation of classroom routines. **Criteria** help you stretch beyond just trying a routine to ensuring that students learn effectively and that you can use the routine to adjust instruction.

5   **Chapter Reflection** provides a chapter summary and prompts you to record your learning from the chapter in a *Learning Journal*. At the end of each chapter we invite you to return to the chapter's Starting Position exercise to reflect on your learning.

We are using this structure deliberately because we feel lesson plans need these parts for you to adjust instruction to meet learner needs and to support students in making learning meaningful.

Start a *Learning Journal*

To record your thinking, you will need a *Learning Journal*. The *Learning Journal* could be a notebook, scrap pieces of paper or sticky notes placed in each chapter, or a digital file. You might draw (see Figures B.1 and B.2), make lists, or write out your thinking or collect pictures on your cell phone to document your learning while reading this book. Box B.1 provides an example of a *Learning Journal* with the suggested prompts from each chapter. You will benefit from keeping a *Learning Journal* to track how your thinking develops as you read and try out the decision-making framework and ALL-ED routines. As you will learn in Chapters 1 and 3, reflection is an essential part of learning and differentiated instruction, so we encourage you to test the *Learning Journal* routine with yourself before implementing the routine with students.

Box B.1. Example Teacher *Learning Journal* from Reading Chapter 1

ALL-ED Classroom Routine Directions: Learning Journal

Research consistently demonstrates that self-regulated learners (SRL)—students who reflect on their thinking; set appropriate goals and plan for learning; monitor progress toward those goals; and adjust or regulate their thinking, motivation, and study habits—are more likely to achieve academic success than those who do not (Pintrich & Zusho, 2002; Zimmerman, 1990). Research on SRL largely presumes that self-regulatory skills are learned skills that can be modified and improved, thus making it an ideal target for intervention at any age level. One way you can promote and prompt SRL skills is through keeping a *Learning Journal*.

Strengths of this routine:

- Prompts SRL skills
- Provides a record of thinking that can be used for reflection and goal setting
- Encourages reflection on the types of experiences that impact learning
- Supports learning by looking at evidence of learning in student work
- Offers a means for teachers to learn from students
- Communicates to families, peers, teachers, and students themselves their interests, growth, and understanding of the purpose of learning activities.

Implementation Directions

Objective: Reflect on learning and plan next steps.

Starting Position: Work from one or more previous lessons.

Criteria

- *Must Haves*: Examines the work carefully, explains reasoning or why something was interesting and useful to you as a learner.
- *Amazing*: Makes connections to previous learning experiences.

Action Pattern

The teacher identifies in the directions:

- **Rules:** Look back at previous reflections and notes before adding a new journal entry
- **Time:** 15 minutes for each entry

Reflections

- After four or five entries, reread the journal entries from the beginning. Consider patterns in your learning, including what might the entries tell you about yourself as a learner and what are the next steps for your learning.

Sample Teacher Learning Journal for Engaging the Extremes: Chapter 1

Chapter 1

Objective: Why do classroom routines promote motivation and effective learning?

   Criteria—In my notes I plan to:

1   Identify the parts of motivation and how motivation relates to context.
2   Explain how we learn using research from cognitive sciences.
3   Try out a classroom routine that fosters elaboration to increase memory.
4   Adjust instruction by defining four task structures and using more than one task structure during learning activities.

Figure B.1: Starting Position: Best and Worst of Times of Motivation

My Own Notes—*List, Write, Draw* a story to answer these questions

1   What was most interesting and useful for you in this chapter?
2   Why was this interesting and useful?
3   How does this connect to what you know about meeting the learning needs of all learners?
4   What research from this chapter could you use to explain or support decisions to adjust instruction?

Figure B.2: Driving Forces: Motivational Factors of Student Learning

Get Started

With your *Learning Journal* in hand, you are ready to get started understanding dilemmas from the classroom, examining research theory, and implementing ALL-ED classroom routines to ensure that all learners are learning every day.

Chapter 1

Classroom Routines, Motivation, and Effective Learning

Overview

Objective:

Why do classroom routines promote learning?

*Think: <u>Underline</u> the most **familiar** word in this Objective.*

Criteria:

Use the following criteria to increase the quality of your answer to the chapter question. Try to "Take It Up a Notch" or expand your answer by reading the chapter to add these details.

- Identify the meaning of
    - ABC+M
    - Motivation
    - WERMS and
    - Cognitive science on effective learning.

- Explain the connections between research and the ALL-ED framework.
- Try Classroom Routines:
    - Plan—Choose Questions and Record Student Responses.
    - Teach—*List, Write, Draw, Rumors,* or *FQA.*
    - Adjust Instruction—React to student responses.

Starting Position: List, Write, Draw

Start your thinking about motivation by reflecting on times when you felt motivated using the ALL-ED Classroom Routine, *List, Write, Draw.* Think about a time when you felt motivated. Make a list, draw a sketch, and/or write a few notes or sentences of a story to capture your thinking about a "best time" when you were totally motivated. Now think of one of the "worst times" when you could barely force yourself to do something. Brainstorm a list, draw a sketch, and/or write about one of the worst times when you were totally unmotivated. From your best and worst list, can you begin to make a few initial observations about what moves you to act? Save this list to refer to as you learn more about motivation, cognition, and durable learning in this chapter and in the Research Roots section throughout this book. (See *Before You Start*, *Learning Journal* for examples drawing from this routine.)

From the Classroom: *The Beginning of ALL-ED*

When Rhonda Bondie was a classroom teacher, like most teachers, she was inspired to reach every child in her class. She knew that her students had divergent experiences, understandings, interests, strengths, and needs. But when she tried to build on these strengths to eliminate gaps in achievement, she found that the planning took an unbelievable amount of time. The extra planning usually led to greater student engagement, but it did not always result in better learning for students, and it was hard to determine what would make learning more effective. She tried to recall research and theories that she learned while preparing to become a teacher, but she did not know how to integrate these ideas in her daily classroom practice. Sometimes she spent her weekends creating appropriate materials, only to find students still disengaged during lessons. As a result, Rhonda routinely met with students during lunch and after school to provide additional help. She felt that students on the other extreme, who needed more challenging work, remained bored or untested. She wondered, "Was daily differentiated instruction possible, and could it lead to effective learning for all students?"

After many years of attending workshops and experimenting in her classroom, Rhonda found that daily differentiated instruction was practical and effective when routines were used to promote student learning. Student autonomy and engagement increased as students relied less on teacher prompting. Even better, she was less tired at the end of the day because classroom routines saved time in planning, giving directions, and managing behavior during lessons. Rhonda was able to teach almost two additional units during the year because she spent less time reviewing and re-teaching. With routine daily differentiated instruction, she left school with so much energy that, for the first time since she began teaching, she could join a gym!

When Rhonda began to partner with Akane Zusho, a researcher of motivation and cognition, they synthesized the research on effective learning and refined her routines using the larger psychological and educational literature. This collaboration ultimately resulted in the development of the All Learners Learning Every Day (ALL-ED) framework, which came about through working with teachers from around the world in implementing the routines with their students. The ALL-ED framework combines years of practical classroom experience with the latest research on learning and cognition.

Rooted in Research: *Theoretical Bases of ALL-ED Framework*

To understand how the decision-making framework and classroom routines promote learning, we summarize the theoretical and empirical bases in Figure 1.1. Focus your attention on the student learning outcomes portion of the figure on the far right. You will see the important outcomes that have been linked with college and career readiness. We believe that *all* students should: (a) develop deep, durable, and flexible understandings of course content; (b) feel empowered to take academic risks; (c) put forth effort and persist in the face of academic challenges (what the social psychologist Angela Duckworth would call grit); and, of course, (d) experience academic success.

Theoretical Bases

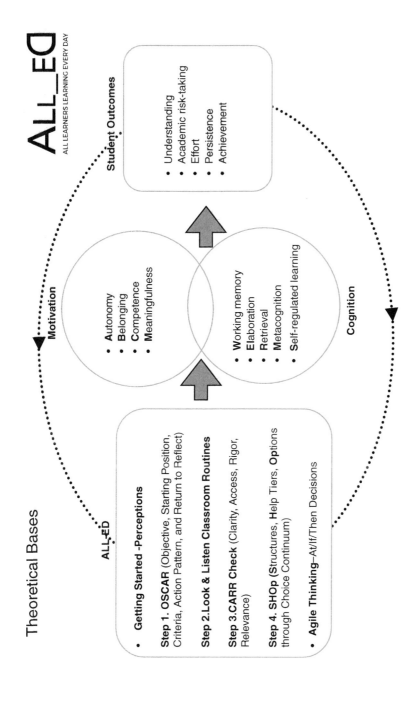

Figure 1.1 ALL-ED Framework Components, Roots in Research, and Expected Student Outcomes.

The center portion of Figure 1.1 represents the research base on learning, which demonstrates that both motivational and cognitive factors are strongly predictive of desired student outcomes. The collective research on achievement motivation suggests that students are more likely to put forth effort, persist, take academic risks, and achieve when they feel autonomous, a sense of belonging with others, and competent, and when they perceive that what they are learning is personally meaningful (Kumar, Zusho, & Bondie, submitted; Turner, 2014). We refer to this as the ABC+M of motivation.

The cognitive research, in turn, suggests that to develop deep and lasting understanding, it is important for students to overcome the limits of working memory by engaging deeper-processing, elaborative, and retrieval-based strategies to interrupt the process of forgetting and consolidate learning, and to overcome illusions of knowing (Brown, Roedinger, & McDaniel, 2014). Research also demonstrates that self-regulated learners—students who are metacognitively aware of how they think; who set appropriate goals and plan for learning; monitor progress toward goals; adjust or regulate their thinking, motivation, and study habits—are more likely to achieve academic success than those who do not (Pintrich & Zusho, 2007; Zimmerman, 1990). ALL-ED leverages what we know about working memory, elaboration, retrieval, and metacognition as well as self-regulated learning (we remember these parts of cognition with the acronym, WERMS) to create effective and efficient learning experiences, all while meeting diverse learner needs.

The far left of Figure 1.1 illustrates how the four-step ALL-ED teacher decision-making framework is rooted in motivation and cognitive sciences that lead to student outcomes. We will not discuss exactly how the specific steps of ALL-ED are linked to this literature just yet—you will find information on that in Chapters 3 to 8. First, the following section delves more deeply into the research on motivation and cognitive science that explains why the routines promote engagement and durable learning.

ABC+M of Motivation

Return to your **Starting Position** for this chapter and consider your responses to the following questions: "What moves you to act? What makes you invest time and energy in one task but not another?" These are the kinds of questions that concern motivational researchers. Researchers generally define motivation as something that influences or explains why a person will start a task, whether a person will approach or avoid a task, how much effort a person will put into a task, and whether or not a person will continue to work on the task once they start (Maehr & Zusho, 2009).

When it comes to understanding the effects on achievement, motivational factors have what researchers such as John Hattie (2009) refer to as a medium "effect size." This means that motivational interventions can improve achievement by roughly half of a standard deviation (Lazowski & Hulleman, 2016). Motivational factors have been demonstrated to enhance achievement in noticeable ways in the real world, and the effects go beyond what a teacher can accomplish in a single academic year.

Motivation researchers have identified the elements of intrinsic motivation as Autonomy, Belonging, Competence, and Meaning (ABC+M). Return to your Starting Position and identify how your description of being motivated relates to

ABC+M. As you read the next section to learn more about ABC+M, notice how your thinking about motivation is confirmed, changed, and maybe challenged.

Autonomy (Perceived Independence)

Research on motivation suggests autonomy is a powerful motivator (Ryan & Deci, 2017). Ryan and Deci (2017), who developed self-determination theory, a dominant theory of motivation, define autonomy as the extent to which individuals perceive that they can accept, endorse, and regulate their own goals or behaviors. When people can decide their own destiny by shaping the environment to meet their specific needs and goals, they develop self-efficacy and competence, which is directly linked with achievement outcomes.

Belonging

Self-determination theory also suggests that humans have an innate desire to form and maintain close and secure relationships with others (Ryan & Deci, 2017). Students feel more motivated when they have a sense of connection and belonging with others, be it their friends, teachers, or caregivers. Research on motivation suggests that feelings of safety and belonging are central to the establishment of an environment that facilitates motivation (Kaplan, Sinai, & Flum, 2014; Maehr & Zusho, 2009). Such feelings of safety can be heightened when students feel that their teachers care and respect them (Wentzel, 2010), and when students are encouraged to work productively and collaboratively in groups (Roseth, Johnson, & Johnson, 2008).

Competence

A core assumption of the research on motivation is that individuals are motivated toward competence. Students are more likely to engage in tasks when they feel confident about their abilities to achieve and when people feel a sense of self-efficacy (Bandura, 1997). Research on motivation consistently finds self-efficacy to be one of the strongest predictors of academic achievement (Linnenbrink-Garcia & Patall, 2016). Research also demonstrates that when students endorse a goal of developing competence (referred to in the literature as having a mastery goal), not only are they likely to adopt a growth mindset (the understanding that abilities and intelligence can be developed (Dweck, 2006)), but they are also more likely to seek academic challenges and take risks (Maehr & Zusho, 2009).

Meaning

Theories of motivation also recognize that perceptions of competence are not always enough to spur action—students must also want to complete the task. Motivational theories largely assume that students are more likely to approach and engage in academic tasks when they have personal meaning for them. Research suggests that the quality of motivated behavior is higher when students find the task and/or subject domain important, interesting, and useful (Wigfield & Eccles, 2000). Such values are more predictive of outcomes such as choice and subsequent course enrollment. In Figure 1.2, we summarize Ten Facts About Motivation that are useful reminders of why students may feel motivated.

Ten Facts About Motivation

1   Motivation is changeable—it is not a personality trait. Altering the task or the general learning environment can change it.
2   When you are placed in a setting where you feel autonomous (or empowered), competent, and that you belong, you are more likely to feel intrinsically motivated.
3   Competence is at the core of motivation. When you feel like you can do the work, you are more likely to do it.
4   Students are more likely to be intrinsically motivated when they know what they know and do not know. There is a symbiotic relationship between motivation and self-regulated learning.
5   But … sometimes it is not enough to feel like you can do the work. You must also value it in some way—maybe it is something that interests you or something that you find useful for future goals (e.g., job, college).
6   When students perceive the task to be relevant to their lives, they are more likely to value the task.
7   The quality of behavior is generally much better when an individual feels intrinsically as opposed to extrinsically motivated. You are more likely to put in more effort, persist longer, and learn more when the source of the motivation is yourself and not others.
8   Although other people can be powerful motivators, it is generally better to decrease social comparison if you want *all* students to be motivated. Social comparison generally works as a motivator for stronger students; for weaker students, it is usually a deterrent. Do not set others as the standard; set the task as the standard (e.g., do not grade on a curve).
9   Rewards can be tricky. Simple extrinsic rewards generally do not promote lasting motivation. If you want to sustain motivation, it is much more important to find ways to get students to value the task and feel more competent about what they are working on. Rewards can backfire if they are not equitable (so everyone feels like they all have a chance to get them), if they do not make students feel competent about what they are doing, and if students do not feel in control. We recommend posting specific quality criteria to help students find value and increase feelings of competence with assigned tasks.
10 Given this research, ALL-ED classroom routines are central to fostering motivation.

Figure 1.2 Top Ten Considerations about Motivation in ALL-ED.

We believe that when instruction is adjusted to meet learner needs within the learning community and focused on building deep, durable, and flexible understandings, then all students will feel ABC+M every day in our lessons. Table 1.1 displays a summary of how the elements of motivation relate to our goals for all students in a learning community.

Table 1.1 Elements of Motivation ABC+M

All Learners Feel

Autonomy	Belonging	Competence	Meaning
Empowered to take ownership of their learning.	They are valued members of a learning community.	Capable of pursuing rigorous learning.	Learning is interesting and important.

Durable Learning and WERMS

In addition to hoping students will feel motivated throughout our lessons, we also strive for all learners to develop learning that is both flexible and durable in daily lessons. When learning is flexible, students revise, expand, and even unlearn to further their learning. Students expect their learning to grow and change. When learning is durable, it sticks and is not easily forgotten. To understand durable learning, it is necessary to understand how memory works. More than half a century of research in the cognitive sciences has established that learning depends, in large part, on the interaction between two specific memory systems—working memory and long-term memory. According to Alan Baddeley, the man who coined the term, *working memory* is the "memory system that allows us to 'keep things in mind' when performing complex tasks" (Baddeley, Eysenck, & Anderson, 2014, p. 13)[1]. Long-term memory is the memory system that holds all of our knowledge. From a purely cognitive perspective, learning can be defined as a process of encoding (getting in) and retrieving (getting out) information into and out of long-term memory (Baddeley et al., 2014). Durable learning, in turn, is learning that gets consolidated in long-term memory.

Working memory. Working memory is important because it plays a central role in the encoding process. It is also involved in most, if not all, academic tasks (Pickering, 2006). At least until students have automatized the process, reading, for example, relies heavily on working memory. To read, beginning readers have to juggle multiple things in working memory. They first recognize the letter, connect the letter to its sound, put the sounds together to form a word, put multiple words together to form a sentence, remember the meaning of each word and the sentence as a whole, and then connect the meaning of sentences. Reading is, indeed, a very complicated process.

Test your working memory using the puzzle shown in Figure 1.3 (to get the most out of this, do not look ahead to the answer later in the chapter). The task is one that many elementary school teachers are familiar with—a spelling test but with a twist. Study the symbols associated with the letters for two minutes—you will be asked to complete a spelling test using the symbols in just a few minutes. Are you ready? Go!

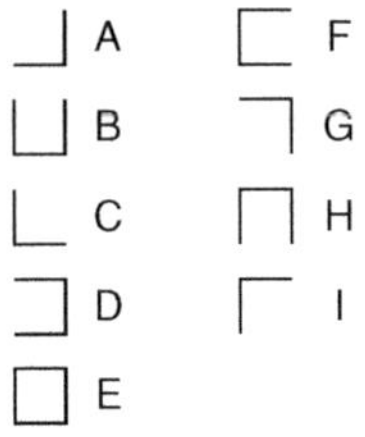

```
  ⌋ A      ⌈ F
  ⌊⌋ B     ⌐ G
  ⌊ C      ⊓ H
  ⌋ D      ⌈ I
  ⊔ E
```

Figure 1.3 Symbols for Spelling Test.

Okay—two minutes are up. What strategies did you use to remember the symbols? There are, of course, many ways to memorize things—the most common is what cognitive scientists call the rehearsal strategy, which is essentially repeating things over and over again. Some of you may have attached meaning to each symbol, employing a strategy known as elaboration. Others of you may have used additional strategies to help you keep the symbols in your working memory.

Decades of research on learning and memory has established that how we encode information in working memory matters (Brown et al., 2014). For example, despite its popularity among students and teachers, research shows that repeating information over and over until it is perceived to be "burned into memory" (what researchers refer to as **massed practice**) is not a very effective way to learn, if you define learning as not just acquiring new information but also being able to apply it later—a concept known as **transfer**.

Are you now ready for the spelling test? Using just the symbols, "spell" the words shown in Figure 1.4.

CEDE

DEAF

HIGH

CABBAGE

HEADACHE

Figure 1.4 Spelling Words.

How did you do? How confident are you that you spelled the words correctly? Were some words easier than others? If we asked you to repeat the spelling test at the end of the chapter, how do you think you will do? Have the symbols been stored in your long-term memory? In general, among other factors (i.e., how attentive you were to the task), research on memory would predict that your performance would depend, in large part, on what kinds of strategies you used.

Elaboration: Research on memory consistently demonstrates that *elaboration* is a much more effective strategy than rehearsal. When students give new material personal meaning by connecting it to what they already know, or organize it into a mental model or **schema**, the learning is much more durable (Brown et al., 2014). Why is this more effective? Because by attaching meaning to new information, we are far more likely to consolidate (i.e., organize and solidify) information and therefore less likely to forget it. As any student will attest, repeating information over and over may delay forgetting for a short period of time, but generally not for much longer (Baddeley, 2004). For example, the schema for the spelling test we just did is presented in Figure 1.5. Can you connect this figure to the symbols we gave you previously?

A	B	C
D	E	F
G	H	I

Figure 1.5 Schema for Spelling Test.

Now, if we asked you to repeat the spelling test, how well do you think you will perform? Most likely, very well—just like a student who has extensive prior knowledge (i.e., elaborate schemas) on a given topic.

Several of our routines were designed with this basic cognitive principle in mind, including *Fact, Question, Answer (FQA)*. FQA is a group learning routine designed to help students remember the meaning of a text by attaching the meaning of the text to a previous experience (see Figure 1.6). As you can see, part of the *FQA* routine involves students of mixed abilities working in groups, sharing a fact from the text, and then changing it into a how or a why question. Then, each student takes turns answering the question using their own experiences (i.e., elaborating).

ALL-ED Classroom Routine Directions:
Fact, Question, Answer (FQA)

Based on the cognitive science of elaboration, *FQA* challenges students to bring personal meaning to a text. In the discussion, one at a time, each student states a fact from the text. The students choose one of the three facts to discuss. The students change the fact into a how or why question. Then each student takes turns answering the question based on their own experience, not using words from the text. The process repeats until the group has completed the routine with three different facts. Finally, students reflect on the most meaningful connection to each of the facts that was heard in the group.

Strengths of this routine:

- promotes making meaningful connections
- encourages collaboration
- provides a means for students to receive feedback on evidence or quotes selected from a text
- allows students to explore and play with a text
- invites creativity
- requires listening to and thinking about the responses of others.

Implementation Directions

Objective: To understand and remember the facts from a reading.

Starting Positions (individually and then in small groups)

Individually: Students identify facts of a text that they want to remember. Students may be asked to identify facts that support the main idea or a particular perspective; the identifying task should align to the goal of the lesson. The teacher may assign required facts that must be remembered and then students can choose two additional facts on their own.

Groups: The teacher assigns students into groups of three with a range of student reading levels in each group. The teacher designates where in the room each group of three will meet with the students sitting or standing knee to knee and eye to eye—so that it is easier to hear each student in the group.

Criteria

- *Must Haves*: Connection to personal experience must add meaning, answer/response must include the word "because."
- *Amazing*: Answer/response to the question uses vocabulary from the class word wall.

Action Pattern

The teacher identifies in the directions:

- **Roles**: Speaker and Listeners
- **Turns**: The teacher assigns one student in each group to "Go first" stating a fact from the text, and then the student who will go second and third.
- **Rules**: "Add or Repeat" students can repeat an answer from a previous student or add a new response.
- **Time**: The teacher times each round of *Fact, Question, Answer* so that all groups move through the routine at the same pace.

1 *Fact*: One at a time, read the fact to be remembered (Rule: "Add or Repeat"—facts can be repeated or new facts added).
2 *Question*: As a group, restate the fact into a why or how question.
3 *Answer*: One at a time, answer the how/why question using personal experience (no quotes from the text).
4 Reflect through an Open Discussion: As a group, discuss which personal connection is most memorable and why. Group members take turns being the recorder, who writes down the fact and the most memorable connection on an index card with the group member's names following the Open Discussion.
5 Repeat: Repeat *Fact, Question, Answer* until at least three facts have been turned into questions and each person has provided a connection.

Reflections

1 Create a list of the most meaningful connections to each of the facts that was heard in the group. Use the Criteria to determine the most meaningful connection.
2 Answer the questions, "What is this text about? How does this text relate to our lives?"

FQA also ensures equity by offering each student opportunities to share their ideas. In addition, the "Add or Repeat" rule enables students who need to find a quote, to participate in the discussion by using a quote that another student has offered. Students use elaboration and the support of a structured collaborative discussion to encode the meaning of the text. While the students are engaged in *FQA*, the teacher is free to listen, observe, and record student thinking and vocabulary use. This enables teachers to make decisions in the moment about how to correct misunderstandings and how to tailor the next part of the lesson to further student learning. *FQA* is a great example of how ALL-ED classroom routines are rooted in research and implemented in a practical manner designed for student variability. *FQA* is also an example of practicing retrieval, our next area of focus.

Retrieval: Considering the way our memory is set up, we are far more likely to forget things than to remember them. We can at most juggle only about four bits of information in our working memory at a time, and unless we do something to keep that information active in our working memory, it is only retained for a few seconds (Baddeley, 2004). Some of you may have experienced this with the spelling activity above. We intentionally tried to interfere with your working memory by inserting text you had to read before letting you proceed to the spelling test. Considering that the window for getting information into long-term memory from working memory is quite short, the more time passes, the less likely we are to be able to do this. This is also why some students who are slow at pronunciation or counting often have difficulty with reading or doing arithmetic; by the time they are ready to work on the higher order task of reading or arithmetic, they may have already forgotten the word or the number. Learning is more about finding ways not to forget information than about remembering. Studies show that we forget about 70% of what we have just heard or read (Brown et al., 2014).

Recent cognitive research has therefore focused on finding more effective ways to counteract this natural process of forgetting. First, studies demonstrate that having prior knowledge on the topic helps a lot. When you can tie information to a **schema**, like the schema for the spelling activity we just completed, you are much less likely to forget it because that information has meaning (APA, 2015; Mayer, 2011). Now that you know the trick to the activity, how likely is it that you would forget the symbols? Probably not very likely. In the same way, having extensive schemas on a topic helps with the processing (i.e., encoding) of information. Similarly, in the reading example, reading comprehension usually becomes easier for students as soon as they have automatized phonics, freeing up more working memory capacity to devote to meaning.

Apart from the research on prior knowledge and encoding, studies have also found that learning is more effective when we increase the frequency of retrieving knowledge from memory, what psychologists refer to as the **testing (or retrieval–practice) effect**. When we practice retrieving information from long-term memory, it helps us to re-remember it, and ultimately not forget it as easily. For example, *FQA* asks students to repeat factual information from the text; when students are doing this, they are essentially engaging in retrieval practice.

It is important to note that the quality of retrieval makes a difference; to be most effective, studies show that retrieval must be repeated over and over again, spaced out over time, and effortful. Repetition is important for consolidating knowledge and automatizing skills, but it is also important to space out our learning to allow for some forgetting to occur so that when we try to remember information, it is not always easy. Doing the *FQA* routine once is likely to aid students' memory of the reading, but doing the *FQA* routine spaced out over time would be even better.

Metacognition and self-regulated learning: When we perceive a task as easy, we often fall prey to what psychologists refer to as the **illusion of knowing**—or the perception that we know more than we actually do (Brown et al., 2014). Illusions of knowing (and overconfidence, which often accompanies illusions of knowing) impede learning. When we think that we know something, we are less likely to take action to remediate our understanding—after all, we already know it! In most cases, we are very poor judges of our abilities. As the Nobel Laureate Kahneman (2011) notes in his book *Thinking Fast and Slow*, we have an "almost unlimited ability to ignore our ignorance" (p. 201). How many times have you encountered that flabbergasted student who was so convinced that he knew the material that he could not possibly fathom why he did so poorly on the exam?

Such students essentially lack what researchers refer to as **metacognitive awareness,** or awareness about their thinking. Metacognitive awareness is the hallmark of a self-regulated learner—a learner who, upon being given an assignment, thinks about what she knows about the topic, what she did in the past to succeed on similar assignments, and her goals for the assignment. Such a learner monitors his progress toward his goals when working on the assignment and adjusts his strategies when he finds that they are not working. A learner with metacognitive awareness reflects on her work and thinks about what she could do better next time (Zimmerman & Schunk, 2011).

Not surprisingly, research on self-regulated learning finds that such students typically perform well in school. John Hattie (2009) lists metacognition as among the top factors related to academic achievement. The use of metacognitive strategies—including planning how to approach a task, evaluating progress, and monitoring understanding—was determined to have a large effect size. Skills related to self-regulated learning have always been considered critical for academic success; however, we would argue that these skills are perhaps even more imperative now. Standards like the Common Core State Standards (CCCS) and the Next Generation Science Standards (NGSS) collectively emphasize the development of real-world, higher-order thinking skills, making training in self-regulated learning (SRL) not only important but a necessity (White & DiBenedetto, 2015). See Figure 1.6 for a summary of the research on cognition.

Top Ten Considerations About Cognition (WERMS) in ALL-ED

1   Durable learning is learning that sticks. It largely depends on the interaction between two specific memory systems—working memory and long-term memory. Working memory is involved in all academic tasks (like reading and math) that has multiple steps.

2   We can at most juggle only about four bits of information in our working memory at a time. Unless we do something to keep that information active in our working memory, it is only retained in working memory for a few seconds. Thus, effective learning involves learning how to overcome the limits of working memory.

3   One way to overcome the limits of working memory is to use deeper-processing cognitive strategies, like elaboration. The more meaning you attach to information you are trying to learn, the more likely it is that you will not forget it.

4   Prior knowledge (or having elaborate schemas) aids in the processing of information because it can help make the incoming information more meaningful.

5   You are less likely to forget information if you increase the frequency of retrieving knowledge from memory—or, what psychologists refer to as the testing (or *retrieval–practice*) effect. To be most effective, retrieval must be repeated over and over again, be spaced out over time, and be effortful.

6   Illusions of knowing (and overconfidence, which often accompanies illusions of knowing) impede learning. Students with metacognitive awareness (i.e., students who know what they know and do not know) are less likely to fall prey to illusions of knowing.

7   Students with metacognitive awareness are also more likely to regulate their learning. Upon given an assignment, they are more likely to think about what they know about the topic and their goals. Self-regulated learners are also more likely to monitor their progress toward goals and adjust their strategies when they find that they aren't working. Upon completion of the task, they are also more likely to reflect on their work and think about what they could do better next time.

8   Research on transfer further suggests that in order for learning to be flexible and durable, you need to know when and how to use that knowledge. It is not enough to know about a topic—you need to be able to do something with that knowledge. Building metacognitive awareness and self-regulation is one way to promote transfer.

9   Research demonstrates a positive association between motivation and cognition. Students who feel ABC+M are much more likely to use effective cognitive strategies that lead to durable learning.

10   Given this research, ALL-ED classroom routines are central to fostering durable learning.

Figure 1.6 Top Ten Considerations about Cognition (WERMS) in ALL-ED.

Importance of Context: Thus far, we have argued that both motivational and cognitive factors are predictors of important learning outcomes. Learning is enhanced when students feel autonomous, belonging to a learning community, competent, and find meaning in their learning (ABC+M). Research on cognition (WERMS) further suggests that self-regulated learners who use more effective encoding strategies to interrupt the process of forgetting are less likely to fall prey to biases related to overconfidence and illusions of understanding, and are more likely to ultimately achieve higher levels of learning.

What we have not said is that both motivational and cognitive processes are highly dependent upon context. Often, we hear from teachers that "my students are simply not motivated." There is a tendency for teachers to think of motivation as a personality trait—students either have it or they do not. Although it is certainly possible to identify students who appear more or less motivated in a classroom through their behavior, it is important to note that *motivation is NOT a personality trait. Altering the task or the general learning environment can change it.* Recall the students that appear unmotivated in your class. If you take them out of your classroom and put them in a setting where they are working on something that they love—an athletic field or their workplace—what are they like? In a different context, you may see a totally different student. Again, motivation is not a personality trait.

Similarly, research on self-regulated learning assumes that it is a teachable skill. Skills associated with self-regulated learning are learned skills that can be modified and improved, thus making it an ideal target for intervention at any age level. Research suggests that students are more likely to regulate their learning when they have adequate resources available, including time, effective and supportive teachers and peers, as well as access to supplementary learning materials. Students are more likely to become self-regulated when they are prompted to do so, either directly (through instruction) or indirectly (through feedback or activity prompts). Research shows that periodic self-assessments that ask students to reflect on what they know or do not know about a topic (to overcome illusions of knowing), and their depth of knowledge about key points promotes regulation of learning. Research further suggests that metacognitive training is most effective during small group instruction (Hattie, 2009).

Return once more to your Starting Position routine *List, Write, Draw* and review your memory about an experience where you felt motivated or unmotivated. Can you explain using the research from this chapter why you felt motivated and unmotivated? If you could change something in your story, what would you change that might increase the support in that context for your motivation? Use the routine *List, Write, Draw* to gather notes as you read the next chapters.

ALL-ED Classroom Routine Directions:
List, Write, Draw (Individual Routine)

Before an activity begins, teachers activate student prior knowledge and gather information about what students know and questions they have about the topic. *List, Write, Draw* is an individual routine designed to provide options for students to record their memories. The options make writing about memories easier so that the focus for students is thinking about the topic. Any options that are available and easily used by students in your setting could be used, such as *Type, Picture with Caption,* or *Collage* if you are using a computer. The goal is to facilitate all students making a quick visible recording of their thinking on the topic. This routine can be used as an introduction to a topic, a check for understanding in the middle of a lesson, or story being read aloud. It can also be used as a reflection at the end of the assignment reflecting on what the student will remember from completing the learning task and why that part is memorable.

Strengths of this routine:

- takes little time
- is fun—students like sharing because students choose different options
- shows key points that are on the minds of students.

Implementation Directions

Objective: Record your thinking with details.

Starting Positions (individually)

> *Individually*: Ask students to think "in their head" about a question or a prompt. For example, "Think of a time when you (related to the topic—maybe how you learned _____ or when you were motivated ...)." You might ask the students to summarize a lesson using *List, Write, Draw* capturing the most important points. Or to describe a part of a story or a character.

Criteria

- *Must Haves*: Answers the prompt, includes details.
- *Amazing*: Answer/response to the question uses vocabulary from the class word wall, includes how you felt.

Action Pattern

The teacher identifies in the directions:

- **Rules:** Must use the whole time to add to your response, so if you finish your drawing then add words or if you finish writing then add a sketch. When you think that you are finished, then reread what you have written or drawn and add two more details. Continue until time is called.
- **Time:** About two to four minutes.

1   Ask students to *List, Write, Draw* to answer the prompt.
2   Remind students that when they think that they are finished to reread and add two more details.

Reflections

3   Ask students to reread what they have written and circle the most important part.

This routine can be followed by a table discussion and then *Domino Discover* to gather the most important parts (circled) of the responses.

Applying Research to Classroom Practice

As Marvin, an exemplary science teacher, noted, "motivation fuels learning, whereas cognition puts the brakes on learning like a parachute on a drag racecar." When we are designing learning experiences, we want to both foster motivation and to pay attention to how cognitive limits may enhance or create constraints for effective learning. Although the acronyms facilitate your memory of ABC+M and WERMS, we have designed recommendations from this research into classroom routines to facilitate learning so that you can focus on implementing the routine. For example, you could begin with a simple habit of recording student responses at least once in every lesson. The student responses could be answers to any question that is asked that could have multiple answers or explanations. This teacher habit can be used with many different classroom routines and has many benefits. For students, it provides a means for them to reflect on how their thinking has changed because of learning in a lesson or unit. Teachers use the responses to adjust instruction by answering specific student questions or grouping students by similar or different answers. Recording student responses also draws the teacher's attention to the effectiveness of questions. The quality of a question is revealed in what is done with the answers. Recording student responses is a great place to begin agile teacher thinking.

There are many ways to record responses without adding too much time to a lesson. We organize the possibilities into three categories, **Share-Out, Gather and Group**, and **Around the Room**. The differences are important because the way responses are recorded makes a difference in how students receive feedback and how quickly teachers can use the responses to adjust instruction. For example, each table can summarize individual responses into a table response that is shared by a table reporter or written largely on a paper for the routine, *Show and Share*, without any speaking. Responses can be written by each table or group and posted on the board or typed into a digital document. *Show and Share* takes very little time; the teacher gathers responses at the group level, not from individuals. For feedback, groups generally can notice how their responses were similar or different than other groups.

There are at least three different ways to record responses. Each method results in a different collection of student responses. Remember that the teacher habit is to record student responses visibly at least once during every lesson. You will need a variety of methods for recording responses considering the time allowed in the lesson, length of student responses, feedback you would like students to receive, and organization of collected responses for adjusting instruction. Students may respond to questions in a variety of forms, such as: writing, drawing, speaking, moving, and building. The method of gathering student responses will need to fit for the form as well as the length of student responses.

Methods for Recording Student Responses

1   Share-Out—Purpose: Assess student responses so that students see how their ideas are similar or different from those of other students. Ideas should be shared from all members of the class. Avoid calling on hands as a first routine for gathering student responses. Begin with a group or individual routine and then call on hands for additional responses. Routines that use the *Share-Out* method are *Domino Discover* and *Show and Share*.

2   **Gather and Group**—Purpose: When you need student responses to be grouped into patterns to determine the next steps of the lesson or student groups, then *Gather and Group* should be used instead of *Share-Out*. The difference is that in *Gather and Group*, individual student responses are sorted into categories as part of the gathering process. This enables teachers to respond to the patterns during lessons rather than taking student responses home, sorting them, and then returning a day or two later to respond to student differences. In addition, because individual student responses are written down and saved, both teachers and students may return to original responses for reflection. The routine, *Rumors*, uses the *Gather and Group* method.

3   **Around the Room**—Purpose: When you need students to generate responses on a focused topic or question through discussion in small groups and students need written feedback on their responses, then *Around the Room* is the most efficient method. For *Around the Room*, you will post a topic, photograph, data table, question, map—any prompt that you would like students to discuss and record their responses. Students form small groups at each station, discuss, and document their responses on chart paper or a laptop. Then students rotate, reading the responses of other groups and contributing feedback to the original responses. This rotation continues "around the room" until students have participated in discussion on the needed topics. Together as a class, you and your students can look for patterns across student responses to the different prompts. This is a great way to introduce or review units, a time in the curriculum where you both want to activate student knowledge and get them remembering what they know and at the same time further student knowledge through peer discussions. The teacher benefits from the time to listen to student conversations around the room. The routine, *Idea Carousel*, uses the *Around the Room* method.

Domino Discover or *Show and Share* should be used first before calling on hands to collect responses from students. In these routines, every student shares their response in small groups, or representatives share responses from each group to the whole class. The opportunity to hear from each individual or individuals via a group representative sends a message to students that their ideas are valued in class. For students, *Domino Discover* and *Show and Share* build feelings of ABC+M through exchanging and building on the ideas of peers. Students know that the teacher is interested and values the responses of everyone because everyone is heard and the responses are recorded on paper, the board or in a digital document. Hands can be called on for additional responses following the routine. Teachers can only adjust instruction based on the student needs that they perceive. *Domino Discover* and *Show and Share* are essential routines because while furthering student learning, teachers listen and observe students to consider their strengths and needs for effective learning.

Gather and Group routines of *Rumors* and *Sort and Post (or Place)* usually take more time than the *Share-Out* routines, such as *Domino Discover* and *Show and Share*. However, students receive more oral practice and feedback, and teachers finish with student responses sorted into groups versus one big list. These routines can be used at any time in the lesson, beginning, middle, or end. Anytime you want to find out what students are thinking and then use the thinking to form groups, the *Gather and Group* routines are the most efficient routine.

ALL-ED Classroom Routine Directions: Rumors

Rumors is a group learning routine where students write their individual responses on a sticky note or paper, share their responses with another student, listen to the partner's response, and then exchange or swap responses. Students continue sharing and swapping with other students to listen for patterns among the responses for a designated amount of time or number of "response swaps." Students must read the response each time before exchanging. At the end, students generate labels or categories of patterns that they perceived from their exchanges. The responses are sorted into categories, ending with patterns among student responses and the ability to see individual student responses.

Strengths of this routine:

- gets students on their feet and moving
- everyone has to engage in conversation
- requires students to listen and repeat the ideas of others
- allows many students to talk at the same time, no waiting for a turn
- patterns or groupings may be used to further instruction.

Implementation Directions

Objective: Exchange ideas to find similarities and differences.

Starting Positions: Ask students to jot down an idea on a sticky note or piece of paper along with their name. Ideas include:

- note three questions, put a star next to the most urgent to get answered
- sum up how you are feeling in a word
- identify a next step for learning
- list one strategy used to review for a test.

Note: Use only one idea at a time for *Rumors*. Ask students to star the most important question or idea if they have written more than one. Students will share the one question or idea with a star during *Rumors*.

Criteria

- *Must Haves*: Uses the word "because," explains with detail, includes visual representation of ideas.
- *Amazing*: Makes connection to previous unit or word, uses vocabulary from word wall.

Action Pattern

Directions: The teacher identifies in the directions:

- **Roles:** Speaker, Listener
- **Turns:** Simultaneously, all students pair up, then take turns being the speaker and then the listener.

- **Rules:** Students must read what is written on the rumor (they cannot just exchange or swap rumors without sharing them)
- **Time:** Three minutes

1   Invite students to join you in an open space with their completed Starting Position on a sticky note or piece of paper.
2   Tell students there are a lot of rumors going around about _____ (whatever the topic was for the rumor). Ask students what they know about rumors (e.g., they spread quickly and people repeat what they heard from other people).
3   Tell students that we are going to spread our rumors by going up to someone, reading our rumor, listening to their rumor, and then exchanging rumors. Then each person goes up to another student and does the same thing again. Give the directions for the action pattern Listen, Read, Exchange. Students can use the name written on the rumor when they tell a rumor—"I heard from Marvin that … ".
4   Allow students to exchange ideas with as many people as possible in three minutes.
5   Stop the rumors. Ask a student who is currently holding a rumor that they think is similar to other rumors to read the rumor out loud. Post the rumor on a whiteboard or chart paper and then ask other students to post their rumor next to it if it could be in a group with this one. Ask students to read their rumor out loud as they post them in a group.
6   Encourage students to give the group of similar rumors a name. Ask for a very different rumor—and start a second group. Invite others to post similar rumors to make a second group and brainstorm a name for the new group of rumors.
7   Continue adding groups until all rumors are collected.

Reflections

1   Discuss what our rumors may tell us about our learning, questions, and ourselves.
2   Adjust instruction based on results from *Rumors*. For example, group students by similar rumors for a discussion or save original rumors and then have students return to their rumor after several lessons to reflect on how their thinking has stayed the same and/or changed.

Around the room routine, *Idea Carousel*, is particularly useful when you feel many students may not have an answer to your question. The collaboration allows students to learn from their peers and generate ideas collaboratively. Usually following the *Idea Carousel*, all students will be able to individually answer the question. *Idea Carousel* is a great routine when introducing or reviewing a topic, because students don't form individual responses to begin. Usually, it makes sense to assign the groups or to ask students to move to the prompt that they are ready to answer—this pushes students to begin at a place where they feel the greatest confidence and are more likely to participate because they have an idea to share. Students have plenty of time to practice speaking during *Idea Carousel* and the teacher gains essential listening time. You will notice a pattern for the structure of the routine always beginning with an objective, then offering criteria to monitor the quality of responses, and ending with reflection. Review the Research Roots in this chapter and notice how the structure of these routines prompts self-regulated learning. The structure of the routines leverages the recommendations from this research. By building on basic principles of motivation and cognitive science, ALL-ED provides teachers with a decision-making framework that will transform the learning climate into one where *all* students feel motivated to learn, both on their own and with others, and achieve durable learning outcomes.

Try Classroom Routines:

Precise, Effective, Efficient Learning for All

Plan: Choose Questions and Record Student Responses

Examine an upcoming lesson plan. Identify at least one question that you will ask where you could use a routine to record student responses. You will want to choose a question where student responses matter. For example, you may want to know if all students remember five vocabulary words, realize the steps to solving a problem, can infer a response to an abstract question, or remember what was read the day before. Then, recording student responses enables you to gather that information. Select a question that has multiple answers and that student responses matter, in terms of the next part of the lesson.

Teach: Rumors or FQA

To embark on your journey toward agile teacher thinking, consider simply recording student responses at least once during a lesson. For example, you might ask a big question, such as, "How does the energy from the sun get into the food that we eat?" or, "What will you remember from today's lesson?" As students raise their hands and are called on, you, a co-teacher, or a student can record the responses. These recorded responses act as a Starting Position, and can be used to help students to recognize their own growth. Routine recording of student responses during every lesson provides students a point to return to for reflection. Visible, written student responses provide students with additional benefits. For example, students needing longer language processing time or support with working memory can use the written list to understand student responses. Students who are simply sitting where it is hard to hear their peers can now read the written responses. Recorded responses provide all students with a means to engage in thinking instead of being confused because they missed what was said in class. Most importantly, this routine also offers teachers an opportunity to check for student understanding while lessons are in progress.

Choose one of the five routines to record responses to implement once in every lesson, *Domino Discover* (Chapter 2), *Show and Share* (Chapter 5), *Rumors* (Chapter 1), *Sort and Post (or Place)* (Chapter 5), and *Idea Carousel* (Chapter 7). These routines have many benefits for students, including promoting reflection, goal setting, and accountability while giving value and importance to student responses. At the same time, this routine provides teachers with needed data to clarify perceptions and then adjust instruction. For example, before a mini-lesson the teacher makes students record one question about the topic from each table and then adjusts instruction during the mini-lesson to answer the questions. This routine requires no planning time or any additional materials and expands teacher perceptions of student Starting Positions (including their questions) to adjust the lesson to the students who are in the classroom at that moment.

Adjust Instruction: React to Student Responses

Use the student responses that you have recorded in some way during the lesson. For example, you might add to the list of responses new ideas that emerge during the lesson. You might ask students which ideas from the recorded responses were talked about in class. If questions are recorded, then you might ask students how the questions were answered in the mini-lesson. If students are using *Must Have*-required vocabulary words in their responses, then you can adjust instruction to review other words or words that stretch students. Recording responses will give you a signal as to possible adjustments to instruction to spend time more strategically and to maintain a written record summarizing student learning.

Checklist to Try Routines in Your Teaching

See https://www.routledge.com/9780815370819 for additional resources: *Domino Discover* Step by Step Directions.

Plan	Teach	Adjust Instruction
❏ Plan to record student responses to at least one of your questions in every lesson. Plan possible ways to use student responses in the lesson.	❏ Rumors, FQA, or Domino Discover	❏ React to student responses during the lesson.

Quality Criteria to Implement Classroom Routines

Must Haves	Amazing
• Classroom routine is implemented on a regular basis, either daily, weekly, or is tied to a specific type of instruction, such as a mini-lesson, independent practice, or review. • Identify criteria for high quality work when assigning at least one task in every lesson (for example, the teacher might say before asking students to share their ideas with a partner, called an *Elbow Exchange, Must Haves* for high quality listening means that you can repeat what your partner said to you; *Amazing* listening means that you can repeat and build on or ask a question about your partner's idea).	• Look at student work or student responses before planning the next lesson. • Record what students said that surprised you during the routines every day for at least one week. • Return to recorded responses to notice growth with students. • Use recorded responses to tailor instruction by answering questions that were raised or assigning a task or question related to their responses.

Chapter Reflection

Chapter Summary

In this chapter we explored why classroom routines promote student engagement from a motivational standpoint and from a cognitive perspective. We described the genesis of the ALL-ED framework and roots in both classroom practice and research. We synthesized motivation research into autonomy, belonging, competence, and meaning (**ABC+M**) and cognitive science into working memory, elaboration, retrieval, metacognition, and self-regulated learning (**WERMS**) for teachers to use as tools to plan more effective instruction and understand how learning happens. We encouraged you to try out routines that are rooted in science, yet practical to implement on a daily basis, such as establishing a Starting Position, the elaboration routine, *FQA*, and Recording Student Responses.

Learning Journal: Record Important Takeaways

Create a *Learning Journal* to track your thinking about meeting the needs of diverse learners by recording in a notebook or computer file answers to the following four questions:

1   What was most interesting and useful for you in this chapter?
2   Why was this interesting and useful?
3   How does this connect to what you know about meeting the learning needs of all learners?
4   What research from this chapter could you use to explain or support decisions to adjust instruction?

Save these responses for reflection after reading more of this book and trying out ideas in your classroom. We will answer these same four questions at the end of every chapter.

Return to Your Starting Position

Return to your preliminary first draft answer to our chapter question, "Why do classroom routines promote learning?" Add new ideas or revise in another way. Circle the most important part and save to return to after Chapter 4: Step Two: Look and Listen and Chapter 6: Step Four: SHOp Adjustments to see how your thinking both stays the same and changes as you read and try routines in your classroom.

Note

1   You may be wondering what the difference is between working memory and short-term memory. It's essentially the same thing, if you conceptualize working memory as a memory system that involves the temporary storage of information. But, as its name denotes, you often do more than simply store information in working memory. Often you are engaging in strategies to keep information in there so that you can do something with it later. For example, in the spelling activity, you have to keep the symbol–letter connection in your working memory in order to actually perform the spelling test. This is why cognitive scientists now prefer to use the term "working memory" over "short-term memory." There are other more complicated aspects of working memory (e.g., episodic buffer, phonological loop, visuospatial sketchpad, central executive) that we did not review here that also distinguish it from short-term memory.

Chapter 2

The Changing Extremes in Our Classrooms

Overview

Objective:

Why do we need to adjust or differentiate instruction?
  Think: Circle the most <u>important</u> word in the Objective.

Criteria:

Use the following criteria to increase the quality of your answer to the chapter question. Try to "Take It Up a Notch" or expand your answer by reading the chapter to add these details.

- Identify ways students vary, which create opportunities and obstacles to student engagement in your subject area.
- Explain research that describes the ways that students vary.
- Try Classroom Routines:
  - Plan—*Traction Planner.*
  - Teach—*Domino Discover.*
  - Adjust Instruction—*Inclusive Directions.*

Starting Position: Jot Notes—Perceptions of the Extremes

Begin by reflecting on your students within the context of your subject area. Identify a specific task used in lessons such as independent reading and surround the task with a brainstorm of ways that students vary that impact learning. Think about all of the things that students have and bring to the task as well as things that they might need to learn:

- Consider their interests that relate to this task.
- Surround the task with student strengths.
- Break the task down and consider all of the things that students would need to learn or have before even beginning this task.

Use this exercise to begin to examine the many variations and dimensions of student characteristics (experiences, strengths, needs, interests, understandings) that impact learning in your subject area (see Figure 2.1).

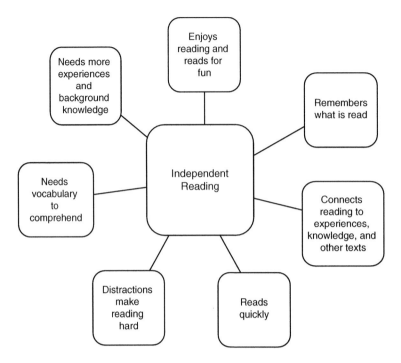

Figure 2.1 Independent Reading Brainstorm of Student Variability.

Reread your networks of student variations. To learn more about this approach to making our own perceptions about student variability visible in relation to our curriculum, try the *Traction Planner* routine. Consider how the extremes of your network begin to answer our chapter question, "Why do we need differentiated instruction?" Take a moment to jot down your draft answer. We will return to this question at the end of this chapter and at the end of this book to reflect on how your thinking has been confirmed, challenged, or changed.

From the Classroom: *What Are the Extremes?*

Near the end of the school year, one of Ms. Ford's favorite annual activities is to play a video from the first day of school where her sixth-grade students individually state their names and what they hope to learn. The initial goals recorded on this video serve as a starting position to help students reflect on their learning over the year. The students scream with laughter as they recognize how much they have changed in just eight months. Of course, the physical changes are dramatic from the beginning to the end of each school year. Students have grown, their voices have changed, and often their hair or dress styles are new. After spending a year together, they also now recognize the myriad ways in which they are different and unique in their knowledge, language, interests, childhood experience, family, culture, and special skills.

This story of the sixth-grade video illustrates just how much students are constantly changing in a variety of ways, and at differing rates. When we aim to adjust instruction to meet the academic needs of all learners, we must remember that students are continuously changing, and that, along with differences, students share common experiences. The amount of time we have at school for learning is set, as is much of the curriculum. The varying starting positions and rates of change among students, along with a fixed amount of class time and required learning standards, create a tension for teachers. How do you provide instruction that is appropriate for each individual student within time and curriculum constraints? We find that impactful teachers have their fingers on the pulse of the class. They monitor student learning by considering the interactions among students and themselves during lessons, and the relationships between students and the curriculum. This perception is vital because it is the beginning—the impetus for why adjustments are made to instruction.

Rooted in Research: *Identifying the Extremes*

Diversity in Our Classrooms

Research generally confirms teachers' perceptions about shifts in the overall diversity of the K–12 student population. When it comes to ethnic diversity, according to a recent report released by the U.S. Department of Education (2014), the percentage of public school K–12 students who identified as White fell to under 50%, whereas the percentage of Hispanic and Asian students increased (Musu-Gillette et al., 2016). The percentage of public school students who were non-native speakers of English was higher in 2014–2015 than a decade ago, making up roughly 9% of the student population. Not surprisingly, the percentage of English as a New Language learners varies by state—West Virginia has the fewest number (only 1%), whereas almost a quarter of the student population in California are English as a New Language learners. In 2014, about 14% of the English as a New Language student population were identified as having learning disabilities.

In terms of the overall population of students receiving special education services, approximately 13% (or 6.6 million) of the public school population received services in 2014–2015, with more male students receiving special education services under the Individuals with Disabilities Education Act (IDEA) than female students, and more American Indian and Black students receiving services than White students. An overwhelming majority of students receiving special education services (95%) were enrolled in regular schools. Moreover, there was a dramatic increase in the percentage of students who spent most of their time in general education classes, from 33% in 1990 to 62% in 2014/2015—an increase of 29 percentage points. There is limited recent data available on students considered to be gifted and talented, although in 2006, approximately 6% of the overall public-school population in the United States was identified as gifted (Snyder & Dillow, 2015).

The National Assessment of Educational Progress (NAEP, 2015), more commonly referred to as the Nation's Report Card, is useful in providing an overall picture of U.S. students' academic achievement. NAEP assessments are administered periodically to a nationally representative sample of fourth, eighth, and 12th-grade students in nine different subject areas. Examining the 2015 achievement results for the core subjects of reading and mathematics helps us understand variability in achievement within and across grades.

First, in terms of reading, 36% of fourth-grade students, 34% of eighth-grade students, and 37% of 12th-grade students performed at or above the proficient level on the reading assessment in 2015, indicating solid academic performance.

By contrast, 31% of fourth-grade, 24% of eighth-grade, and 28% of 12th-grade students performed below "basic" levels (NAEP, 2015). As for mathematics, 40% of fourth-grade, 33% of eighth-grade, and 25% of 12th-grade students performed at or above the proficient level, whereas 18% of fourth-grade, 29% of eighth-grade, and 38% of 12th-grade students performed below the basic level. When the data is disaggregated by specific groups, students receiving special education services and English as a New Language learners generally perform below the basic level of proficiency across all grades in both reading and mathematics.

These results suggest a trend toward increasing academic diversity in U.S. schools. The NAEP assessments attest that there is a substantial percentage of elementary, middle, and high school students who are not meeting grade-level standards of mathematics and reading proficiency. These data confirm that not all students are learning in school every day. It is important to note that these trends are not unique to the U.S. context. Results of large-scale international assessments like the Programme for International Student Assessment (PISA), which focuses on issues of equity, also speak to variability in achievement scores. In reporting the results of the 2015 assessments, the Organisation for Economic Co-operation and Development (OECD) who oversees PISA made the following conclusion: "Clearly all countries and economies have excellent students, but few have enabled all students to excel" (p. 6). Indeed, they reported that only a handful of countries were able to get four out of five 15-year-olds to achieve basic levels of proficiency in science, reading, and mathematics. These included Canada, Estonia, Finland, Hong Kong (China), Japan, Macao (China), and Singapore (OECD, 2016).

Danger of Perceiving General Extremes

To achieve our goal of engaging the extremes, it is important to understand the nature of the extremes and especially the extent of variability that exists in academic proficiency in our nation's schools. As the statistics above demonstrate, teachers are confronted by considerable academic diversity, which speaks to the urgent need for differentiated education (Fuchs, 2006). However, research also suggests that differentiated instruction is relatively uncommon in most classrooms, particularly in large urban school districts that face considerable linguistic, cultural, and academic diversity. In the face of such a challenge, most teachers opt for a one-size-fits-all instructional approach, only selectively attending to student differences, or focusing more on academically competent students. Findings from numerous studies indicate that children who perform at lower levels of achievement receive less differentiated instruction than students who perform at higher levels, which may increase achievement gaps between the extremes (Fuchs, 2006).

It is in this context that we interpret the statistics presented in the previous section. Although the NAEP data clearly show specific achievement patterns with certain groups outperforming others, we fundamentally believe that a major contributing factor is lack of targeted instruction and not that certain students are more capable than others. Proponents of universal learning design (UDL) support this belief:

> Advances in neuroscience and education research over the past 40 years have reshaped our understanding of the learning brain. One of the clearest and most important revelations stemming from brain research is that there is no such thing as a "regular student." Instead, learning is as unique to individuals as

their fingerprints or DNA. The notion of broad categories of learners—"smart–not smart," "disabled–not disabled," "regular–not regular"—is a gross over-simplification that does not reflect reality. By categorizing students in this way, we miss many subtle and important qualities and strengths. Science shows that individual qualities or abilities are not static or fixed; rather they are continually shifting, and they exist in relationship to the environment.

(Hall, Meyer, & Rose, 2012, p. 2)

It is important to keep in mind that the extremes of achievement differences are not enduring, stable characteristics of an individual or groups of students, and that targeted instruction can go a long way in closing achievement gaps. A recent study found that 71% of the variability in student engagement could be attributed to class-room rather than student variables (Cooper, 2014), underscoring the importance of looking beyond student traits when it comes to understanding academic engagement.

Although statistics are useful in allowing us to better understand the range in academic ability that exists in our schools, they do not tell us anything about specific students, and there is an inherent danger in extrapolating these results to individuals. As the research on UDL would attest, variability or heterogeneity within groups of students is the norm; an "average" score cannot adequately capture the profiles of every member of that group. Just because students are English as a New Language learners, or are identified as having a disability, does not necessarily mean that they will struggle with *all* academic tasks; similarly, this does not mean that gifted students do not have their own share of challenges, even academic ones. We all have our strengths and weaknesses, and these attributes are likely to change depending upon the context. This is why we advise implementing frequent individualized assessments for *all* students in a learning community, not just those who are struggling.

Teacher Perception and Thinking

With this in mind, consider what Carol Dweck (2006) would call a growth mind-set—thinking not about what certain students or groups *cannot* do but rather to think about what *all* students *can* do, and what changes you need to make in your curriculum and your practices to achieve this goal. Can you think of the educational system, the curriculum or the lessons, rather than students, as having "disabilities"? (Hall et al., 2012). Researchers of UDL suggest that traditional curricula are "disa-bled" in the sense that a curriculum only works for certain kinds of students who can decode print-based text or physically turn pages. Some would argue that the educational system, too, is currently set up to advantage certain learners over oth-ers. Research on culturally relevant pedagogy (Ladson-Billings, 1995), for example, suggests many minority students do not perceive school and schooling as validating, liberating, or emancipatory (Kumar et al., submitted). What changes do you need to make to your instructional practice to ensure fair and equal access so that all students achieve at the proficient level? Can you shift your thinking from teachers to teaching (Hiebert & Stigler, 2017) and from students to learning?

Teacher Expectations

Among the major contributions of the last century of psychological research on learning is the research on teacher expectations. *Teacher expectations matter.* In the first study on teacher effects—now aptly referred to as the Pygmalion experiment

(Rosenthal & Jacobson, 1968)—teachers who were simply told that their students were likely to "bloom" expected more of these students, and these bloomers, consequently, were found to achieve at higher levels. Building on this initial study, researchers have since examined how teacher expectations affect teacher behavior.

There is empirical evidence to suggest that teachers generally interact less with and provide less wait time and praise for low-expectation students (Brophy, 1985), ultimately undermining their motivation and subsequent achievement. In contrast, teachers with high expectations for their students are more likely to engage in motivationally supportive practices intended to promote a warm classroom climate (Rubie-Davies, Peterson, Sibley, & Rosenthal, 2015). They are more likely to believe in and employ non-ability grouping practices (flexible grouping), promote self-regulated learning (i.e., goal-setting and support in monitoring progress toward goals), and provide choice and autonomy to all students (Rubie-Davies et al., 2015). These are all practices emphasized by ALL-ED.

We are all biased in some way, shape, or form,[1] and we do not mean to suggest that some teachers are more biased than others. Even the most successful, well-intentioned educators are capable of falling prey to teacher expectation effects. The good news is that teacher expectations, like academic ability, are not fixed. Interventions for teacher expectations demonstrate not only that these beliefs are malleable, but training teachers in the practices of high expectations can promote student achievement. For example, Rubie-Davies et al. (2015) trained a subset of New Zealand teachers in flexible grouping, student choice, and goal-setting and found that these teachers' students obtained higher mathematics scores than teachers who did not receive this training. In a similar way, our approach to differentiated instruction supports teachers in establishing high expectations for all students.

Teacher Decision-Making Framework – ALL-ED

Now that you have some background about the extremes, let's return to your starting position at the beginning of the chapter to consider again: what are the extremes that we are aiming to engage? Students do not fall into clear levels such as high, medium, and low because there are too many variables involved in learning activities, and students vary on more than one critical dimension. For example, during a reading activity, students may vary on their current reading level, creating extremes related to access and rigor for students engaged in the same task. Factors such as lack of regular attendance and cultural background knowledge also impact student understanding of the text regardless of their independent reading level. The ways that students vary have connections or dimensions that matter for learning. During the course of the year as students grow, the ways in which they vary are constantly changing. Teacher effort to perceive student variability must therefore be a continuous process where teachers learn about students with some depth and make connections among students and the teacher. In addition to learning from students, teachers need to revise their understanding of students to reflect changes in students.

When we think of engaging everyone in our diverse classes, we imagine a three-dimensional network, with new connections lighting up continuously. Academic diversity is a dynamic network of strengths, needs, and interests that both facilitate and sometimes block or challenge learning within different contexts. These student characteristics are situational, related to the individual learning task, and not fixed attributes of a learner. Strong causal conversation skills with friends might facilitate project work in small groups, but might pose a challenge for students responding to academic questions spontaneously during a structured literature discussion or when giving a speech for an audience. Being adept at academic writing in Spanish might present both a strength and a challenge when writing in English because of the different cultural expectations for the structure of a written text.

Student characteristics on the extremes are specific to the task and the topic being taught. Because the extremes are related to each learning task, teachers are in a continuous cycle of perceiving student strengths that facilitate learning and eliminating or avoiding challenges to effective and efficient learning. Classroom routines enable teachers to find time during daily lessons to listen and observe students as they learn, continuously perceiving student strengths and needs, and recognizing the ever-changing student extremes within the context of specific learning tasks. This ability to listen and look is vital to ensuring all learners are learning every day, because teachers can only respond to what they perceive in the classroom. Learning from students is a foundational teacher habit essential to differentiating or adjusting instruction. All adjustments to instruction are based on teacher perception of student learning needs, so routine efforts to notice, expand, and revise our perceptions of students are necessary before we begin to make instructional decisions.

The Classroom Routines highlighted in this chapter, *Jot Notes*, *Traction Planner*, and several routines to support the daily teaching habit of recording student responses all increase our awareness of our knowledge of students and invite us to draw on student strengths in our lesson plans. For example, you might revise one activity or question each week to learn more about your students. The activity could be a question on an exit card, an opportunity to draw a picture, or a three-minute individual conference where students share something they enjoy outside of school. Students could be asked to place a stamp or a sticker on their work to show a skill that they used, such as thinking, listening, or focusing. Another way to learn from students is to ask students to teach you or the class a game that they know or how to say something in a language that they speak. Finally, by saving records of student responses, you, as well as students, can notice patterns in their thinking, language, and understanding. The responses provide a means to learn more about students and precisely adjust instruction to meet learning needs.

Classroom Routines provide necessary observation and listening time to help teachers expand their perceptions of students in every unit throughout the year. This is a shift from getting to know students in the first unit of the year and then jumping into the curriculum, to an intentional, planned effort to continuously learn from and about students to strategically build new learning onto the foundations that are present. Our perceptions inform our expectations, so making our perceptions visible to ourselves and pursuing learning with and from our students is fundamental in providing precise, effective, and efficient differentiated instruction.

Try Classroom Routines

Precise, Effective, Efficient Learning for All

Plan: Traction Planner

In planning, the *Traction Planner* prepares our thinking prior to unit and lesson planning to recognize our own and student characteristics that can strengthen or challenge learning. The traction planner asks teachers to jot down the objectives for a unit or topic of study in the center of the circle. Then the teacher brainstorms student strengths that connect to the objectives. The attention is focused on passions of both the teacher and the students, listing all the things that might be interesting, valuable, useful, and meaningful about these objectives.

ALL-ED Classroom Routine Directions: Traction Planner—Teacher Planning

This planner is designed to focus our attention on the strengths that **students and teachers** bring to a unit of study. The *Traction Planner* helps teachers envision practical, concrete ways to increase the relevance of a unit of study. (See Figure 2.2.)

Strengths of this routine:

- reflects teacher perceptions
- sets frame or lens for planning
- can be adapted and completed by students.

Implementation Directions

Objective: Root the new learning of a unit in strengths (planning like an environmentally conscious land developer).

Starting Position: Complete the *Jot Notes* activity (Starting Position for this chapter).

Criteria

- *Must Haves*: Connections to Objectives are reasonable.
- *Amazing*: Connections include a wide variety of skills, strengths, and interests shared by individuals as well as groups of students.

Action Pattern

The teacher follows these directions in planning:

1 Identify the goals for the unit of study: the core understanding, knowledge, and skills that students will learn.
2 Build new learning from a base of student strengths and student and teacher passions related to the goals of the unit of study.
3 Consider connections from the goals of the unit to student everyday life and the importance of this topic for both now and the future.
4 Identify student needs and learning the hardest part of the unit. Use the information from two and three to support student needs and learning the hardest part of the unit.

<u>**Reflections**</u>

1   Share your *Traction Planner* with a colleague asking them to add at least two ideas to your planner of additional strengths, skills, and interests of your students and yourself that connect to your topic.
2   Connect these ideas and possibly revise to strengthen connections, the major assessments, or activities in the unit.

Traction Planner

Unit Title _____

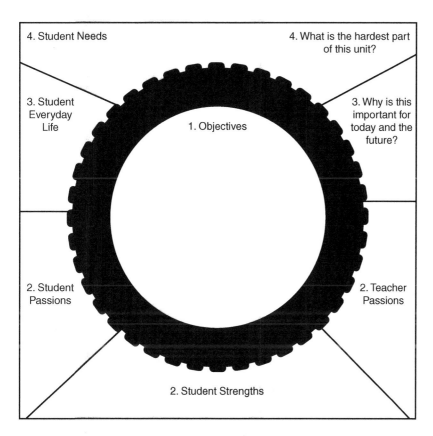

Figure 2.2 Traction Planner

It is important to consider strengths and passions with a wide scope. Some characteristics may be less valued during lessons, such as texting or talking with friends, but include those and any other ideas that relate to the objectives in this brainstorm. Literally, you are rooting the objectives in the strengths and passions that you and your students bring to the classroom to help you see how learning will build on previous learning and offers traction to launch new understanding.

After rooting the objectives for a unit of study in teacher and student strengths, then you will make connections between the objectives and student everyday life and predict how mastering these objectives may be useful for the students' futures. Finally, you will identify the hardest part of the unit and learning needs for accomplishing these objectives that you can already predict using what you already know about your students. This *Traction Planner* supports teachers in building on strengths, leveraging previous learning to gain new learning, and identifying from the onset where time will be needed to meet student learning needs.

Teach: Domino Discover Before Calling on Raised Hands

After asking a question and providing time for students to discuss their responses at a table or in a small group, tell students that they will hear a response from each table from one reporter. As reporters speak, everyone else will be a listener, listening for a teacher-identified goal for listening, such as patterns, vocabulary words, text evidence, or other teacher-tailored instruction. Each person in the group prepares to be the reporter, perhaps by jotting down one response and two backup ideas. The reporter's responses should be brief so that each group can be heard and listeners can remember what was said. The teacher calls on one reporter from each group, enforcing the "Add or Repeat" rule; responses can confirm something that was already said, but the reporter has to acknowledge who said it, or responses can contribute a new idea. Record student responses as each group shares on a list visible to all students. Reminding students of the listening goal helps students discuss and organize responses. Following the *Domino Discover*, allow students to raise their hands to add additional ideas. Invite students to offer compliments to groups by referencing posted criteria for high quality responses.

Why use *Domino Discover* before calling on raised hands? *Domino Discover* promotes inclusive equitable engagement in classrooms where students have diverse learning needs, because teachers ensure that all students have an equal opportunity for their voice to be heard. Engagement increases as every student knows that they will have a turn to share their thinking, or that their ideas will be represented by a group reporter. As engagement increases so does thinking, because all students are accountable to think about a response to questions. This gives students more opportunities in class to purposefully use academic vocabulary and to gain immediate feedback on their ideas. Finally, *Domino Discover* provides an efficient means to collect and organize formative assessment data from the class that teachers can use to tailor instruction to better meet the needs of students.

ALL-ED Classroom Routine Directions: Domino Discover

Domino Discover equitably gathers responses from all members of a class or group. In *Domino Discover*, representatives from each group (Table or Group reporters) share out a response while the teacher records answers on chart paper, chalk/whiteboard, or projected slide or document. Additional responses are gathered from individual students following the representatives.

Strengths of this routine:

- equity in gathering student responses
- students practice using oral language, vocabulary, and listening

- students learn from many students in the class
- students are up, moving, and having fun
- students have a reason to listen.

Implementation Directions

Objective: To find patterns and surprises among student responses.

Starting Positions: Individuals consider a response to a question. You may use the *List, Draw, Write* routine.

Criteria

- *Must Haves:* Uses the word "because," explains with detail, includes visual representation of ideas.
- *Amazing:* Makes connection to previous unit or current events, uses vocabulary from word wall.

Action Pattern

Directions: The teacher identifies in the directions:

- **Roles:** Speaker and Listeners
- **Turns:** Teacher selects students who will go first and second in each group, establishing the direction for each member of the group to take turns sharing their response one at a time.
- **Rules:** "Add or repeat"—students can add new ideas or repeat another student. This supports the speaker—when someone is the speaker and they need a response to share (for example, if a student was absent or late and doesn't have the Starting Position to share out) then someone in the group can let the group member use their response—this rule ensures that all students practice speaking on the topic.
- **Time:** Each student speaks for a set amount of time (ranging anywhere from ten seconds to two minutes, depending on the length of the response and class time).

1 State a reason for listening or an Objective.
2 Decide who will share first in the group (individuals sharing at a table or reporters sharing a response to represent their group).
3 Point to the person that will go second, establishing the direction for each person to share one after another.
4 Take turns completing the task until everyone has gone, one after the other, like dominoes falling.
5 Ask each person in the group to share their response (usually the Starting Position).
6 Record student responses (capture responses on the board/chart/computer).

Reflections

1   Take a few minutes to notice patterns and surprises that learners noticed as well as pose questions.
2   Ask students to generate compliments to reporters using specific criteria.
3   Ask students for feedback about the process, suggestions, adjustment, or new rules for the next *Domino Discover*.
4   Adjust instruction based on student responses.

Adjust Instruction: Inclusive Directions

Use *Inclusive Directions* to adjust group learning routines to fit learner needs in addition to structuring the routine with OSCAR. There are four parts to *Inclusive Directions*: roles, turns, rules, and time. We refer to this as *Inclusive Directions* when each of these parts are identified, because being specific with students increases clarity of the outcome and behaviors expected. In addition, these parts can be adjusted to fit learning needs. For example, you can assign students who were absent to take the last turn in sharing a response with their small group. You might also state a rule of "Add or Repeat," meaning that students could repeat a response spoken by another student or add a new idea. In this way, all students can meaningfully participate in the group discussion, whether absent or present the day before. The more specific you are with roles, turns, rules, and time, the greater the possibilities for challenging and engaging all learners. As discussed above in the research section, roles involve designating who will be the listener and the speaker. A recorder and/or a reporter or group representative may be added to share the results of the group's collaboration with the class. Managerial roles, such as materials gatherer or clean-up, should be used before or after a group learning routine but not during. During group learning routines, the roles should be essential to furthering discussion. There always needs to be a reason to listen to a speaker or students will not know what to listen for and remember.

"Turns" means to simply identify who is going first as the speaker in each group. This resolves problems with social loafing and wasted time, as students negotiate who is going to go first. The turns should always be assigned by the teacher to reach an instructional goal. For example, there may be times when you would want to assign a student with a question to begin. There may also be times when you want a student with a correct and complete answer to begin. By assigning a student to start the group conversation for a particular reason, teachers can move group discussions efficiently toward the instructional goal.

Rules are made to ensure rigor and access for all students. For example, a rule of "Point and Repeat" enables students who are still forming a response and those who are new to speaking in English to simply point to a student to have that student repeat what they said. In this way, every student can engage in the group's discussion. As the year progresses, rules can change to ensure the routine maintains rigor for students. So, our rule of "Point and Repeat" might shift to "Point, Repeat, Repeat" or "Point, Repeat, Add or Repeat" to ensure that all students are using academic oral language in the group discussion.

Finally, time is always designated to ensure equity in opportunities, to share ideas in the class, and to protect time to think about responses before being required to reply. Time may be kept by the teacher using a watch, or a timer may be used.

Time should always be designated and kept for each individual to share and for all group members to think about what was heard before moving on to more sharing. There should also be free discussion time during every group learning routine. Keeping time enables a teacher to shorten time when students are just developing their responses, so that students can give a partial response and be successful. It also enables a teacher to extend time to foster longer explanations from students. Another advantage to keeping time is that group learning routines never run over the time allotted in a lesson, because time is kept for each part of the routine.

Teachers use the four parts of *Inclusive Directions*—roles, rules, turns, and time—to ensure equity and engagement for all learners during small group discussions. There are sample dilemmas in Chapter 8 where you can practice adjusting roles, turns, rules, and time to eliminate challenges and increase rigor and student learning from the group routine.

Checklist to Try Routines in Your Teaching

See https://www.routledge.com/9780815370819 for additional resources: *Domino Discover* Step by Step Directions, Knowing Your Students, and Printable *Traction Planner*.

Plan	Teach	Adjust Instruction
❏ Traction Planner	❏ Domino Discover	❏ Inclusive Directions

Quality Criteria to Implement Classroom Routines

Must Haves	Amazing
• Notice student strengths in planning and in the classroom. • Increase time spent reflecting in planning and in the classroom. • Share the results of these routines with a friend and discuss your observations about student responses. • Shift task structure on a daily or weekly basis, or tie a specific structure to a type of instruction, such as a mini-lesson, independent practice, or review.	• Implement an activity or question aimed at learning from and about students in every lesson. • Stretch your thinking and perceptions about students. • Stretch student perceptions about themselves. • Encourage student ownership by asking students to assist in recording responses or managing the collection.

Chapter Reflection

Chapter Summary

In this chapter we answered the question, "Why do we need to adjust or differentiate instruction?" To accomplish this objective, we identified our starting positions with the *Jot Notes* routine to consider teacher perceptions of student characteristics that vary widely, creating extremes that are challenging to engage within time and curriculum constraints. We examined statistics that speak to the increasing range of student ethnic and academic diversity, which confirms teacher perception of the wide range and diversity of student strengths and needs that impact effective learning in every lesson. We provided classroom routines to launch daily differentiated instruction. For planning instruction, we highlighted how the *Traction Planner* routine can build our awareness of the relationships between student characteristics that we perceive and the required curriculum. We also described how shifting structures allows teachers to listen to and observe students, while students receive feedback on their thinking from peers. By using shifting structures, you began to develop agile teacher responses to student needs as learning occurred during lessons. We encouraged you to adjust instruction by planning to learn from your students in every lesson before you began teaching. Finally, we asked you to return to your starting position of how your perceptions of students reflect on learning and plan the next steps toward ensuring all learners are learning every day.

Learning Journal: Record Important Takeaways

In your *Learning Journal*, track your thinking about meeting the needs of diverse learners by answering the same four questions we presented in Chapter 1:

1   What was most interesting and useful for you in this chapter?
2   Why was this interesting and useful?
3   How does this connect to what you know about meeting the learning needs of all learners?
4   What research from this chapter could you use to explain or support decisions to adjust instruction?

Save these responses for reflection after reading more of this book and trying out ideas in your classroom.

Return to Your Starting Position

Return to your chart of student characteristics that impact learning in your subject area. Add and adjust characteristics that may be important when planning instruction. Consider how these characteristics might change and how you along with the students will notice the changes throughout the school year. Consider ways to document student characteristics through student work, photos of learning, and video to facilitate noticing changes in a way similar to our opening story.

Now, go all the way back to our chapter question, "Why do we need differentiated instruction?" Reread your preliminary first draft answer to our chapter question. Consider how your answer has been confirmed, changed, or challenged after reading this chapter and trying out the classroom routines in your planning and practice with students. Add new ideas to your answer or revise it in another way. Circle the most important part and save it to return to after Chapter 8. Now that we know why we need differentiated instruction, let us turn our attention to our next chapter, step one of our framework, **Identify OSCAR.**

Note

1 For those of you who are interested in further exploring your biases, we would recommend looking into the implicit association test. https://implicit.harvard.edu

Chapter 3

Step 1
Identify OSCAR

Overview

Objective:

What are the adjustable parts of every lesson?

Think: Make a list of the parts of lessons from your school's lesson template, a curriculum guide, or of lessons that you remember from your own schooling. Put a star next to a part that is usually consistent for all students.

Criteria:

- Identify the adjustable parts, OSCAR, in a lesson or activity.
- Explain the research of self-regulated learning in connection to adjustable parts.
- Try Classroom Routines:
    - Plan—Identify OSCAR in lesson plans.
    - Teach—*Think, Talk, Open Exchange (TTO)*.
    - Adjust Instruction—Criteria Checklist.

Starting Position: Exploring Successful Learning

Take a moment to think about a successful learning experience that you have had in the past. Use the individual routine *List, Write, Draw* to record your successful learning experience. Describe in detail what you were learning, where you were learning, who was there and teaching, why you were learning, how learning was happening, and when you were learning and for how long. Underline the parts that explain why this experience was successful. Share your experience with a friend or a colleague to determine if there are common qualities in learning experiences that successfully engage all learners. Continue asking others about their experiences until you can compile a top ten list of qualities that ensure that all learners are learning. Compare your list to the list we compiled by asking classroom teachers. We will return to this list at the end of this chapter.

Qualities of Experiences Where All Learners Are Learning Relevant Content

- Meaningful topic
- Captures interest
- Safe risk-taking

- Clear expectations
- Known product
- Community
- Engaging
- Physical or active
- Goal oriented
- Visible progress
- Ongoing feedback

From the Classroom: Oscar Teaches Us How to Engage the Extremes

Remember Oscar? We described him in the introduction to this book—he's the student from the Bronx who felt like he "knew nothing" when he didn't understand lessons. Remember Oscar's teacher, Ms. Ford? She's the dedicated teacher who we found literally sweating, running from student to student offering help. In this chapter, we return to Oscar's story to address the question, "How can we ensure that Oscar never leaves class confused?"

What Are the Adjustable Lesson Parts of Every Lesson?

Think for a moment about the driver's seat in a car. Car seats adjust to ensure that all drivers, who vary on many different dimensions, can reach the controls. We can use the parts of lessons, like the levers in car seats, to make adjustments to ensure a good fit for learners. To find these parts or levers, just think of the letters OSCAR, the name of our student. OSCAR is both our student and his name is a mnemonic for the adjustable parts in every lesson: O stands for Objective, S stands for Starting Position, C stands for Criteria, A stands for Action Pattern, and R stands for Reflections. We can extend the range of students able to engage in every learning activity by adjusting one or more of these parts.

Objective

The Objective is the goal for the lesson or activity. Goals are sometimes written as "*Students will be able to* ____" where the teacher fills in what students will learn in the lesson. Or goals may be written from the student perspective as learning targets, such as "*I can* _____." Regardless of how the goal is written, it should be visible to students like a destination on a map—clear, visible, and meaningful to achieve. Objectives may be broken down into parts, creating opportunities for students to set goals specific to their needs within the required standards. Objectives should be *clear, accessible, rigorous, and relevant* (CARR) for all students. Teachers can use the reflection questions in the Objective Planning Chart (see Table 3.1) to revise objectives from lesson and unit plans to increase the ways learners can relate to and use the objectives as a vehicle for engagement.

Starting Position

The Starting Position is simply taking a moment to note where you are before embarking on a journey or before trying to make a change. Think about any time that you have made a change in your life; noting a starting position was essential.

Table 3.1 Objective Planning Chart

Objective	
Clarity	Is the objective stated in words memorable for students? Why does this objective matter?
Access	Are attainable parts identified within goals?
Rigor	What are the challenging parts of the objective? What kind of thinking is required to accomplish this objective?
Relevance	What will students find interesting, important, and valuable in this objective? How does this objective leverage student strengths? How will students use the objective throughout the lesson?

Table 3.2 Starting Position Planning Chart

Starting Position	
Clarity	What questions do students have about this topic? Are there misunderstandings I need to address? How will the starting position alert students who have an "illusion of knowing"?
Access	Will they all understand the vocabulary?
Rigor	Are the starting positions the same for all students? How will I intrigue students with more comfort or knowledge with this topic?
Relevance	What is their prior knowledge? How will students feel confident about learning the topic?

Before starting an exercise program, for example, it is often useful to note your starting weight and resting heart rate so that you can judge how daily exercises impact those important markers. When you embark on a trip, noting a starting position enables you to measure the distance that you have traveled. When using a GPS, a starting position allows the GPS to recommend alternate routes.

In much the same way of these examples, starting positions provide students with a necessary marker to measure their learning. In the classroom and as we have modeled at the start of every chapter, starting positions can be as simple as asking students to circle three familiar words or star the hardest question. A simple pre-assessment where students are given two minutes to start a worksheet on their own and note progress before finishing by working at a table with peers is a common starting position that we often use in lessons. Starting positions can be completed individually or in groups to activate and further background knowledge. In addition to being essential for student learning, starting positions provide a vehicle for teachers to adjust instruction. For example, student responses to starting positions may be gathered so that teachers can make in-the-moment adjustments, such as asking students to raise their hand for the problem that looks the most challenging and then adjusting to model that problem on the board (see Table 3.2 *The Starting Position Planning Chart*).

Criteria

Criteria are the qualities that you want to see in students' work. Quality criteria help students know the requirements or *Must Haves* and *Amazing* qualities that challenge students, especially early finishers, to go beyond the requirements. *Must Haves* ensure that all students are focused on reaching the required standards. *Must*

Table 3.3 Criteria Planning Chart

Criteria	
Clarity	How will students know the criteria needed for high quality work? Will they use a chart, checklist, rubric, model, or other tool?
Access	What are the *Must Haves* (i.e., those things that all students should be able to do or understand by the end of each activity/lesson)? What adjustments will be needed to ensure that all learners are able to use the criteria to guide their work? (e.g., Should some images or example student work be provided along with the language in the rubric? Or should key vocabulary be defined with images?)
Rigor	How will students be challenged to reach beyond the *Must Haves* for *Amazing* criteria?
Relevance	How will students receive feedback and self-reflect on the qualities in their work, process for learning, and plans for next steps?

Haves may include, for example, required vocabulary, the word "because," using sentence structures, or supporting with evidence. *Amazing* criteria may include using advanced vocabulary, providing alternate strategies or perspectives, and including all group members in a response. *Amazing* criteria provide room to extend expectations ensuring that all students are challenged (see Table 3.3 *The Criteria Planning Chart*).

Action Patterns

Action Patterns are the steps of the lesson plan. What makes an action pattern different is that classroom routines (individual and group) are attached to the types of instruction that occur regularly, such as introduction to new units, mini-lessons, review, experiments, tests, team challenges, and discussion circles. Teachers use the same action pattern to save time spent on giving directions and transitions during lessons. This also helps students like Oscar to focus their attention on what they are learning because the directions are known, freeing up working memory. Routines work like a dashboard in a car because routines enable students to learn without teacher management or direction, freeing the teacher to look at the dashboard. Routines are also used to collect responses from students on key elements similar to the way a dashboard displays data on critical features needed for effective driving (see Table 3.4 *The Action Pattern Planning Chart*).

Table 3.4 Action Pattern Planning Chart

Action Pattern	
Clarity	How do I ensure that *all* students are participating (and that there is no socializing with friends)?
Access	How can I make sure that students feel comfortable participating (and that they feel like they can participate)?
Rigor	How much time are students focusing on listening, speaking, writing, reading, and thinking? How many parts are involved in this routine? Do the parts fit together in more than one way?
Relevance	How can I promote productive group collaborations where students help each other learn?

Table 3.5 Reflections Planning Chart

Reflections	
Clarity	How will students know what to look for and monitor in their learning?
Access	How will students remember feedback that was offered and/or apply the feedback in their learning?
Rigor	How have students used Criteria (including both *Must Haves* and *Amazing*) to monitor and improve their process and products?
Relevance	How have students documented their progress and plans for next steps?

Reflections

Reflections are when students go back to their starting position and describe how their thinking has stayed the same, been challenged, changed, or added to during the lesson. Reflections are like a photo album of a trip, documenting the journey and providing a starting place for future trips. When teachers explicitly teach OSCAR to students in lessons, they are literally giving students a steering wheel enabling them to take greater responsibility and independence in pursuing their own learning. At the same time, OSCAR provides the adjustable parts that teachers use to engage, value, stretch, and inspire every learner (see Table 3.5 *The Reflections Planning Chart*).

Let's Help Oscar

Now that we've identified the elements of OSCAR, let's return to our problem of practice—"*How can we ensure that Oscar never leaves class confused?*" In this section, we detail exactly what we did using OSCAR, to solve this problem of practice. In much the same way, you, too, can apply the OSCAR framework to help other students like Oscar in your class.

First, we imagined success—we imagined Oscar leaving class with clarity; being able to describe what he had learned. Then we thought backwards from that vision all the way to Oscar's current starting position of feeling like he missed everything that happened in class. By moving backwards from our vision of Oscar's success, we were able to identify the required parts needed for him to increase clarity on the subject matter and access to promote his engagement in the learning activities. For example, we knew that Oscar would need to be clear on the learning objective, literally beginning with the end goal clearly visible in his mind. Then he would need to figure out his starting position so that he could build metacognitive awareness by clarifying what he already knows about the objective. To begin his journey toward self-regulation, we also thought that he would need to reflect on the distance between his starting position and the objective. In this way he could return to his starting position to reflect by describing how his position has changed as a result of the lesson.

Second, we realized that we needed to find a way to accomplish this efficiently during daily lessons. So we developed a routine that required little verbal teacher direction to reduce the effort Oscar had to spend on understanding what to do during the lesson, freeing up important and limited working memory space, and increasing his time using English to talk about math. In collaboration with his teacher, we decided to implement a group learning routine called *Think, Talk, Open Exchange (TTO)* before and after every mini-lesson to increase clarity and access for all students.

During *TTO*, students meet in assigned groups of three (triad stations) with mixed abilities in language, background knowledge, and math skills. The teacher simply puts up a sample problem for the day's lesson and the students in their triad stations complete the *TTO* routine, taking turns around in a circle pointing out one thing that was familiar, such as an equals sign or the number two, and something new or surprising, such as an unknown variable or a negative sign. Following a round where each person shares one idea, the students have a short discussion to list things that they think they know about this problem.

To ensure that all students can participate, the teacher asks students who have something to share to speak first. She also set a rule of "Add or Repeat" so that students can repeat or confirm the idea shared by another student or add a new idea. Newcomers are encouraged to use the rule, "Point and Repeat," where they point to a student who has spoken before and that student repeats what was said. In this way, all students can engage in the small group of three.

Because this routine is completed before and after a mini-lesson in the same assigned groups, the teacher is free to listen and observe students talking about math. For example, important misunderstandings are revealed through these short three- to five-minute discussions, such as the teacher heard students using the word "two" instead of "squared." After the mini-lesson, the groups form again for a quick round where each student shares the most important thing that they learned and the group has a short conversation to discuss patterns in their learning and any surprise takeaways from the lesson.

Oscar now has a good idea of what the lesson will be about before the lesson begins and he knows that if he gets lost with the English spoken during the lesson, his triad station partners will repeat the most important points during *TTO* helping him understand what was missed during the lesson. The five minutes of *TTO*, a structured group learning routine, decreases the time that the teacher spends reviewing and answering questions, so the lesson fits into the 40-minute period.

Never Leave Class Confused

TTO in assigned triad stations provides a routine way for Oscar to understand the objective, identify his starting position, and return to the starting position to reflect on his learning from the lesson. Without making any other changes to the lesson, *TTO* routinely stretches the teacher's ability to adjust instruction to reach students on the extreme range of fluency in English. Oscar no longer leaves confused. In addition, the teacher reports teaching more lessons each week because she spends far less time explaining and repeating information to the whole class. Most importantly, students are engaged in talking about math in every lesson. Designing for the edges seemed to benefit everyone in the class, including Ms. Ford.

ALL-ED Classroom Routine Directions: Think, Talk, Open Exchange (TTO)—Group Structure

Think, Talk, Open Exchange provides time for each student to share a response with two peers. When students have longer responses, it is helpful to form groups of three or "triad stations" to share responses. *TTO* ensures equity and opportunity for every student to use academic vocabulary in class. *TTO* is different from *Domino Discover* (Chapter 2) because after each student has spoken, students discuss their responses in an unstructured conversation called Open Exchange. During Open Exchange, students gain greater clarity when peers answer questions or review the main points from a reading or mini-lesson, or describe connections to the lesson to develop greater meaning. The teacher listens and observes students talking during *TTO*. Often, *TTO* is preceded by an individual routine to develop a response to share such as *List, Write, Draw* (Chapter 1) or *Criteria Checklist* (Chapter 3) to reflect on their work before sharing. *TTO* is often followed by a *Domino Discover* to gather one response from each group of three students. Gathering responses from each group takes less time than gathering from each individual student and there are fewer responses for teachers to synthesize to determine how to adjust instruction next. Strengths of this routine:

- promotes critical thinking
- encourages collaboration
- requires students to use and develop language skills
- engages students because the talk part is non-threatening so students are inclined to participate
- serves different purposes such as clarifies student confusions, corrects homework, checks for understanding, and generates ideas efficiently through this routine.

Implementation Directions

Objective: Build understanding through discussion.

Starting Positions (individually and then in small groups):

Individually: Students complete a learning activity such as a *List, Write, Draw* or *Criteria Checklist* to prepare a response to share with a small group.

Groups: The teacher assigns students into groups of three with a range of student skill and background knowledge levels in each group. The teacher designates where in the room each group of three will meet, with the students sitting or standing knee to knee and eye to eye—so that it is easier to hear each student in the group.

Criteria

- *Must Haves*: Answers the prompt, explains your thinking.
- *Amazing*: Answer/response to the question uses vocabulary from our word wall.

Action Pattern

The teacher identifies in the directions:

Roles: One Speaker, Two Listeners, One Timekeeper (can be the facilitator for the entire group or one of the listeners. It is useful to set a timer so that no one has to watch a clock.)

Note: *Whenever a participant's task is* **to listen** *then the participant* **cannot talk.**

- **Turns:** The teacher assigns one student in each group to "Go first" stating a fact from the text and then the student who will go second and third.
- **Rules:** "Add or Repeat" students can repeat an answer from a previous student or add a new response.
- **Time:** The teacher times each round so that all groups move through the routine at the same pace.

Starting Position: Initial Thoughts

1   Prepare initial thoughts to share with the group.

Actions: Think—Talk—Repeat—Open Exchange

1   **Determine** who is going first in small groups sitting knee to knee and eye to eye, or standing in a huddle with toes facing in.
2   **Think:** Direct students to think about what they will say if they are the speaker and why they are listening if they are the listener.
3   **Talk:** Speaker: describes a response to a question, the most important ideas from a lesson or a text, a summary, or a memory of an experience. Listener: listens without interrupting, paying attention to a specific purpose such as listening for patterns and surprises, vocabulary words (we call vocabulary words buzzwords), feelings, or connections to important ideas or other units. Only the speaker talks during this time period. If the speaker finishes before the time is up then the group uses the extra time to think.
4   **Think:** Everyone takes time to think about what they heard. During think time learners may jot down questions, record connections, patterns, and surprises, and take notes.
5   **Repeat steps two through four** (changing roles so that everyone has a chance to be the Speaker).
6   **Open Exchange:** Discuss patterns in what was shared. Ask questions to clarify and probe ideas. The only rule is that everyone must both give and take ideas.

Reflections

Individually: Return to the initial thoughts in the starting position. Reflect on how the *TTO* confirmed and added to thinking. Annotate and revise starting position to add, confirm, and change the record of thinking based on learning through *TTO*.

Whole Class: Use a *Domino Discover* to quickly collect one summary response from every group of three or triad station. Use this list of recorded responses to adjust the next steps of instruction in the lesson.

The *TTO* structure is based on the Micro Lab Protocol from the National School Reform website. http://www.nsrfharmony.org/protocol/doc/microlabs.pdf

OSCAR *in Every Lesson*

So, the first step to engaging all learners in inclusive classrooms every day is to see OSCAR in every lesson. Begin by envisioning a student who is currently leaving class confused or bored as a successful learner. Then identify the five adjustable parts: objectives, starting position, criteria, action pattern, and reflections to determine where a routine shift will engage all learners. In Oscar's case, our first step was to envision Oscar's success and the desired result of our instruction—Oscar never leaving class confused. Second, we identified the adjustable parts of the lesson. We kept everything consistent and only identified the opening and closing of the mini-lesson as places where some students needed greater clarity. Third, we adjusted the actions of the mini-lesson for a better fit for all learners. In this case, we added *TTO* before and after a mini-lesson as a routine action pattern. We used this routine action pattern reliably when mini-lessons were being taught. We ensured that Oscar never left class confused through *TTO*.

It is important to note that the first move was not to make two versions, an easy and a hard, of a worksheet, or to put Oscar on a computer program to practice basic skills even though we might use those strategies to develop specific skills in an occasional lesson. Instead, our initial approach was to implement a routine that would reliably adjust instruction to better fit Oscar's need for additional clarity and access on days when instruction included a mini-lesson. Oscar benefitted from this routine as well as his peers.

Rooted in Research: Self-Regulated Learning

OSCAR *Prompts Self-Regulated Learning*

OSCAR and the adjustable parts of lessons stem from the research on self-regulated learning (SRL). As we indicated in Chapter 1, self-regulated learning is commonly defined as a process where learners actively monitor, control, and regulate their thoughts, feelings, and behaviors to achieve self-set learning goals (Pintrich & Zusho, 2007; Zimmerman, 2008). Theoretical models typically describe the process of self-regulated learning in terms of specific phases (see Figure 3.1).

The process of self-regulated learning begins with the planning phase; during this phase, the self-regulated learner activates prior knowledge about the task at hand, and makes decisions about how to go about working—in other words, she sets goals. This phase is followed by the monitoring and control phases, which occur when the self-regulated learner is actually working on the task. During these phases, the self-regulated learner will monitor the extent to which he feels that he is making progress toward his learning goals, and when found wanting, change his strategies to stay on track. The last phase is the reflection phase, which occurs after the task has been completed, whereby self-regulated learners consider how well their strategies worked, and what changes need to be made to improve their performance in the future.

It is important to note that researchers do not necessarily assume that all learning occurs in the explicit manner depicted in Figure 3.1. Of course, there are instances where learning can occur more implicitly without following these phases, and earlier phases may come before later ones. Nevertheless, it is a useful method to summarize the theory and research on SRL, and to observe how OSCAR corresponds to these theoretical models.

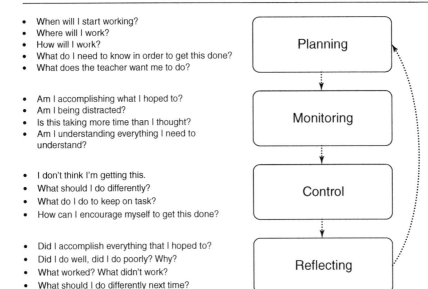

- When will I start working?
- Where will I work?
- How will I work?
- What do I need to know in order to get this done?
- What does the teacher want me to do?

- Am I accomplishing what I hoped to?
- Am I being distracted?
- Is this taking more time than I thought?
- Am I understanding everything I need to understand?

- I don't think I'm getting this.
- What should I do differently?
- What do I do to keep on task?
- How can I encourage myself to get this done?

- Did I accomplish everything that I hoped to?
- Did I do well, did I do poorly? Why?
- What worked? What didn't work?
- What should I do differently next time?

Figure 3.1 Theoretical Model of Self-Regulated Learning.

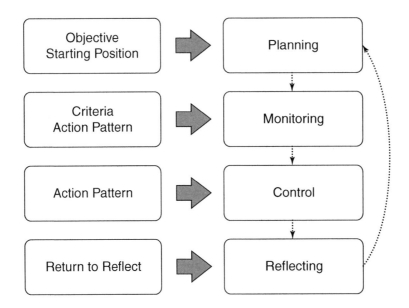

Figure 3.2 Relationship between OSCAR and Self-Regulated Learning.

Figure 3.2 depicts the relationship between OSCAR and our theoretical model of SRL. When the objective of the lesson is clear, accessible, rigorous, and relevant and when the starting position is made observable, it assists Oscar to plan and set appropriate goals more effectively. The quality criteria and the action pattern, in turn, helps Oscar monitor and control his learning—to observe whether or not he is making progress toward his goals, or whether or not he needs to make some adjustments. Finally, the action of returning to reflect helps Oscar evaluate his learning and determine next steps. In short, OSCAR helps Oscar become a self-regulated learner (see also Figure 3.3 *Top Ten Facts about SRL*).

Top Ten Facts about Self-Regulated Learning (SRL)

1   Self-regulated students—that is students who reflect on their thinking, set appropriate goals and plan for learning, monitor progress towards those goals, and adjust or regulate their thinking, motivation, and study habits—are more likely to achieve academic success than those who do not (Pintrich & Zusho, 2007; Zimmerman, 1990).

2   SRL skills are learned skills that can be modified and improved, thus making it an ideal target for intervention at any age level.

3   The use of SRL-related strategies (e.g., goal-setting, monitoring, evaluating) should improve performance in any subject domain (e.g., reading, writing, mathematics, chemistry, biology, psychology, and even physical education) and at any grade level. Younger students may need more support with regulation.

4   Students who feel more confident (but not overconfident) about the subject and their academic skills are more likely to use self-regulatory strategies. Asking students to self-assess and monitor their progress helps to develop their perceptions of competence.

5   For students to regulate their learning effectively, they must also have adequate knowledge about the task and its requirements, the subject domain, and knowledge of strategies.

6   Students are more likely to regulate their learning when they have adequate resources available, including time, effective and supportive teachers and peers, as well as access to supplementary learning materials.

7   The use of SRL strategies is strongly associated with a growth mindset. Students who believe that intelligence is changeable are more likely to use SRL strategies.

8   Students are more likely to regulate their learning when they are prompted to do so, either directly (through instruction) or indirectly (through feedback or activity prompts). Specifically, research shows that periodic self-assessments that ask students to reflect on what they know or do not know about a topic, and their depth of knowledge about key points promotes regulation of learning.

9   Differentiated instruction is easier when students support the effort by assessing their progress, seek help when needed, and pursue learning goals independently.

10 The ALL-ED routines and OSCAR are central to fostering self-regulated learners.

Figure 3.3 Top Ten Facts about Self-Regulated Learning (SRL).

Try Classroom Routines: Precise, Effective, Efficient Learning for All

Plan: Identify OSCAR in a Lesson Plan

Read a lesson plan that you are about to teach. Identify how students will be able to see OSCAR and begin to identify places where instruction could be adjusted to meet diverse learner needs by asking yourself the following questions in Table 3.6.

Table 3.6 Identify the Adjustable Parts of Every Lesson

Adjustable Parts of Every Lesson	Is this part consistent for all students or are there adjustable parts? Note everything does not have to be adjustable. Adjust parts to increase clarity, access, rigor, and relevance.	How and when are students asked to think with or use this part of the lesson to help them learn?
Objective	Are there specific achievable parts within the objective that can be identified and accomplished as milestones during the lesson?	What are students asked to do with the objective? What type of thinking is required when students are working specifically with the objective? For example, are they copying the objective from the board or are they thinking about a time when they remember working on this objective before or circling a surprising word in the objective and then explaining their surprise to a partner?
Starting Position	Will all students be able to engage in the starting position task? If not, then how could the task be adjusted to ensure all students are able to engage?	What activity in the lesson serves as the starting position? This could be the opening activity or the exit card from the day before. The starting position could be feedback from a test or project or a pre-assessment. A short free table discussion with a recorder taking notes could serve as a starting position for a group of students.
Criteria	What are the required qualities or *Must Haves* and the *Amazing* criteria for the products that students produce during the lesson? Products could be questions, discussions, problems, solutions, actions, writing, and feedback.	Are there *Must Haves* and *Amazing* criteria that are attainable by all students?
Action Pattern	How are individual and group learning routines used during the lesson?	When in the lesson are students working autonomously either individually or in groups so that the teacher is able to listen and observe learning?
Reflection	When during the lesson are students prompted to reflect to monitor their learning and evaluate their process and product in relation to the objective? Would some students need help or prompts to be able to use the criteria to reflect on their learning?	How will students measure progress and use this reflection to plan next steps?

Teach: Criteria Checklist

Criteria Checklist. Making visible to students criteria to guide the quality of their work prompts self-regulated learning, increases student autonomy, and provides levers to adjust how students are focused on learning through a common activity. Required and optional criteria increase access and rigor for all students when completing common tasks and assignments. Start with stating the *Must Haves* or the criteria that are required and necessary to accomplish the objective. Think beyond these criteria to *Amazing* criteria designed to extend and challenge learners. Include options or choices in the *Amazing* criteria to enable teachers to assign challenge criteria to specific students or groups of students. Invite students to ensure that all *Must Haves* or required criteria are in their work and at least one *Amazing* criteria.

ALL-ED Classroom Routine Directions: Criteria Checklist

Visible criteria for quality enable students to monitor their work and establish a vision for the objective that they are trying to accomplish. *Must Have* criteria identifies the requirements. *Amazing* articulates possibilities for going beyond the requirements. Many times students who have mastered a skill wait for a challenge during lessons. If optional *Amazing* criteria are always articulated in every task then there is always the opportunity to stretch all learners. *Amazing* criteria can be assigned to some or individual students. Students should be asked to use posted criteria to give compliments and suggestions to each other. A purpose for listening during a *Share-Out* routine can be to listen for the *Must Have* and *Amazing* criteria heard in student responses.
Strengths of this routine:

- promotes reflection by comparing a product to criteria
- focuses students on learning from assignments, rather than working to finish
- prompts self-regulated learning
- supports building student feelings of competence
- challenges all students

Implementation Directions

Objective: To use criteria to further learning by finding evidence of quality in your own work.

Starting Position

- Students need a completed or in-progress assignment and criteria.
- *Individually (or with a partner or group):* Students examine the criteria to determine which criteria they will look for in their work.

Criteria

- *Must Haves*: Annotates work for evidence of assigned criteria, explains why evidence shows use of criteria.
- *Amazing*: Annotates work for *Amazing* criteria, explains how annotated evidence could be revised to strengthen or improve the quality, considers adding useful criteria.

Action Pattern

- **Rules:** Must annotate or make suggestions of what should be there to achieve criteria, Offer compliments before suggestions.
- **Time:** Ten minutes for review, five minutes for discussion, five minutes for next-step planning.
- Practice identifying evidence of criteria in sample student work as a whole class or small group.
- Review own work and annotate evidence of quality criteria.

Reflections

- Check in with a partner to confirm accuracy.
- Make plans for next steps.

This individual routine encourages the habit of reflection and using criteria to revise or improve learning.

Action Pattern

- **Rules:** Annotations must refer to actual evidence in the student work.
- **Time:** One to five minutes depending on the length or the work and the number of criteria.

  1 Model the offering compliments and suggestions tying specific criteria to evidence when looking at student work.
  2 Ask students to review their work underlining evidence of a specific criteria.
  3 Ask students to explain why their evidence meets or is working toward the criteria.
  4 Invite students to share their evidence and annotations of quality criteria with peers.

Reflections

- Ask students to set a next step or goal for their next assignment based on their work in this task.
- Use next steps and strengths and needs from this self-assessment to adjust instruction.
- Check self-assessments for accuracy and offer feedback to students.

Adjust Instruction

Notice the difference in these directions, "Complete problems one through five" and "Complete problems one through five, go back to read your work, and circle two vocabulary words that were used that a reader should notice," or "When you think you are finished, then read your work and put a star next to the most interesting answer." Students could routinely "read their work and put a number next to evidence of a quality criteria that they see in their work" as the last step in every assignment. We call this specific action in directions, "Assigning to reflection instead of completion." Assigning to reflect rather than to finish helps students see evidence of their abilities and growth in every assignment. This is an easy first step toward adjusting instruction without making anything new or giving different assignments. Prompting students to routinely reflect promotes effective learning, supports the teacher's perceiving student differences, and provides an opportunity within every assignment for small adjustments of criteria to focus student attention on individual needs.

Checklist to Try Routines in Your Teaching

See https://www.routledge.com/9780815370819 for additional resources: Identify OSCAR in Lesson Plans.

Plan	Teach	Adjust Instruction
❏ Identify OSCAR in your lesson plan visible to your students during lessons.	❏ Think, Talk, Open Exchange (TTO)	❏ Incorporate Criteria Checklist into every lesson. Regularly post Criteria (*Must Haves* or *Required*) to guide students in high quality work. Include *Amazing* criteria (additional or optional) to extend and challenge all learners.

Quality Criteria to Implement Classroom Routines

Must Haves	Amazing
• Classroom routine is implemented on a daily or weekly basis, or is tied to a specific type of instruction, such as a mini-lesson, independent practice, or review. • Identify criteria for high quality work when assigning at least one task in every lesson (for example, the teacher might say before an *Elbow Exchange*: *Must Haves* for high quality listening means that you can repeat what your partner said to you; *Amazing* listening means that you can repeat and build on or ask a question about your partner's idea).	• Return to recorded responses to notice growth with students. • Use recorded responses to tailor instruction by answering questions that were raised or assigning a task or question related to their responses.

Chapter Reflection

Chapter Summary

In this chapter, the story of Oscar helped us identify the adjustable parts of lesson plans. We examined how to increase clarity through an action pattern of a group learning routine before and after a mini-lesson. This resulted in Oscar never leaving class confused. This approach was different than engaging Oscar through an easier version of an activity because this approach can be offered to Oscar routinely every day, not just when the teacher has time to create additional activities. In addition, this recruits Oscar actively in monitoring his own learning, capitalizing on the research of self-regulated learning to engage a student on the extremes of achievement in math. Use these suggestions to try these ideas using classroom routines to engage all learners in your own planning and practice.

Learning Journal: Record Important Takeaways

Continue your *Learning Journal* to track your thinking about meeting the needs of diverse learners by recording answers to the following four questions:

1   What was most interesting and useful for you in this chapter?
2   Why was this interesting and useful?
3   How does this connect to what you know about meeting the learning needs of all learners?
4   What research from this chapter could you use to explain or support decisions to adjust instruction?

Save these responses for reflection after reading more of this book and trying out ideas in your classroom. We will answer these same four questions at the end of every chapter.

Return to Your Starting Position

Return to your reflection of a successful learning experience. Can you identify OSCAR in this experience? What was the objective or goal of the activity? Were you aware of your starting position before you began to learn? How did you know that you were doing good work? What criteria for quality were you aware of? Were you able to use routines to facilitate learning, so you could repeat a process so you could focus on what you were learning, and not the how, or the steps that you were doing? When did you reflect to realize that you learned? Circle one part of your story where adjustments were made to make learning a better fit for you or other learners.

Now, think all the way back to the research on motivation in Chapter 1. Can you remember what ABC+M represents? Autonomy, Belonging, Competence, and Meaning. Go back one more time to your story, annotate with an A times or things that helped you feel independent or autonomous, B for moments where you felt belonging to something beyond yourself, C for competence, noting when and what made you feel capable, and M the reason why this learning was meaningful to you. Add details of how ABC+M was present in your learning experience or note if ABC, and/or M was missing for you. Save this reflection on successful learning to return to in Step Four SHOp Adjustments.

Chapter 4

Step 2

Look and Listen through Classroom Routines

Overview

Objective:

How do teachers know when to adjust instruction?

Think: What are things that you adjust in life (for example, car seats, sound volume, pant hems, speed when driving)? What signals you to make adjustments?

Criteria

- Identify the purpose of a structured group learning routine—gather, help, or collaborate.
- Explain research roots of *Inclusive Directions* to promote engagement, specifically behavior, cognitive, and affective engagement, and to address social regulation. Explain how dashboards and shoulders along the road provide needed formative assessments that are the basis of adjustments to instruction.
- Try Classroom Routines:
  - Plan—*Define* the four structures used in lesson plans.
  - Teach—*Elbow Exchange*.
  - Adjust Instruction—Use two or more structures.

Starting Position: Thinking Minutes

Measure the Teacher's Time to Think—Examine a lesson plan noting where the teacher is *not* giving directions, offering feedback, or managing student actions. Approximately how many minutes during a lesson is the teacher specifically observing and listening to student learning? Look at another lesson plan and notice patterns of when thinking time for teachers is noted in the lesson plan, if any. Our argument is that it is difficult, maybe impossible, for teachers to respond to student learning during lessons with minimal time to think and reflect on learning or make adjustment to instruction.

From the Classroom: The Need for Dashboards and Shoulders along the Road

Once the day begins, Ms. Ford is on her feet until 4 p.m. when the after-school program ends. She takes thousands of steps each day. There are times when she is simultaneously teaching, collecting field trip notices, providing a tissue to a student with a cold, and passing out materials. It is completely amazing to watch. To keep students motivated, she sometimes moves so fast through questions and answers that she can't remember what things were said. There is so much going on that lessons are often a blur of actions, as Ms. Ford races to provide information, offer feedback, and manage students. She is constantly talking with only short breaks when students respond to her questions. Ms. Ford wishes she could put a lesson into slow motion, offering more time to listen to students and think carefully about their responses.

Picture our student Oscar and Ms. Ford, our teacher, driving along in a driver education car. They depend on the dashboard to monitor many different key data points and processes that impact progress toward the destination. Dashboards are designed to give the driver current information to monitor key controls such as speed, temperature, and fuel. A quick glance to the dashboard offers a summary of key features that can be used to make adjustments in driving to help the driver reach the destination. A blinking red light on a dashboard may require a driver to pull off onto a shoulder along the road to reflect and investigate problems that appear on the dashboard. On the shoulder, a driver might check under the hood and even crawl under the car to see what is happening beneath the surface, examining the connections and how the parts are working together.

Like drivers, Ms. Ford and Oscar also need dashboards to monitor learning as it unfolds in the lesson. Gauges for student variables such as background knowledge, strengths, questions, and interests provide teachers with the information needed to adjust lessons to meet learner needs. Finding time to check the dashboard during a lesson is challenging because you are usually presenting information, giving feedback, or managing students. However, structured classroom routines provide a dashboard where your role is to look, listen, and think. For example, using the *Rumors* group learning routine to gather student responses to a question on a sticky note or an individual routine of asking students to rank the most important idea learned in a mini-lesson provides quick gauges to monitor student learning.

Teachers also need shoulders along the road in every lesson to examine problems occurring as learning unfolds. A shoulder enables you to look under the surface to understand the roots of student responses and how students are making connections. You may use a shoulder in a lesson plan to determine why students need an idea repeated, how students are building understanding, and who is confused but not asking questions. Shoulders along the road help you make effective and efficient decisions during lessons because you are not only observing and listening to students as a check for understanding but you have time to think and make decisions to increase the effectiveness and efficiency of instruction. Longer routines such as small group discussions and peer feedback routines provide shoulders along the road during lessons where you have enough time to observe students, assess how individuals are progressing toward the objective, and then make decisions about adjustments to the next part of instruction.

Think back to OSCAR and the adjustable parts of every lesson. You can plan to use structured individual or group learning routines during the Objective, Starting Position, Action Pattern, and/or Reflections parts of the lesson. The routines will both foster student autonomy while providing an opportunity to observe student responses. For example, examine the lesson plan agenda depicted in Figure 4.1. Notice how this teacher has identified structured individual and group learning

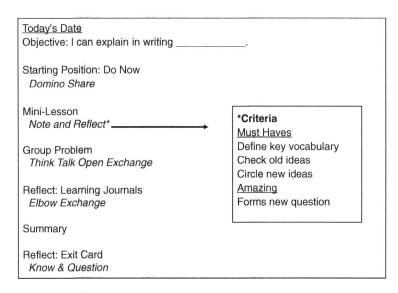

Figure 4.1 Lesson Agenda with Routines Identified for Each Step.

routines during each part of this lesson agenda—providing the opportunity to *Listen and Look* for problems as well as student strengths throughout the lesson.

Criteria for Activities That Provide a Dashboard or Shoulder Along the Road

- Students enjoy the routine.
- Students find the routine useful in furthering their learning.
- 100% of students are engaged and able to learn autonomously.
- Every student is capable of completing the actions in the routine (although not always correctly).
- Teachers are *not* providing directions, feedback, or management.
- Teachers are free to listen, look, and think.

Defining Structures for Tasks

In order to use task structure as a shoulder along the road, you need to have clearly defined classroom routines including the purpose of the structure, roles, procedures, and the help resources that are available. Students and teachers need specific roles for each task structure. This enables you to be both observer and listener during a lesson. To begin, you should define the routines for the four different learning structures used in a typical lesson. When the structures are clearly defined, you can alternate learning structures to clear up confusion among students, provide review and practice for durable learning, and offer help to many students simultaneously during lessons every day.

Each part of the lesson from the Objective, Opening Activity or Starting Position, Mini-Lesson and Practice Time or other Action Patterns, and Closing or Reflection and Criteria should use more than one of these structures to provide the support needed to effectively serve diverse learners. In every structure, help resources are provided and students are taught how to ask for help or use the help resources. The known way to ask for help supports student autonomy, risk taking, and normalizes mistakes and revision as an expectation during learning because help resources are routinely provided and used by students.

Once the structure is identified and given a name, students can transition from one structure to another with little time because the expectations are consistent and known by everyone (again aiding those students with working memory issues). This supports students learning English as a New Language (ENL) or students who need more time for auditory processing because directions are only needed for the content of the lesson being taught—the behavioral actions of the task structure are always the same.

Defining, teaching, and identifying the task structure being used for tasks during lessons is critical to adjusting instruction. Changing the structure for a task requires no new materials, but each structure offers different levels of learner independence and types of help resources enabling teachers to use this simple change to adjust instruction. In addition, you can facilitate intrinsic motivation by alternating these structures to increase student feelings of autonomy or independence, belonging, competence, and meaning. (See Table 4.1 *Defining Structures*.)

How Do Dashboards and Shoulders around the Road Fit into Lessons?

Let's take a look at the agenda for a lesson displayed in Figure 4.1. You see that the teacher has listed the individual or group learning routine that will be used under each step of the lesson. Because the routines are used regularly, the teacher offers minimal directions, only stating adjustments such as rules or who is going first based on the particular lesson taking place.

Let's get even closer to the *Action Pattern* in our next sample agenda in Figure 4.2 where we can see how individual and group learning routines surround the mini-lesson. The action pattern for the mini-lesson includes a group-learning routine, *Elbow Exchange*, prior to the mini-lesson; an individual routine during the mini-lesson, "Note and Question"; and finally a return to the *Elbow Exchange* to review, retrieve, and measure learning from the mini-lesson. The teacher uses the individual and group learning routines to gather responses like a dashboard to monitor learning as it unfolds in real time. In Chapter 6: SHOp Adjustments, we will share how these responses are used to adjust instruction both during and

Table 4.1 Defining Structures

	Independent Task	Group Learning	Table Talk or Free Discussion—Work Time	Explicit Instruction
Physical Set-Up	Eyes on own paper	Sit knee to knee and eye to eye	Sit where you are	Home Base Seats
How	Work alone	Roles Turns Rules Time	Work collegially	Listen, Look, Note, Question, Connect
Supports/ Help	Use classroom resources for support.	Use classroom and peers as resources for learning.	Use classroom, peers, and teacher as resources for learning.	Use board and note organizer.
Additions				

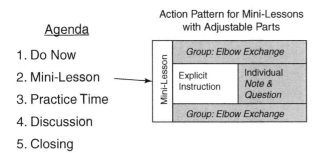

Figure 4.2 Sample Agenda with Action Pattern for Mini-Lesson.

after the mini-lesson. At the same time that the teacher is creating a dashboard, the learners are using the routines to gain peer feedback and adjust their understanding before and after the mini-lesson ensuring all students are better prepared for the instruction and have an opportunity to review what was learned before going on to the next part of the lesson.

Why Individual and Group Learning Routines Are Essential

There are four types of task structures typically used in lessons: explicit instruction, table talk or free discussion, and individual and group learning routines. It is important to consider how the structures foster different types of student engagement and autonomy as well as how teacher time for thinking differs. During explicit instruction you are speaking and providing information to students. This structure requires you to focus on what you are saying, how you will respond to questions, and what to say next. During explicit instruction, it is challenging for you to observe and listen to students. During table talk or free discussion, students may be working independently or collaboratively. It is a relaxed work time and the teacher is usually circulating to offer feedback and prompt students to stay on task. However, during individual and group learning routines, the role for the teacher is distinctly different. Figure 4.3 illustrates how structured individual and group learning routines increase student engagement and autonomy, while at the same time offering you an opportunity to think.

A teacher stating the objective for a lesson is using a structure of explicit instruction. In this example, there is low student engagement and low student autonomy. To increase engagement the teacher may ask students to talk about the objective at their table. However, during a free discussion structure, such as "talk at your table," not all students will participate in the short discussion. So, while engagement has increased for most students, some students may continue to not participate.

To increase autonomy and student engagement, you might follow explicit instruction with three routine structures: an individual, small group, and then the whole class gathering responses of representatives of each group to provide both a dashboard and to promote student engagement and understanding. You could state the objective (explicit instruction), ask students to individually write down the most important word that they heard in their notebook (individual), and have each student share their most important word quickly, one person at a time around their table group. You might then call on a representative from each table to share out one important word from the objective before heading into the lesson. This process

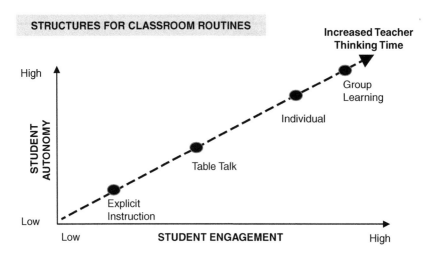

Figure 4.3 Relationship of Structures for Tasks by Level of Engagement and Autonomy.

takes about the same amount of time as calling on hands. It also increases both student autonomy and engagement while offering you a summary of student thinking about the objective. You could adjust the next part of the lesson based on student responses. This illustrates how using more than one structure for tasks can increase student autonomy while providing teachers time to observe, listen, and think about student learning during lessons.

Clearly, there are times when explicit instruction is the most effective way for students to learn. Relaxed work time or table talk provides a great opportunity for teachers to offer feedback to students, but not thinking time for teachers while they are speaking to students. In addition, explicit instruction and table talk are not effective monitors of student learning because students engage in a variety of ways. During work time, students might work alone, collaboratively with a friend, or copy from another student. Only structured individual and group learning routines provide the dashboard and shoulder along the road for teachers to investigate problems.

Rooted in Research: Student Engagement

In this section, we unpack the research roots of Figure 4.3, although we save the research on autonomy for Chapter 7. Corresponding to the figure, we begin by first briefly reviewing the research on engagement, followed by a discussion of studies that address how task structures impact engagement and learning. We conclude with a brief summary of research related to the dashboard that brings us back to the overarching question of this chapter—"How do teachers know when to adjust instruction?"

Engagement and Structures

All too often, we see classrooms where not every student is actively participating in the lesson. Participation and academic learning time are key indicators of what researchers refer to as *behavioral* engagement. Engagement theories recognize behavioral engagement (e.g., paying attention to the teacher, responding to the teacher's questions, completing assignments) as a fundamental and necessary component of academic success (Christenson, Reschly, & Wylie, 2011) .

Nevertheless, behavioral engagement is not the *only* aspect of engagement (Fredricks, Blumenfeld, & Paris, 2004). In fact, most models of engagement point to the importance of feeling a sense of attachment or belonging, even enjoyment of the work. Engagement researchers refer to this aspect of engagement as *affective* or emotional engagement (in this book, we typically refer to it as motivation). Theories of engagement also emphasize the importance of *cognitive* engagement. Indicators of cognitive engagement include using deeper-processing study strategies (i.e., elaboration) and self-regulated learning—essentially strategies associated with WERMS. Researchers conceptualize engagement as having three basic components: behavioral, affective, and cognitive. To be truly engaged, students should not just be going through the motions; they must also be invested in their work emotionally and cognitively. This research is the basis for Chapter 1 and our ALL-ED theoretical framework, which lays out the importance of encouraging the habit of paying attention to both student thinking (WERMS) and feeling (ABC+M).

Explicit instruction and table talk are much less likely to result in active engagement among all students than individual and group learning routines, as you can see in Figure 4.3. An examination of the research indicates why this is so. We can begin by first comparing explicit instruction to individual learning routines, considering that these task structures are completed by the individual student. We can then compare the remaining more social-based structures—table talk and group learning routines.

Explicit Instruction versus Individualized Routines. As mentioned above, we define explicit instruction as a teacher-directed task structure where the teacher is speaking and providing information to students, and the students are listening, if they are behaviorally, affectively, and cognitively engaged. Of course, there are certainly times when explicit instruction is necessary, and there is no doubt that an effective lecture *can* result in learning. However, cognitive science research demonstrates that it is unlikely that a lecture (i.e., explicit instruction) will result in the same level of learning for *all* students all the time without some proper adjustments.

Not every student comes into a lecture with the same level of prior knowledge needed to understand a topic and we know that prior knowledge greatly impacts how a student processes new information (APA, 2015; Mayer, 2011). If students know something about a topic and the new information to be learned is in line with their prior knowledge, then students can simply add the new knowledge into their existing schema (researchers refer to this as conceptual growth). However, if students know very little or believe something that contradicts the information to be learned, then they must transform or revise their schema in some way (researchers refer to this as conceptual change), which typically taxes working memory. Not surprisingly, it is much easier to achieve conceptual growth than conceptual change. Like most people, students are much more reluctant to let go of familiar beliefs, even if they are wrong (APA, 2015).

Students not only differ in their level of prior knowledge, but they also differ in terms of how efficiently and effectively they process information—in short, they differ in WERMS. In order to process information in working memory, students must first perceive the auditory and visual stimuli (i.e., what the teacher is saying or showing), and pay attention to the instruction. However, as all teachers know, not all students do this—some students may have biologically-based processing difficulties related to perception or attention, whereas other students may simply not have the interest or motivation to engage emotionally in the task. Whatever the reason, the information never reaches working memory, impeding learning.

Even if the information reaches working memory, students vary in terms of their ability to retain the information in working memory long enough for the information to make its way to long-term memory. Self-regulated learners are much more likely to have the strategic knowledge to process information more effectively as they are generally aware of how they think and they often use more deeper-processing encoding strategies, or engage in retrieval practice (Roedinger, 2013). Students who are not self-regulated learners lack these skills. By providing explicit instruction, learning gains are more likely given individual differences in processes related to cognitive engagement.

Individual routines, by contrast, have been designed with the cognitive principles of durable learning in mind, and offer students confidence to complete a task. Little cognitive effort is placed on figuring out what actions to do because the actions are known and visible elements of the routine. Students use individual routines as tools to accomplish a thinking purpose, such as remembering, evaluating, organizing, making connections, and using evidence to make an inference—critical tasks that promote durable learning. For example, the individual routine, *List, Write, Draw* activates background knowledge and records initial student ideas. Individual routines are typically implemented with one or more self-regulated learning prompts intended to encourage students to set goals, to monitor and evaluate their progress toward those goals, and to evaluate both the process and outcomes in an effort to set new goals. The complete cycle of self-regulated learning may not be included in the actions of an individual routine; however, you will always find in our individual routines some kind of self-regulatory prompts to promote effective learning.

Table Talk versus Group Learning Routines. There is good reason why group learning—whether cooperative or collaborative—continues to be encouraged in schools. Various meta-analyses point to the benefits of cooperative group learning (compared to competitive and individualistic goal structures) on student achievement in all subject areas and across all ages (Hattie, 2009; Roseth, Johnson, & Johnson, 2008). Researchers even concluded in one study, "If you want to increase student academic achievement, give each student a friend" (Roseth, Fang, Johnson, & Johnson, 2006, p. 7).

As you may have experienced, group learning does not always result in learning across *all* group members. Social loafing, where some students exert less effort when working in groups than when they work alone, is a common complaint. Off-task behaviors are another common problem teachers encounter when they have students working in groups. We can turn to the research on collaborative learning to identify several factors that address these problems and facilitate learning and successful group products (Hmelo-Silver & Chinn, 2016).

Effective groups are deeply engaged in tasks—emotionally, cognitively, and behaviorally. They typically find the task to be interesting, and are motivated to discuss issues related to the task. This is likely to result when students are working on authentic tasks of the discipline, using the norms and standards of that discipline—what some researchers refer to as disciplinary engagement (Hmelo-Silver & Chinn, 2016). Engagement is also enhanced when the task requires positive interdependence, or input from all group members to achieve a common goal (Roseth et al., 2008). The task cannot be completed successfully by one person because task completion is dependent upon students actually interacting and talking with each other.

Effective groups are also characterized by mutual respect and the use of high-quality social and cognitive strategies (Hmelo-Silver & Chinn, 2016). Nothing derails learning more than group members who undermine or disparage others in the group. Groups are more effective when members take turns, offer encouragement of alternative perspectives, refrain from dominating the conversation and seek equal input from all. Research by Noreen Webb and her colleagues (e.g., Webb, 2013) also points to the importance of group members listening and responding to each other's ideas in constructive ways. Effective groups utilize high-level cognitive strategies such as helping each other summarize, elaborate, and refine each other's thoughts and ideas, or helping each other plan or revise their work, rather than simply telling each other the answers with little to no explanations. SRL researchers refer to such processes as co-regulation or shared regulation (Hadwin, Jarvela, & Miller, 2011). Groups that are effective are more likely to listen, value, and build on the contributions of each member, as they work toward a common goal (Hmelo-Silver & Chinn, 2016).

Now let's compare how table talk and group learning routines relate to student engagement, considering the above research on group learning. Both structures clearly involve students talking to each other, but they differ in important ways. With table talk, students are usually directed by the teacher to simply discuss a topic with a partner or two, with little or no guidance on what and how to discuss. Group learning routines, on the other hand, are much more structured and are specifically designed to promote productive group collaborations. It is our contention that table talk, given unspecified directions and vague expectations, is much more likely to result in behaviors that prevent productive collaborations and overall student engagement than group learning routines.

More specifically, ALL-ED group learning routines are characterized by what we refer to as *roles* and *rounds*. In line with the research on effective groups and positive interdependence, ALL-ED group learning routines, much like a jigsaw, call on each member of the group to take on specific roles to accomplish a common goal. As such, the group work can only be successfully completed when each group member carries out their role, for example, in the case of math problem-solving, as an illustrator, an expression writer, or a model builder (see Figure 4.4).

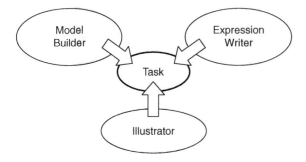

Figure 4.4 Roles for Math Problem-Solving.

In addition to roles, rounds prompt everyone in the group to take turns completing the same task in a circle, helping to ensure even participation by all group members. Thus, rounds facilitate productive collaborations (Kuhn, 2015) by ensuring that every member of the group has a chance to talk, listen, think, and respond to each other in a specified amount of time. For example, in *Think, Talk, Open Exchange (TTO)*, a fundamental ALL-ED group routine, students take turns sharing their own viewpoint one at a time in a circle. The viewpoint could be as simple as a summary of their understanding and questions of today's lessons, their current learning goals and progress they are making, or their understanding of an assignment, the steps required, and qualities expected. After each speaker, all students take a few seconds to think about what they heard. Students are challenged to listen for patterns and surprises in student responses.

Dashboards and Formative Assessments

Finally, a brief comment is warranted on the notion of dashboards and formative assessments brought up in this chapter. Just as students need time to plan, monitor, and reflect on their understanding, teachers need an opportunity to monitor, adjust, and reflect on their instruction. The idea of the dashboard is supported, in part, by the research on decision making. Up to this point, we have discussed cognition mostly in terms of WERMS. In his book, *Thinking Fast and Slow*, Kahneman (2011), an expert on decision-making, makes one additional distinction that is directly relevant to our dashboard idea.

In describing how people think, he distinguishes between two systems: System 1 and System 2. System 1, according to Kahneman, operates at an instinctual level—automatically and quickly with no sense of overt control. System 2, on the other hand, operates more slowly—it's essentially the system that controls WERMS. In his book, he claims that one of the reasons why we often make poor decisions is because we generally let System 1 run the show.

> When all goes smoothly, which is most of the time, System 2 adopts the suggestions of System 1 with little or no modification. You generally believe your impressions and act on your desires, and that is fine—usually. When System 1 runs into difficulty, it calls on System 2 to support more detailed and specific processing that may solve the problem of the moment. System 2 is mobilized when a question arises for which System 1 does not offer an answer.
>
> (Kahneman, 2011, p. 24)

Applying this to the problem of differentiated instruction, what he is essentially saying is that one of the reasons why teachers may not differentiate instruction as much as needed is because we let System 1 take over during instruction. Without overt reminders that students are not getting what we are saying, we are happy to give in to our first reaction and assume that they are understanding everything we are saying. Usually, it is not until we assign some kind of summative assessment that we see that our initial reaction was wrong, and by that time it's often too late. Oscar has already left the classroom thoroughly confused.

To that end, formative assessments—assessments that gather evidence of student learning to guide instructional decisions—are critical. Rather than an actual test per se, researchers consider formative assessments as a process; a process that involves the establishment of learning goals and progressions of learning, which are used to monitor student knowledge and understanding in order to provide timely feedback to students (Mandinach & Lash, 2016). Research indicates that timely feedback is one of the most powerful influences on academic achievement. Hattie (2009) lists it in the top ten factors associated with student achievement. He further maintains that effective feedback answers three main questions: (a) Where am I going? (b) How am I going? and (c) Where to next?—questions that are ostensibly addressed through formative assessments, and through our notion of the dashboard.

The emerging research on formative assessments notes several trends. First, the roles of students and teachers shift in classrooms that routinely use formative assessments—from one that is more teacher-directed to one that is more student-centered. As Mandinach and Lash (2016) note, "The classroom environment necessary for formative assessments is collaborative and supportive; students must be comfortable with questioning and constructive feedback. Students not only engage in assessment activities with their teachers, they also may be involved in self- and sometimes peer-assessments" (p. 393). Step One: Identify OSCAR establishes the elements needed for formative assessment: an objective starting position in order to measure progress, criteria to measure quality, and reflection to make the learning meaningful and set new goals.

Second, although timely feedback has a large effect on achievement, the unique effects of formative assessments on achievement are not always large (Mandinach & Lash, 2016). Researchers attribute such findings to difficulties associated with defining what types of assessments are considered to be formative. In addition, there is evidence to suggest that many teachers have no trouble collecting or interpreting formative assessment data, but they do not always know what to do with that information. We contend that one factor that may prevent teachers from taking appropriate action is the lack of time to deeply and thoughtfully look and listen and let System 2 take over. The following are some classroom routines that can help you not give in to System 1.

Try Classroom Routines: *Precise, Effective, Efficient Learning for All*

Plan: Defining Four Structures for Learning During Lessons

There are at least four different learning structures used in a typical lesson. When the structures are clearly defined (see *Example Chart Defining Four Task Structures*), teachers can alternate learning structures to clear up confusion among students, provide review and practice for durable learning, and offer help to many students simultaneously during lessons every day. Each part of the lesson—from the *Opening Activity, Mini-Lesson, Practice Time*, and *Closing*—should use more than one of these structures to provide the support needed to effectively serve diverse learners.

In planning, take time to define for students the expectations for physical location, process for working, and the help resources available for each type of structures used during lessons. Table 4.2 provides suggestions for the parts of each structure that need definitions. Students can contribute to the procedures for the classroom routines. Post the procedures and be sure to teach students how to use the help resources during each different type of structure.

Table 4.2 Example Chart of Defining Four Task Structures

	Independent Task	Group Learning	Table Talk
Physical Set-Up	Eyes on own paper	Sit knee to knee and eye to eye	Sit where you are
How	Work alone	Work collaboratively	Work collegially
Supports/ Help	Use classroom resources for support.	Use classroom and peers as resources for learning.	Use classroom, peers, and teacher as resources for learning.
Add Specifics for Your Setting			

Teach: Elbow Exchange or Group Learning Routine

In practice, begin by implementing one structured group learning routine regularly. We provide step-by-step directions for group learning routines in each chapter. Teachers use group learning routines for three different purposes during lessons. The most common purpose is to gather student responses for a dashboard. In addition, specific routines may be used at times to provide peer help, and collaborate with peers. Simultaneously, as the routines accomplish the teacher's instructional purpose, the group learning routines benefit students by fostering durable learning, building community, providing a vehicle for feedback, and promoting fun.

ALL-ED Classroom Routine Directions: Elbow Exchange

Elbow Exchange offers students an opportunity to clarify and consolidate their thinking. The exchange provides immediate feedback on their thinking during a lesson. The teacher can use an *Elbow Exchange* to take the "pulse" of the class, gaining a general sense of what students are learning and need to accomplish the objective.
Strengths of this routine:

- promotes making meaningful connections
- encourages collaboration
- provides a means for students to receive feedback on their thinking
- provides meaningful practice for using vocabulary and language skills
- requires listening to and thinking about the responses of others.

Implementation Directions

<u>O</u>bjective: To compare responses and build ideas or questions.

<u>S</u>tarting Positions (individually and then in groups):

Individually: Ask students to jot down an initial answer to the question or prepare to share your thinking in a brief informal way (sketch, identify an important word or problem to discuss). *Groups*: Assigns students an elbow partner (literally touch elbows with the partner). Provide students who need movement an elbow partner in another group, enabling the student to get up and walk over to the elbow partner. Consider asking elbow partners to turn so that partners actually sit at different tables. Ask young children to sit in rows facing an elbow partner on the carpet or meet an elbow partner at an assigned number posted on the wall. Assign elbow partners for discussions when students are sitting on the carpet during lessons or watching a demonstration in a science class. Consider the configuration of student seating for different instructional activities and assign elbow partners for each configuration.

Criteria

- *Must Haves*: Answer/response must include the word "because."
- *Amazing*: Uses vocabulary from our word wall.

Action Pattern

The teacher identifies in the directions:

- **Roles**: Speaker and Listeners, possible role ideas listed in Table 4.3

Table 4.3 Elbow Exchange Role Ideas

Elbow Exchange Role Ideas		
Partner 1	*Partner 2*	*Directions*
Questioner	Speaker	Questioner finds out from partner. Speaker shares question or summary.
Summarizer	Detail Adder	Summarizer sums up lesson or main idea of a reading. Detail adder adds to the summary a vocabulary word or connection to a previous lesson, or a question.
Recorder Note-taker	Presenter Summarizer	A recorder jots down notes from a short discussion with an elbow partner. Together they star the most important points or questions in the notes. Then the Summarizer reports out to the class a summary of the discussion.
Problem Solver	Problem Checker	Problem solver shares answer and strategy used to solve a problem. Problem checker monitors if the solution and strategy shared were the same or different than his/her own work.
Word Definer	Word Illustrator	Word definer offers a definition for a vocabulary word. Word illustrator makes the meaning visible by using the word in a problem or sentence, drawing the meaning or suggesting synonyms.

- **Turns**: Assigns partner on the left or the right to be the first speaker. Switch roles so that the person on the right will be the speaker.
- **Rules**: "Add or Repeat" students can repeat an answer from a previous student or add a new response.
- **Time**: Time each partner when sharing to ensure equity.

    1   State purpose or reason for listening during the exchange.
    2   Ask learners to turn to an elbow partner (someone whose elbow is near one of your elbows).

3   Give learners a minute or two to exchange an idea or question.
4   Switch roles.

Reflections

1   Allow the partners to have an "open exchange" or regular conversation to discuss similarities and differences that were heard. Remind students that open exchange is a discussion where the ideas or questions are like gifts; everyone should be sure to give one and receive one in the allotted amount of time.

Adjust Instruction: Two or More Structures

Begin to adjust instruction by planning to use more than one structure for tasks or shifting between at least two task structures for an activity. For example, after asking a question, invite students to record their thinking using the individual routine *List, Write, Draw.* Be sure to enforce an individual routine environment. For example, you might remind students to keep their eyes on their own paper, not to talk with peers, to use the help resource provided by the teacher if they need it, and to finish within the limited time. Then, following a short individual routine, invite students to share their answers through a free discussion at their table. Close the activity by collecting and writing on the board one response from each table. This gets students in the habit of shifting from one task structure to another; individual learning to table talk to group learning to explicit instruction. Later, we will learn how and when to shift structures to increase student engagement, but for now, begin by setting an expectation of clearly defined different structures for tasks.

Checklist to Try Routines in Your Teaching

See https://www.routledge.com/9780815370819 for additional resources: Defining Structures of Learning Tasks

Plan	Teach	Adjust Instruction
❏ Define the four structures used in lessons.	❏ Implement *Elbow Exchange.*	❏ Shifting Structures. ❏ Use *Inclusive Directions*, roles, turns, rules, and time to address challenges and leverage strengths.

Quality Criteria to Implement Classroom Routines

Must Haves	Amazing
• Classroom routine is implemented on a daily, or weekly basis, or is tied to a specific type of instruction, such as a mini-lesson, independent practice, or review. • Look and Listen at least once during every lesson. • Look at student work or student responses before planning the next lesson.	• Directions are adjusted to fit learners with specific needs such as students who were absent or late. • Student feedback is gathered to improve the rules of the routine. • Students and teachers look back at how responses gathered from the routine have changed as the routine has been implemented over time.

Chapter Reflection
Chapter Summary

In this chapter, you considered how a driver uses a dashboard and a shoulder along the road to monitor and investigate signals to solve problems. Similarly, teachers need dashboards and shoulders to know when adjustments are needed to differentiate instruction more effectively, during lessons. We have shown through both research and practical tools and examples how structured individual and group learning routines can be used to promote student engagement. We also learned how to use *Inclusive Directions* to adjust group learning routines to ensure equity, access, and rigor in discussions for all students.

Learning Journal: Record Important Takeaways

Continue your *Learning Journal* to track your thinking about meeting the needs of diverse learners by recording answers to the following four questions:

1   What was most interesting and useful for you in this chapter?
2   Why was this interesting and useful?
3   How does this connect to what you know about meeting the learning needs of all learners?
4   What research from this chapter could you use to explain or support decisions to adjust instruction?

Save these responses for reflection after reading more of this book and trying out ideas in your classroom. We will answer these same four questions at the end of every chapter.

Return to Your Starting Position

Reread your preliminary first draft answer to our chapter question, "How do teachers know when to adjust instruction?" Add new ideas or revise in another way. Circle the most important part and save to return to after Chapter 5: Step 3: CARR Check to understand the challenge.

Step 3
CARR Check

Overview

Objective:

What can adjustments to instruction accomplish?

Think: Review your answer to the Chapter 2 objective: "Why do we need to adjust or differentiate instruction? Consider how this chapter may confirm or contribute to your answer.

Criteria:

- Identify why an adjustment to instruction is needed using a CARR check.
- Explain research roots of Clarity, Access, Rigor, and Relevance.
- Try Classroom Routines:
    - Plan—*Clarity Planner.*
    - Teach—*Sort and Post (or Place)* and *Show and Share.*
    - Adjust Instruction—Goal setting with Criteria.

Starting Position: Challenges to Engaging All Learners

Identify two challenges to engaging all learners in lessons every day that happen most frequently.

- Absent Students
- Range of Skill Levels or Understanding
- Pace or Speed Differences
- Providing Help Makes Task Less Rigorous
- Small Groups Need Teacher Direction and Management to Stay on Task

What challenges are missing from this list? Can you add two more challenges that make engaging all learners in lessons every day difficult in your school setting?

From the Classroom: Understanding the Blinking Red Light

Ms. Ford needs to finish this unit before school vacation. Feeling the pressure of just a few days, she plans engaging lessons that are packed with information and activities. Even after careful planning, on Monday as she moves from the introduction activity into the mini-lesson she sees a few blank faces. She weighs her choices. If she stops for questions then she will not be able to finish today's lesson and could risk running out of time to finish the unit. Only a few students look lost, so it doesn't make sense to stop the whole class from moving forward. Perhaps if she goes on, she can clarify the confusion during the mini-lesson and circulate to answer individual questions during work time. She makes a mental note of the students that she will go to first as soon as she assigns an independent task.

Throughout the lesson, she sees more students with blank faces but now all momentum will be lost if she stops. She assesses that more than half of the class seems to be with her, so they should be able to help peers at their table. So, she pauses for an *Elbow Exchange* for students to discuss the most important thing that they learned today. She tries to circulate to listen to responses, but she spends time explaining to a discussion pair who are confused, and doesn't get a good sense of what students know and what they have questions about. Hoping the discussion has helped, she goes on to finish the mini-lesson. As she speaks, she notices more blank faces and some students have checked out completely. Now she needs to circulate quickly during work time to help students get back into the lesson. If only she had had time to figure out what was behind those blank stares during the *Elbow Exchange*, but how could she listen to students, think about their responses, and teach a lesson at the same time?

In our last chapter, we considered the importance of a dashboard to monitor student learning and a shoulder along the road in lessons where the teacher can pull off to examine the student responses gathered through individual and group learning routines. We discussed that, occasionally, a blinking red light appears on the dashboard during lessons, such as raised hands, heads down on desks, or blank stares. These reactions are usually blinking red lights that express student feelings such as confusion, distraction, or being lost or bored. These red lights warn teachers that attention is needed or the lesson, like the car, could break down.

Sometimes, a quick glance to the dashboard does not provide enough information. The teacher needs to pull off onto a shoulder along the road with a longer classroom routine to provide more time to think about student responses. In cases such as these, teachers can use a thinking routine called a CARR Check to determine why adjustments to instruction are needed or the cause of those blinking red lights during lessons.

The CARR Check

The thinking routine, CARR Check, helps you identify problems as they appear on the dashboard while teaching or planning lessons. We believe in the importance of using agile thinking to monitor and respond to lesson dashboards. Agile thinking is the teacher's ability to identify opportunities and challenges to learning and then to react by adjusting instruction to better fit student learning needs. A CARR Check will help us with identifying opportunities and challenges. The CARR Check helps teachers explore student responses collected in lessons and student work or data during lesson planning. You can answer the CARR Check reflection questions in Table 5.1 to better understand the type of adjustment to instruction that is needed. The questions determine if the challenge is related to student clarity, access, rigor, or relevance to the topic or task. You should aim to achieve CARR for every student. Often, this reflection happens when you observe and listen to students learning

Table 5.1 CARR Check Questions for Teacher Reflection

C	Clarity	Is this task clear to *all* students? Are the words understandable by all students? Are students expected to understand vocabulary that may be vague, have multiple meanings, or are in unfamiliar contexts?
A	Access	Could *all* students complete the task independently and feel capable?
R	Rigor	How much effort is required of different students? What would students find complex?
R	Relevance	Would *all* students find this task important, interesting, valuable, and/or useful?

during individual or group learning routines. Then you can make specific adjustments to increase clarity, access, rigor, or relevance.

A CARR Check helps you identify a specific problem that students are experiencing, rather than making a task easier or harder (or slower or faster) and hoping this change helps students. You use a CARR Check to determine with greater precision why you are adjusting instruction. Because there is a specific reason why you are adjusting instruction, you can measure the impact of adjustments to instruction on student learning. For example, if the problem was clarity, then you can measure how engagement changed after adjusting instruction through a partner discussion to increase clarity.

Using a CARR Check to Identify Why Adjustments to Instruction Are Needed

In a lesson after Ms. Ford gives directions, she usually says, "Let's get started," and then about half of the students begin. This is a moment to pull over to a shoulder along the road and use a CARR Check to investigate the problem. First, Ms. Ford looks for and listens to student responses during an individual routine such as *List, Write, Draw* followed by an *Elbow Exchange*. She uses the two routines to evaluate at least one quality of CARR that needs increasing through the next steps of instruction. She may focus on the clarity of student responses or relevance, how students are making meaningful connections to the lesson. She can determine from student responses if she needs to increase clarity and/or relevance in the next part of the lesson for all, some, or individual students based on listening to student responses.

Now let's practice using a CARR Check with the challenges that we identified in the *Before You Read* section of this chapter. We have added more details describing the situation so we can use a CARR Check to determine why adjustments to instruction are needed.

1   **Absent students.** Five students came in late from a field trip to class. You are halfway through a mini-lesson. What do these students need most—clarity, access, rigor, or relevance—to engage them and ensure that all students meet the day's Objectives?

2   **Range of skill levels or understanding.** Some students are bored because they have mastered the skills and concepts being reviewed during the Action Pattern of a lesson. Yet, some students need more practice. All students will be required to pass a common test; without a lot of extra planning or totally different activities, how could the teacher increase clarity, access, rigor, or relevance for all students?

3 **Pace or speed differences.** You are moving the students through a well-planned lesson. The pace is quick and engaging for most students. However, some students got lost early on and have "checked out." How can you re-engage those who are lost, keep the others moving forward, and bring everyone to a Reflection point before the end of the period? Should you focus on increasing Clarity, Access, Rigor, or Relevance? Which part of CARR would be most effective? Which part might be most efficient?

4 **Providing help makes task less rigorous.** You are modeling how to complete a complex task one piece at a time. While the support is really helpful, most students are just mindlessly copying and waiting for you to model the next part. How can you provide support and foster student independence and thinking during explicit instruction? Is this a problem of Clarity, Access, Rigor, or Relevance?

5 **Small groups need teacher direction and management to stay on task.** The students are enjoying working in small groups. Some students are working independently, some students are talking, and many students are waiting for you to come around and give directions. You are repeating the same directions for each small group. How can you make the group learning in the Action Pattern more student-driven? Is this a good use of teacher time during a lesson? For a more effective lesson, would the teacher need to increase clarity, access, rigor, or relevance?

For each of these dilemmas, evaluate why the next steps of instruction could aim to increase Clarity, Access, Rigor, and/or Relevance and discuss your ideas with colleagues. Brainstorm how different situations considering different groups of students, the place in the unit from beginning or end or even the time of the day might change what factor impacts effective and efficient learning. Try to explain why one of these factors needs increasing in a specific class situation to promote effective and efficient learning. In our next chapter we demonstrate how to adjust instruction to increase CARR.

Rooted in Research: Clarity, Access, Rigor, and Relevance

Why CARR Checks lead to better learning

Research on CARR dates back to the 1970s and 1980s, when researchers became interested in documenting the effects of teacher behavior on student learning outcomes (Brophy, 1986; Brophy & Good, 1984). Collectively, these studies of teacher effects (also referred to as process–product studies) sought to examine how teacher variables such as the amount and quality of teaching impacted student outcomes. Overall, these studies suggested that amount of academic learning time—time students spend actively engaged in academic tasks of appropriate difficulty levels—mattered, as did how (or how well) teachers performed common instructional tasks such as giving instructions, asking questions, and providing feedback (Brophy, 1986). Thus, the CARR framework is a useful tool to remind us of these foundational teacher-related behaviors.

Given CARR's origins in teacher-effectiveness research, it is important to recognize the overlap between CARR and direct instruction (Adams & Engelmann, 1996). Not to be confused with explicit instruction or teacher-directed instructional methods such as lectures (see Chapter 4), direct instruction is a systematic approach to teaching, which attempts to control specific process–product factors (like clarity and access) that have been found to be associated with higher student achievement. Hattie (2009) notes that direct instruction has a medium to large effect size on student achievement gains; meta-analyses indicate that its effects are particularly strong for students who score in the lower extremes, such as special education students.

Teachers may focus on increasing Clarity, Access, Rigor, or Relevance one goal at a time. Student responses may be evaluated for clarity of the task or access to the task in one review. However, all of CARR needs to be present for effective learning. For example, research suggests that making the curriculum more academically rigorous alone does not translate into student learning gains. A good example is the AP initiative announced in the 2006 State of the Union Address by Bush to train 70,000 high school teachers to teach AP courses. Evaluations of this initiative generally point to limited empirical evidence that having students take more AP classes alone will lead to long-lasting and strong effects on college outcomes (Roderick & Stoker, 2010). Therefore, a complete CARR Check is advised, but to better understand the research roots of each part we examine CARR separately below.

Clarity

Research on teacher effects confirms that students learn more when teachers are clear and easy to understand (Brophy, 1986; Hattie, 2009; Titsworth, Mazer, Goodboy, Bolkan, & Myers, 2015). Specifically, the results of two recent meta-analyses suggest that there is a moderately strong and positive relationship between ratings of teacher clarity and measures of student learning, particularly affective learning. As Titsworth et al. (2015) point out, "Clear teaching increases the probability of perceived cognitive learning by over 100% and affective learning by another 200%" (p. 407). In other words, when teachers are clear, students are much more likely to express positive emotions and adaptive motivational profiles.

Let's put these findings into context: Have you ever experienced a lesson where you had no idea what the point was? How did that make you feel? You were, like Oscar, probably confused and perhaps even frustrated, and therefore less inclined to engage in the task. Incidentally, the word motivation is derived from the Latin word *movere*, which means to move. Research on flow (Csikzentmihalyi, 2014)—a form of intrinsic motivation where individuals experience a holistic sense of total involvement in a task—suggests that the state of flow is dependent upon *clear* goals and feedback. Csikzentmihalyi (2014), the social psychologist who popularized the research on flow, says that clear goals give direction and purpose to behavior, whereas clear and immediate feedback informs individuals about how well they are progressing and whether to adjust or maintain the present course of action. Hattie (2009) rates teacher clarity among the top five teacher factors related to student achievement outcomes.

Access

One of the guiding principles of motivation is that students are motivated toward competence (Elliot, Dweck, & Yaeger, 2017). As the large body of research on self-efficacy attests, when students feel competent (that is, they feel capable), they are more likely to engage in academic tasks and ultimately achieve.

Unfortunately, however, not all academic tasks are perceived by students to be equally accessible.

Both researchers of motivation and UDL point to the importance of tasks being designed at an appropriate level of challenge. For example, studies indicate that in order for individuals to experience flow, they must perceive a match between their skills and opportunities to use those skills (or perceived level of challenge). Any kind of imbalance will result in some form of negative affect—worry, boredom, even anxiety, so it is important that tasks be accessible. Researchers of UDL call attention to how most curricula are not designed within the zones of proximal development of *all* learners. They note that many academic tasks present students, particularly those at the extremes, with "undesirable difficulties"—or barriers to learning that are unconnected to the actual learning goals of the task. Take, for example, the common practice of requiring students to express their knowledge of a topic in a five-paragraph essay. While the learning goal is to have students convey their understanding of the topic, requiring them to do so in a five-paragraph essay creates an undesirable difficulty for students who have motor difficulties, are English as a New Language learners, or who have problems organizing their thoughts in writing. Thus, the UDL framework—based mainly on neuroscience research—is built around three principles to promote access, specifically, instruction that provides (a) multiple means of representation, (b) multiple means of action and expression, and (c) multiple means of engagement.

Instruction that provides multiple means of representation considers the various ways students perceive and comprehend information. Given this variability, UDL assumes that presenting information in a singular way (i.e., by text or lecture only) will limit access to or unnecessarily exclude some students from the content. To that end, UDL suggests presenting content using multiple formats, including print, graphics, or video. Based on the premise that there is variability in how individuals express their understanding, UDL also promotes providing multiple options for how students can communicate their understanding. Finally, UDL promotes choice and autonomy and self-regulated learning to promote multiple ways to engage with the content.

Rigor

Again, both the research on motivation and UDL recognize the importance of maintaining challenge (Schunk & Pajares, 2005). Csikszentmihalyi (2014) summarizes flow as a balance between perceived challenge and skill. UDL, in turn, maintains that its goal is to balance supports and challenges, specifically "to maintain desirable difficulties while reducing or eliminating 'undesirable difficulties'" (Lapinski, Gravel, & Rose, 2012, p. 10). In the academic context, perceptions of challenge and desirable difficulties are mostly defined in terms of students' opportunities for high-level thinking and active use of knowledge—or, in short, academic rigor (Wolf, Crosson, & Resnick, 2005).

Research on academic rigor often alludes to two dimensions of rigor: (a) the provision of challenging academic tasks, and (b) academic press, or the extent to which students are pressed to explain their thinking or justify their arguments (Cooper, 2014; Wolf et al., 2005). The early research on teacher effects considered provision of tasks at an appropriate level of challenge as one important indicator of an effective classroom manager (Brophy, 1986). Research findings also suggest a positive association between the rigor of a student's coursework (as indicated by the total number of Carnegie credits and AP classes) and college-related outcomes (Roderick & Stoker, 2010). More recently, the Measures of Effective Teaching Project (2010), a large-scale project funded by the Bill and Melinda Gates Foundation, found that students' perceptions of the extent to which their teachers pushed for challenge was associated more strongly with student achievement gains. In this study, students respond with their agreement to statements such as "In this class, we learn a lot almost every day"; "My teacher accepts nothing less than our full effort"; "My teacher asks students to explain more about answers they give" were used to indicate students' perception of challenge.

Empirical research on academic press suggests a link between press for understanding and outcomes related to student motivation and self-regulated learning. For example, Middleton and Midgley (2002) observed a moderately strong, positive correlation between academic press and students' endorsement of learning-oriented mastery goals[1], as well as self-regulated learning. These findings suggest a positive association between teachers asking students questions, such as "Why do you think that?" or "Can you explain that more?" to adaptive learning profiles.

Our definition of rigor, in turn, builds on these frameworks by considering both the provision of challenging tasks (i.e., tasks that require high levels of attention, effort, and thinking), and academic press for understanding (i.e., an emphasis on complexity and use of techniques to probe understanding). Specifically, ALL-ED defines rigor through a formula: rigor equals effort multiplied by complexity (see Figure 5.1). In this equation, effort equals required time of sustained focus for students. Complexity equals the number or parts of the topic, the number of ways the parts can fit together, and the type of thinking required to manipulate the parts (Bondie & Zusho, 2017a).

Our definition helps teachers adjust the rigor to fit student needs while maintaining the complexity necessary to develop critical thinking skills and spark student interest.

Use this formula to guide instructional decision making:

To *increase* rigor, add complexity.
Change the number of parts, ways parts fit together, and/or thinking required. In addition, effort can be changed by decreasing the time.

To *decrease* rigor, increase *access*.
Most frequently, the time is extended to increase access, and the number of parts are reduced. However, to maintain complexity and decrease rigor, then the teacher must increase access by adding a scaffold or support. Access may also be increased by changing the structure of the task and help resources provided (see Chapter 6).

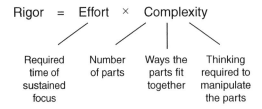

Figure 5.1 Rigor Formula.

Relevance

As we reviewed in the introduction section of this book, one of the guiding principles of motivation is meaningfulness. Students are much more likely to approach and engage in academic tasks when they give personal meaning to them; in other words, when they value the task in some way. Motivational theory points to three main task values. Research suggests that the quality of motivated behavior is higher when students find the task and/or subject domain to be important (what researchers refer to as attainment value), interesting (also referred to as intrinsic interest value), and/or useful (or utility value). Csikszentmihalyi (2014) suggests that simply achieving a balance between skill and challenge will not necessarily sustain flow. He suggests that the extent to which a person is likely to become engrossed in a book is dependent upon not only a match between skill and challenge but also whether or not that book is actually interesting.

Research framed according to modern expectancy–value theory, a dominant theory of motivation, confirms that the way students value tasks strongly predicts choices in activity and subsequent enrollment (Linnenbrink-Garcia & Patall, 2016). For example, studies have found that when it comes to explaining why students pursue certain career paths, values often supersede other motivational constructs in importance. Eccles and Wang (2016) found that occupational values best predicted individual and gender differences in career decisions within STEM disciplines. They found that students, particularly females, were more likely to pursue careers in health, biological, and medical sciences because they perceived those career paths to align with their occupational values related to working with people and altruism.

In light of declining rates of students pursuing careers in STEM, there has been renewed interest in understanding how values impact learning and long-term outcomes such as career choice (Harackiewicz, Tibbets, Canning, & Hyde, 2014; Renninger, Nieswandt, & Hidi, 2015). Given the assumption that task values, particularly utility value, may be more amenable to intervention than internally regulated constructs such as self-efficacy, task value interventions are becoming more commonplace in the literature. Studies demonstrate that interest and task values in STEM can be further developed by directing students to focus on how the topic being learned is relevant to their lives (Harackiewicz et al., 2014).

It is not just the research on motivation that recognizes the importance of tasks having relevance. Cooper (2014) proposes that student engagement is highly dependent upon connective instruction—a category of teaching practices that promote emotional connection to the content being taught, the teacher, and the instruction of the class. Connections to the content are heightened when students sense the work that they are doing is personally meaningful; connections to the teacher are developed when teachers get to know their students; and connections to the instruction occur when students are provided opportunities to develop their competence and learn from mistakes. When it comes to engaging adolescents, Cooper demonstrates that connective instruction that recognizes students as people and honors their interests, perspectives, and experiences is crucial—perhaps even more so than rigor and lively, student-centered teaching practices.

Relevance is also at the core of the research on culturally relevant and responsive pedagogy (Gay, 2010; Ladson-Billings, 1995). For example, Gay (2010) defines teaching as "using the cultural knowledge, prior experiences, frames of reference, and performance styles of ethnically diverse students to make learning encounters more relevant to and effective for them" (p. 31). The main premise of the research on culturally relevant and responsive pedagogy is that educational practices and curricula have a Eurocentric bias, and therefore lack meaning for many marginalized students of color.

Four Reasons to Adjust Instruction: CARR Check

You can use a CARR Check for Clarity, Access, Rigor, and Relevance to identify why an adjustment to instruction is needed. You can use a CARR Check considering individual students, groups of students, and the whole class generally. A CARR Check is useful because each element addresses the needs of students on the extremes for different reasons. For example, increasing Clarity by using a group learning routine to recall directions and plan a strategy to solve the assigned problems supports students who vary on many different dimensions. The CARR Check helps teachers analyze the relationships among the students and the curriculum, in one practical, efficient, and memorable thinking routine.

Return to the Classroom: Practicing the CARR Check

Let's practice a CARR Check again with another example. The objective in this science lesson example is for students to write a definition and an example description of genetic disease citing evidence to support their claims from a nonfiction reading. To start the lesson, a CARR Check tells Ms. Ford that students understand the objective by student responses including many interesting questions students hope to answer by reading about genetic diseases. Students are invited to choose a nonfiction narrative approach such as an article describing a story of a boy living with a genetic disease, or a logical reference approach such as an article from a science text book about genetic diseases. Students will answer the same five questions after reading no matter which article they choose to read. Students seem excited to choose their reading. When Ms. Ford glances at the dashboard, these student responses suggest that Clarity and Relevance are very high so far in the lesson.

However, soon Ms. Ford notices a "blinking red light flashing on the dashboard" when students do not engage in reading the article that they selected. Many students are not reading independently at the level of the texts. Because they cannot understand, or the text is too easy, some begin to talk. Others jump to the task of answering the five questions without reading the article, while a few begin to read and annotate as she had assigned all students to do. The students are clear on the task, and Relevance is increased by asking students to choose the text that interests them. However, a CARR Check helps Ms. Ford realize that Access and Rigor remain problems, preventing many students on the extremes of independent reading levels from successfully engaging in this task. So, now that Ms. Ford has identified the problem, she needs to take her CARR understanding to the SHOp for an adjustment to engage all learners. We will learn about SHOp adjustments in our next chapter.

Try Classroom Routines: Precise, Effective, Efficient Learning for All

Plan: Clarity Planner

We encourage you to summarize a unit of study using our *Clarity Planner* to help make OSCAR visible. This is available at https://www.routledge.com/9780815370819. The *Clarity Planner* enables teachers to think with clarity and agility about the topic being taught in a unit by matching the Objective and Goals to the Assessments and Feedback. The *Clarity Planner* makes it possible to see the core measures of learning for a unit on one page, enabling teachers to plan, reflect, and revise the variety of assessments, feedback, and timing prior to the launch of the unit. By anticipating teaching time in between each assessment, noting how many lessons are needed and available given the school calendar, teachers can ensure that units are not rushed at the end and ample time is given for the hardest parts and necessary practice. The *Clarity Planner* makes visible Objectives, Starting Positions, Criteria, and Reflections, which are key features of lessons that are adjustable to learner need and that promote lasting learning for all.

ALL-ED Classroom Routine Directions: Clarity Planner

Purpose: To enable teachers to think with clarity and agility about the content being taught in a unit and how students and teachers will see and promote growth toward mastery. The *Clarity Planner* makes it possible to see the core measures of learning for a unit on one page and is used by teachers to plan, reflect, and revise the variety of assessments, and learning goal/assessment, match and the feedback cycle for a unit of study. By anticipating teaching time in between each assessment, noting how many lessons are needed and available given the school calendar, teachers can ensure that units are not rushed at the end and ample time is given for the hardest parts and necessary practice.

<u>O</u>bjectives (teacher learning goals for this planning tool)

- I can state the objectives for a unit in clear, accessible, rigorous, and relevant terms for all students.
- I can make precise and explicit connections between the objectives and the assessments students complete in a unit of study.
- I can articulate *Must Haves* and *Amazing* criteria for each assessment.
- I can plan a variety of types, forms, and sources of feedback throughout each unit.
- I can support students in knowing what an assessment measures and monitoring how criteria are being used.
- I can plan where help resources, such as extra time, practice, and different activities will likely be needed before teaching the unit.
- I can see relationships among this unit, the students, and myself (connect to *Traction Planner*).

<u>S</u>tarting Position: Complete *Traction Planner* (Chapter 2).

<u>C</u>riteria

Objectives

Must Haves

- Articulates clear objectives (understanding, knowledge, and skills) that are student-friendly and that would make sense to someone who isn't an expert on the topic.
- Objectives are written as statements that describe desired learner outcomes in precise, measurable, and obtainable terms.

- Objectives are attainable by *all* students and also challenge your strongest students.

Amazing

- Objectives are likely to pique the interest of all your students.
- Objectives will not only foster inquiry and understanding but will also promote transfer to other domains.

Assessments

Must Haves

- The link between objectives and assessments are clear. The *Clarity Planner* helps students understand how the assessments are tied to the objectives and will help them regulate their learning.
- Clear criteria for requirements, *Must Haves*, and for going beyond, *Amazing*, expectations are identified and provide guidance toward qualities students could point to in their products and responses.

Amazing

- There is also evidence that a variety of methods are used for students to represent their learning (varying communication modes as appropriate to the content).

<u>A</u>ction Pattern

Complete Traction Planner prior to the Clarity Planner.

Step One: Make Visible the Unit Plan

A. Place objectives in the center of the circle. Include content and skill objectives in center of circle. An objective example is "I can write a five-paragraph persuasive paper." Number each goal. The objectives must be memorable for students (review research on memory from Chapter 1). If a unit has too many objectives to fit into the circle consider dividing the unit into several small units or create combination objectives that include smaller objectives as criteria or parts of the objective.

B. Identify a large-scale understanding goal that relates to the unit. Write this in sentence or question form (Essential Question) and label this goal A.

C. Identify major assessments that students will complete in the unit and place the names of these assessments around the outside of the circle, numbering the assessments in the order that they are completed.

Step Two: Connect the Learning Goals to the Assessments

Write the number of the Objective next to the assessment that assesses the Objective. Only write the numbers of Objectives that students will get feedback on from the assessment.

Step Three: Create Tools for Students to Set Goals, Monitor Progress, Receive and Apply Feedback, and Reflect on Learning.

For each assessment, identify or create a tool that prompts student self-regulated learning (See Chapter 1).

Most curriculum materials already have rubrics, checklists, and reflection prompts that can be used. Students can also use *learning journals* or performance summaries (see image to right).

Step Four: Reflect on Clarity and Opportunity

Consider the following questions:

Are all objectives assessed in at least one assessment? How many times in the unit are objectives assessed? Should certain goals be assessed more than once to show growth? Is there a variety of types, forms, and sources of feedback throughout the unit?

Step Five: Plan for Time

Note how many lessons are required and are available given the school calendar between each assessment.

Step Six: Plan for Differences

Ensure all students can attain or make progress toward each goal. If necessary, break goals down into parts and determine where each part will be assessed to show progress toward a goal.

Annotate the multiple ways students are acquiring, practicing, and demonstrating their learning.

Note how students will be grouped.

Identify where supports and extensions will be needed.

Mark if an assessment will be differentiated and associate the learning goals assessed.

Mark where there will be time for students to practice a skill that they need as individuals.

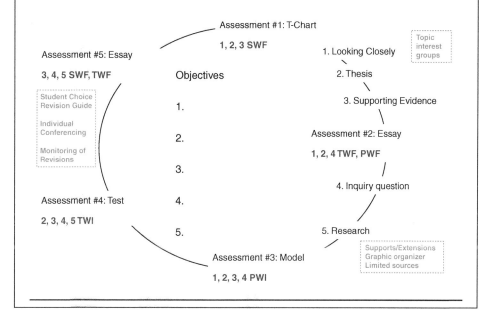

Teach: Try Out Sort and Post (or Place) or Show and Share (Monitoring Routines)

1 Use the *Criteria Checklist* routine (Chapter 3) for students to annotate criteria of quality shown in their work. You will increase student clarity by asking students to annotate their work for *Must Haves* and *Amazing* qualities, such as circling key vocabulary words or a particular strategy. Students can use these reflections to identify next steps for their learning. This enables students to use criteria to reflect on objectives promoting self-regulated learning.

2 Use the *Sort and Post (or Place)* routine (Chapter 5) to create a monitoring chart to develop student autonomy and confidence in themselves as learners.

The more students know themselves, the more they can understand the best way to reach success. Sometimes adjusting instruction is overwhelming to teachers because we feel that it is something we do for the students. However, students play an important role in ensuring learning fits their needs—just as important as the teacher. Students who know what they need to work on and feel capable of asking for help or pursuing learning independently will help you make sure that all learners are progressing. The learners are one of the most important resources that support you in implementing effective instruction that engages all students. Create a chart that monitors student progress toward completing a large task or mastery of learning objectives, or special skills students are willing to share with others. Ask students to move a sticky note with their name to match their movement in learning through the unit.

ALL-ED Classroom Routine Directions: Sort and Post (or Place)

Often teachers collect formative assessments and spend hours after school assessing exit cards or student responses to form purposeful groups for the next lesson. Sometimes you may want to group students by a skill that they need to develop or by an interest. The *Sort and Post* (or *Place*) routine, asks students to self-assess their response by criteria—for example, an interest or a skill they think this work shows that they need to practice, or the most important question that they would like to answer. Then the students sort their responses by placing their response on desks labeled with categories using words or pictures where their response fits. If student responses are on sticky notes, then students can place their response under the label on chart paper divided into columns. Students may place their response under a specific step where they have a question. This is different from *Rumors* in that students are not reading and listening to each other's responses. In this routine, students are not receiving feedback on their ideas or practicing academic language; however, the responses are visible for students to view their response in the context of ideas from their classmates and the responses are sorted for the teacher to adjust instruction.

Strengths of this routine:

- saves time after school sorting responses
- prompts students to think about their response
- encourages students to help each other
- does not require discussion.

Implementation Directions

Objective: Organize student responses into categories helping both students and teachers know where students are in a process or in their learning.

Starting Position: Students complete a response to a question or a self-reflection on their learning.

Criteria

- *Must Haves*: Answers the question, explains placement into category.

- *Amazing:* Uses vocabulary words from the word wall, makes a connection to a class activity, reading, or comment spoken by another student.

Action Pattern

Directions: The teacher identifies in the directions:

- **Roles:** Observers
- **Turns:** Simultaneously, all students *Sort and Post (or Place)*
- **Rules:** Look carefully for patterns and differences paying attention to each person's work.
- **Time:** Two minutes

  1 Place categories or topics on columns on chart paper or label desks.
  2 Ask students to sort their responses by placing or posting their response in the most appropriate category.

Reflections

1 Ask students to make observations about what this sort might mean for our class and themselves.
2 Adjust instruction based on student responses by forming groups or providing targeted instruction based on the student response.

Variation: A digital version of sorting exit cards might be, *Type In and Tag*, using an online form or spreadsheet. Digital files have the advantage of easy storing and sorting and the disadvantage of less oral language practice and feedback for students.

ALL-ED Classroom Routine Directions: Show and Share

Show and Share gives students an opportunity to learn from a quick glance at the ideas of others. At the same time, the teacher quickly views all students' work to gain a general assessment of student learning. This is used when time is limited prohibiting a *Share-Out* and when the student work or response would lose details if an oral summary was given (for example seeing a math problem showing the work to get to the answer versus hearing the answer). *Show and Share* is helpful when students are learning English as a New Language because they can see a model of what is being discussed, and associated words.

For *Show and Share*, students show their answer without speaking by holding up a paper while sitting at their table; post answer on a chart paper or a whiteboard; submit answer via technology such as an iPad laptop or cell phone; or upload a digital picture to shared digital folder.

Strengths of this routine:

- takes little time
- everyone participates at the same time
- requires no language or speaking

- the silence focuses learners
- students gain clarity on the assignment from viewing the work of others.

Implementation Directions

_O_bjective: To find patterns and surprises among student responses.

_S_tarting Positions: Individuals consider a response to a question. You may use the *List, Write, Draw* routine.

_C_riteria

- *Must Haves*: Uses the word because, explains with detail, includes visual representation of ideas.
- *Amazing*: Makes connection to previous unit or world, uses vocabulary from word wall.

_A_ction Pattern

Directions: The teacher identifies in the directions:

- **Roles:** Observers
- **Turns:** Simultaneously, all students share at one time
- **Rules:** Look carefully for patterns and differences paying attention to each person's work; Keep silent, no talking, only looking
- **Time:** One to three minutes

  1 State a reason for looking at each other's work, for example, to notice patterns and differences, or direct students to add two new ideas, you might say, "The purpose of sharing responses is *Plus Two*—to gather two new ideas that you can use when you revise your own work, or spark questions such as, "What do you see in others' work that raises a question for you?"
  2 Direct students that on the count of three, they will show their work to their peers in silence. During the *Show and Share*, there is no talking, just looking for the purpose stated in Step 1.

_R_eflections

  1 Return to individual work to make a revision or compose a question.
  2 Allow students to share their learning from the *Show and Share* at their table or with an assigned elbow partner.
  3 Adjust instruction based on your observations of student work from the *Show and Share*.

  - *Variation: Fist to Five*—Multiple choice responses can be shared by asking students to show a response using their fist to represent zero and their fingers for different numbers. Students raise their arm with their hand in a fist. After the teacher calls out a question, each student responds by changing the number of fingers showing on their hand, one through five, to reveal their answer.

Adjust Instruction: Goal Setting with Criteria

Ask students to routinely set goals when beginning a task. The first step is to make the purpose of tasks, problems, and questions visible to students. This increases clarity and allows students to set goals because they know why they are working on the task. In addition to labeling tasks to identify a purpose, quality criteria (*Must Haves* and *Amazing*) support students in monitoring how their work is progressing and set goals for revising as part of learning. Finally, reflections on the learning process enable learners to set goals to accomplish in a future task.

To begin, develop the teaching habit of **labeling the assignments** and individual problems with the learning objective. Share that objective with the students so that they know specifically what the assignment will help them learn. For example, Assignment #1 is working on past tense verbs with some irregular verb practice, Assignment #2 is working on irregular past-tense verbs with some past-tense verb practice, and Assignment #3 is using both past tense and irregular verbs in your writing. Because tasks are labeled, when students complete a pre-assessment to determine their next steps for learning, students can choose the labeled assignment that meets their learning needs. At times, students may be given assignments with blanks for students to write in what they think the objective is for the problems. In our research, even children as young as five years old have been able to tell us the objective for a task of a game that they are doing. This teaching habit of making the objective of tasks visible recruits students in setting goals for their learning and fosters the disposition to look for ways to practice skills that they hope to develop.

During learning, you can begin to adjust instruction by prompting students to set goals using *Must Have* and *Amazing* criteria, a rubric, or checklist that is already made and ready for use with students. Consider rubrics that you already have in your curriculum. Think of how you can use criteria from just one box to post criteria for daily tasks. In this way, when it is time to use the rubric, the students are already familiar with most of the criteria on the rubric. Another way to assist students with using criteria to monitor their work is to use a group learning routine rubric (see Figure 5.2). A group learning rubric helps students practice high quality skills.

	Needs Practice	*Have Parts*	*You've Got It All*
Listening	I can't remember anything anyone said.	I can remember most of my group members' comments, but I didn't really think about what they said.	I can summarize what each person said and make connections between what was said and things we are learning.
Speaking	I didn't confirm or contribute or exchange ideas.	I spoke my ideas, but was too quiet for my group to hear me.	I exchanged ideas with my group loudly and clearly.
Vocabulary	I did not use specific vocabulary.	I used vocabulary, but I didn't really know what the words meant.	I used the vocabulary to describe what I was talking about.
Thinking	I didn't really think about what was said in my group.	I can identify patterns among my group members' thinking.	I can identify patterns among group members' thinking and the topic we are learning.

Figure 5.2 Example Rubric for Group Learning Routine Participation.

Directions: Before group learning, choose one criteria that you plan to really work on in today's discussions and place a check next to the row. Determine what actions you will take to accomplish this goal. After the discussion, circle the description that best describes your actions. Provide evidence of what makes you circle that description.

After completing (and sometimes during if it is a long project), students use a Pluses and Wishes chart (see Figure 5.3) to monitor their feelings about the process of group learning routines. These tools can be especially useful when you are beginning group learning routines with your students and the practice with rubrics may help them use the rubrics related to curricular tasks more efficiently.

Directions: Reflect on your discussions today and complete the chart below. Read your completed chart and place a star next to the most important idea.

+ **Pluses** List things that really helped you learn today	* **Wishes** List ways to make learning more useful to you

* Note: English as a New Language Learners or students developing literacy skills might check or circle pictures or words that are filled in by the teacher. The class and the teacher can collaboratively make this chart, and students can place a post-it note with their name on it next to pluses and wishes that are true for them. In this way, patterns among students can be seen quickly.

Figure 5.3 Pluses and Wishes Monitoring Chart.

Checklist to Try Routines in Your Teaching

See https://www.routledge.com/9780815370819 for additional resources: Clarity Planner and Reflection Rubric.

Plan	Teach	Adjust Instruction
❑ Complete a *Clarity Planner* to match goals to assessments.	❑ Implement a monitoring strategy using routines from Chapters 2 or 3, or label assignments/tasks by purpose.	❑ Goal Setting using an existing rubric.

Quality Criteria to Implement Classroom Routines

Must Haves	Amazing
• Classroom routine is implemented on a daily or weekly basis, or is tied to a specific type of instruction, such as a mini-lesson, independent practice, or review. • Look and Listen for CARR in student responses during a lesson and in student work.	• Make sure that each task has *Amazing* criteria articulated for students. • Assign one *Amazing* criteria to different groups and/or individual students based on needs.

Chapter Reflection

Chapter Summary

In this chapter, we examined how a CARR Check enables teachers to evaluate, in terms of clarity, access, rigor, and relevance, student variability that is facilitating or impeding progress to an objective. We root the CARR Check in research on teacher effectiveness, as well as the research on motivation and cognitive science. Finally, we suggest routines for planning instruction and classroom routines that help teachers Listen and Look during lessons to examine student responses for CARR.

Learning Journal: Record Important Takeaways

Continue your *Learning Journal* to track your thinking about meeting the needs of diverse learners by recording answers to the following four questions:

1   What was most interesting and useful for you in this chapter?
2   Why was this interesting and useful?
3   How does this connect to what you know about meeting the learning needs of all learners?
4   What research from this chapter could you use to explain or support decisions to adjust instruction?

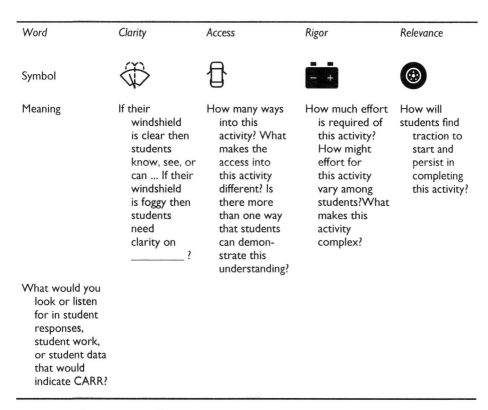

Word	Clarity	Access	Rigor	Relevance
Symbol				
Meaning	If their windshield is clear then students know, see, or can ... If their windshield is foggy then students need clarity on _____ ?	How many ways into this activity? What makes the access into this activity different? Is there more than one way that students can demonstrate this understanding?	How much effort is required of this activity? How might effort for this activity vary among students? What makes this activity complex?	How will students find traction to start and persist in completing this activity?
What would you look or listen for in student responses, student work, or student data that would indicate CARR?				

Figure 5.4 Agile thinking with CARR.

Save these responses for reflection after reading more of this book and trying out ideas in your classroom. We will answer these same four questions at the end of every chapter.

Return to Your Starting Position

Reflect on your own experiences in the classroom. Can you identify a problem and use a CARR Check to explain why an adjustment to instruction is needed? Add a dilemma from your own experience to the list from the beginning of the chapter and use a CARR Check to explain the challenge.

Complete the Agile Thinking Chart shown in Figure 5.4 to consider how you might recognize clarity, access, rigor, and relevance in student work.

Return to your preliminary first draft answer to our chapter question, "Why are adjustments needed to increase student engagement?" Add new ideas or revise in another way. Circle the most important part and save to return to after Chapter 9: Closing Gaps and Extending Learning.

Note

1 Also referred to in the motivational literature as learning goals or task goals. Students who endorse these types of learning goals aim to develop their competence and are more likely to adopt a growth mindset. They view learning for learning's sake.

Chapter 6

Step 4

SHOp Adjustments—Help

Overview

Objective

How do teachers adjust instruction to meet the needs of all learners?
  Think: Make a list of at least three ways that teachers adjust instruction that you already know.

Criteria

- Identify how to adjust instruction using *Structures* and *Help* to increase the range of students able to engage in learning and assess the possible adjustments for effectiveness and efficiency.
- Explain how the research providing help within a community shapes instructional decisions.
- Try Classroom Routines:
    - Plan—Task Analysis.
    - Teach—*Help Desk.*
    - Adjust Instruction—Teach General Help.

Starting Position: Help Resources

Make a list of the help resources on the walls and around your classroom, including wall information, such as charts with learning strategy steps, directions for routines or goal monitoring, student work, criteria charts, and word walls. Think of tools that help students accomplish tasks, such as number-lines, calculators, rulers, timers, tablets, and bookmarks. Consider references such as libraries, dictionaries, and digital textbooks. Do not forget materials such as graphic organizer apps, note-taking guides, rubrics, checklists, paper, pencils, and markers. Finally, and perhaps most important, note the people who provide help in the classroom, including peers and adults. Do not worry if you are not sure if something is a reference (reusable) or a material (consumable). The purpose is to make a list of the help resources so that you can begin to provide, teach, and assign help as a vehicle to adjust instruction (Table 6.1).

  Reread your brainstorm and underline the resources that students are specifically taught how to use, including how to get and put away the resource as well as when to ask to use the resource. Put a star * next to the help resource that your students

Table 6.1 Help in the Classroom. Add ideas to this table to identify help resources.

Wall Information	Tools	Materials	References	People

use most frequently. Use this list of help resources to begin to consider our chapter question, "How do teachers adjust instruction to meet the needs of all learners?"

From the Classroom: "Let's Get Started"— If No One Starts, Then What?

Ms. Ford says, "Let's get started," and less than half of the students pick up their pencil. Immediately, she moves quickly around the room to offer help and encouragement to students. She is repeating the directions, redirecting off-task behavior, encouraging reluctant students, and providing support strategies, such as hints, shortcuts, and word definitions while circulating around the room. Ms. Ford wonders if there is another way to help her students with getting started on tasks.

When students are not engaged in learning, there are at least three problems with the "running to provide help as fast as possible" approach:

1. Many students develop the habit of waiting for help during practice time.
2. The teacher is not really sure why students are not engaged in the task. So, the teacher is either giving the same help to all students regardless of their problem in an effort to circulate quickly or taking time to figure out the problem with each individual, leaving some students unengaged for most of the practice time.
3. There is no time for the teacher to return to students who received help to find out how the help worked or to evaluate how students have applied the feedback given by the teacher.

Clearly, giving directions and then running to help does not foster student autonomy, which is why we recommend a different first step. After giving directions, stand in place for a moment to understand the challenge by observing and listening to students. A CARR Check will enable you to determine if students need greater clarity, access, rigor, and/or relevance. After determining the reason or goal for adjusting instruction, teachers can take the CARR to the SHOp to determine how to adjust instruction. SHOp stands for the three ways teachers adjust instruction to respond to perceived learner needs: *Structures*, *Help*, and *Options*. In this chapter, we briefly review *Structures* and then explain *Help*. We'll focus on *Options* in Chapter 7.

Structures

The S in SHOp stands for Structures. As we outlined in Chapter 4 Step Two: Look and Listen, there are four different learning structures that can be used in every lesson: (a) explicit instruction, (b) table talk, (c) individual learning routines, and (d) group learning routines. We have already discussed how these structures differ in terms of student autonomy and engagement (see Chapter 4, Figure 4.3 *Relationship of Structures for Tasks by Level of Engagement and Autonomy*). In Step Two: Look and Listen, we use only two structures—individual and group learning routines—as dashboards and shoulders along the road, because these are the structures that free the teacher to observe student learning. However, when it comes to adjusting instruction, it is critical to use all four structures. Alternating structures is often the easiest way to adjust instruction because it is simply changing the initial approach to completing a task. Let's look at several examples to see how adjusting structures can help Ms. Ford.

In Ms. Ford's example above, it is likely that only half of the students began the task because they were not clear on what they were supposed to do. To solve this problem, Ms. Ford could change the direction from "Let's get started" to something that all students could do independently and that would help students feel competent such as, "Start by circling the easiest problem and be ready to explain what about the problem makes it easy." Then, she can use a group learning routine like *Domino Discover* to get her students to share ideas, one person at a time around the table, to find the easiest problems and what makes the problems easy. In doing so, Ms. Ford has created an opportunity to look and listen to student conversations. After students share out the easiest problems, she can adjust the structure again by asking students to complete the easiest problem independently or by modeling the hardest problem on the board using the structure of explicit instruction. Adjusting the structure requires no planning or special materials, and helps to foster student feelings of ABC+M, making learning a better fit for students with diverse abilities.

Let's take a look at another way to address the problem of only half of the students starting a task. Ms. Ford can begin the lesson by stating the objective using explicit instruction. Rather than calling on a few hands to read and explain the objective, which may leave most of the class unengaged, Ms. Ford can ask students to individually write down the most important word that they heard in the objective in their notebook. Then, she can use the group learning routine *Domino Discover* to have each student share their most important word quickly—again, one person at a time around the table. Finally, Ms. Ford can call on each table to share out one important word before heading into the lesson.

In this example above, Ms. Ford has essentially created a dashboard monitoring CARR for the lesson objective using explicit instruction followed by an individual, group, and then whole class routine. Note that the time taken to implement the routines is about the same (maybe slightly longer) than the time she would have spent calling on hands or running to help students. She has also improved student engagement by actively involving all students in the lesson, not just the few who she called on to explain the objective.

In addition, during the individual and group learning routines, Ms. Ford has time to observe student understanding, which would not have been possible if she relied exclusively on explicit instruction. The additional time spent on routines can easily be recovered by spending less time clarifying the lesson later. These examples show how there is always more than one solution to every dilemma of student differences. All of these solutions required no additional planning time or changes to the materials or lesson. The lesson was adjusted to fit learner needs by changing and using more than one structure to complete tasks.

It is common to see lessons that are largely dedicated to one structure at a time. For example, we often see 15 minutes dedicated to "I do" (the teacher modeling instruction for students). This is typically followed by ten minutes of "We do" (guided practice), and then 15 minutes of "You do" (independent practice). Long blocks with just one structure for tasks offers little feedback for students. Changing structures frequently allows students to reflect and gain feedback on their thinking throughout the lesson. For example, you can have students individually jot, draw, or write their response to a prompt, compare responses with a partner, and then have them revise their own response.

Shifting structures addresses many dilemmas of student differences, but will not solve every problem. When long blocks of one structure are needed, such as sustained practice time to build individuals' stamina, teachers will not be able to use structures to adjust instruction. *Help* resources (the H in SHOp) may be used to ensure all learners are able to complete the task in the assigned structure. Let's learn more about *Help* resources to consider how we can use *Help* along with and in addition to or instead of Structures to ensure lessons are a good fit for all students.

Help

Deciding to offer help is a natural reflex for teachers and a complex decision. Teachers want to extend a helping hand to support students in their learning. However, teachers do not want to foster student dependence on teacher help or promote low feelings of competence. So, while help is essential for learning, it presents a complex dilemma for teacher decision-making. Research on help-seeking confirms teacher concerns about the importance of offering help that fosters independent learning (see Research Roots). It is important to think carefully about the type of help and approach to offering help to most effectively support learning. Along with structures, help can be adjusted daily to make sure lessons are a good fit for all learners.

Tiers of Help Resources

Help resources are offered in three different tiers, aligned to the different types of differentiated instruction (see Figure 6.1). The largest foundational tier includes *General Help Resources*, which should be made available to all students during Adjustable Common Instruction. In your *Starting Position*, you already brainstormed general help resources in the table at the Starting Position for this chapter. The second tier of help resources are given to *Specific Resources*, offered to groups of students or individuals to strategically close gaps or extend learning. These include supports, scaffolds, and extensions that help learners with a specific task. Finally, *Individualized* help includes assignments aimed at remediation, review, preview, and beyond. Individualized help may include specially designed instruction, accommodations, modifications, and remediation as designated in students' individualized education programs.

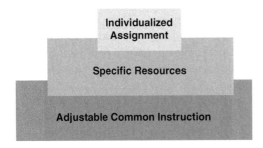

Figure 6.1 Three Tiers of Help Resources.

Table 6.2 General Guidelines of How Help Resources Differ

	General	Specific	Individual
Learners	All	Some (groups and individuals)	Individuals
Use	Many different resources used to accomplish the same and different tasks	Used to accomplish a specific task	Used to develop specific skills for individuals
Approach	Available—Teacher prompted or student selected	Teacher assigned— Systematic teaching by teacher	Teacher assigned— Systematic use by student
Teaching	Teach, Prompt, Provide	Practice and Fade or Independent Use (see section on Specific Resources)	Practice and Check, Periodic or Sustained over time

Let's look specifically at the differences between the learners receiving the help, how the help is used, the teacher's approach to offering the help, and the method for teaching how to use the help resources, as represented in Table 6.2. *Help* can be offered to all, some, or individual learners based on their need. The use of the help resources in relation to the learning task can also be either general or specific to the task. The teacher's approach is to make general resources available to all students, and to always assign specific and individual help resources. You can see that each tier of help requires a different type of teaching.

A useful analogy is to think of help in the classroom as similar to the help resources that swimmers use both when swimming for fun and when they are specifically learning or working on their strokes. Imagine a community pool with three areas: a general swim area, a shallow end or children's pool, and lap lanes. We can remember the different tiers of help by thinking of how swimmers use these different areas. General is the largest tier of help—it's like a free swim area designed for all learners. In the general area, we see many resources available for swimmers to use by their own choice. Different swimmers are using a variety of help resources to accomplish the same task—in this case, swimming for fun. The second tier is assigned for some, either groups or individuals, like our shallow end or a children's pool is used by some swimmers with specific needs. Here, the help is tailored to the needs of a group of swimmers and related to a specific task, such as learning to hold your breath. The third tier is individual help. Lap lanes are great examples where individual students are working toward individual goals using specific help resources. At times, depending on the goal, all swimmers may need one of the different tiers of help. Planning to offer specific help can foster learner competence and independence. Let's dive into the community pool to learn more about each of these different tiers of help.

General Help Resources

In our general free swim area of the community pool, we find all types of swimmers using a variety of help resources for different purposes. Some swimmers may be using goggles, whereas others may be using arm float wings, or a float or life jacket. Still others might be swimming without any help. Whatever the need, the resources are readily available and the swimmers themselves often make the decision to use help resources. In the classroom, general help resources include a wide variety of resources, such as the examples listed in Table 6.3. Compare our table to your Starting Position from this chapter. Are there help resources that you would add to our table?

Table 6.3 General Help Resources

Wall Information	References	Tools
• Word Walls	• Dictionaries	• Calculators
• Goal Charts	• Libraries	• Rulers
• Monitoring Charts	• Textbooks	• Timers
• Strategy Posters	• Timelines	• Software
• Routine Directions	• Digital textbooks	• Apps
• Quality Criteria	• Digital resources	• Number lines
• Student Work		• Counters
Materials		**People**
• Graphic organizers		• Self
• Note-taking guides		• Peers
• Rubrics		• Experts
• Checklists		• Teacher
• Criteria—*Must Have* and *Amazing* Charts		• Support specialists
• Vocabulary lists		
• Sentence frames		
• Answer sheets		
• Digital mind map creators		

There are so many resources available in every classroom that it is often hard for students to determine when to ask for help and what resource would be most effective for the task. One way to assist students in using help is to provide a Help Desk. Thinking back to our community pool, in addition to the three areas, there is a Lifeguard station, a designated place where swimmers can go for help. Just like a Lifeguard station, classrooms can have a designated place for help, such as a Help Desk, where students can seek assistance. Teachers open a Help Desk during work time, where students can go for a help resource. A computer with a video showing the steps to solve a problem can be a Help Desk. An answer key can be posted face-down on the board as a Help Desk where students can get a hint or check their work. The teacher or a student expert might work the Help Desk for a few minutes to offer a short lesson or answer general questions. Students might be prompted or invited to come to the Help Desk for an appointment at a specific time in the lesson. Help Desks support students in feeling comfortable seeking help independently.

Approach to Offering General Help. It is realistic to assume that all, some, or individual students will need at least one form of help during lessons. The approach to offering general help is to teach, prompt, and then provide the help resources (Figure 6.2). After help is taught, the approach for using general help resources should be primarily a student decision, while teachers make the resources available for all students to choose how and when to use.

This first tier of general help resources should be made available for *all* students during each part of lessons, even though not all students will choose to use the help. For example, during the Action Pattern, you might remind students of a problem-solving step chart posted on a wall or to check their spelling using a word wall. This help is available to all students. You can use OSCAR (see Table 6.4) to plan different tiers of help. Planning is important so that help is offered in a manner that fosters student independence.

Let's put structures and general help together to address Ms. Ford's dilemma of getting students started. In this case, Ms. Ford might say, "Pencils down. Before you

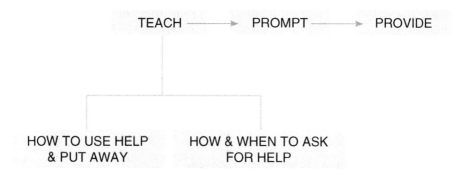

Figure 6.2 Approaches Teachers Use for Providing General Help.

Table 6.4 General Help Resources by OSCAR.

OSCAR	General Help Resources: Possible Choices that Teachers Decide to Provide
Objective	• Box key terms so that students know to listen for those terms in the lesson. • Display images to illustrate vocabulary used in the objective. • Provide samples of student work to show students a progression toward mastery of the objective.
Starting Position	• Use peers, by having an *Elbow Exchange* about a question to spark prior knowledge. • View an individual's ideas in comparison to the ideas of others using a whole group discussion routine. • Provide resources like glossaries and word banks when students are writing an individual response as a starting position.
Criteria	• Annotate a model of completed student work to clarify the expected outcome. • Illustrate criteria with sample student work. • Include Amazing criteria that go beyond by returning to previous units for review and retrieval practice. This enables students who need additional practice to "go beyond" today's lesson by working on an appropriate goal.
Action Pattern	• Identify words that should be heard in student discussions, such as vocabulary words, sentence frames, and accountable talk phrases. • Provide participation rubrics and checklists identifying productive actions, such as sharing ideas with others, asking clarifying questions, building on the ideas of others, and valuing the opinion of others. • Keep time to ensure equity. • Model note-taking using a guide. • Offer answer keys.
Reflections	• Provide students with ample time. Reflections usually get rushed at the end of the lesson. Consider adding stop and reflect moments throughout each lesson. • Provide models of reflective thinking, such as reflections that make connections between the product and criteria, that question results, identify patterns, seek understanding, gather opinions, and consider relationships. • Discuss reflections with peers.

begin, I would like for you to brainstorm three steps to getting started on this task with a partner using an *Elbow Exchange*." Because the *Elbow Exchange* structure is a known group learning routine, Ms. Ford is free to listen to the conversations of student pairs. Then she might adjust instruction by answering a question that she heard, modeling part of the task, or if it seems like the *Elbow Exchange* increased clarity for every student, asking students to pick up their pencils and begin the task individually. By using two structures, first group then individual, most students should be engaged. To get the last few students started, Ms. Ford could call four or five students over to a Help Desk for explicit instruction. In this example, a CARR Check determined some students needed greater clarity, so the SHOp adjustments included changing the structure for the task and providing a Help Desk. When teachers use adjustable instruction, students are not waiting for teacher help and the teacher is not running around the classroom. Rather, the teacher uses SHOp adjustments to engage all learners quickly and efficiently.

Specific Resources: Supports, Scaffolds, and Extensions

While general resources are readily available and can be used for many different tasks, specific help resources in our second tier in Figure 6.7 are used for specific tasks and are assigned by the teacher to some students (groups or individual students) based on perceived needs. There are three different types of specific help resources: supports, scaffolds, and extensions. There are two teaching approaches used in the Specific Resource Help Tier: fading and building independence. In this section, we will learn the differences between the supports, scaffolds, and extensions, and the two approaches to teaching specific help resources.

Let's return to our community pool to understand the difference between supports, scaffolds, and extensions. For specific help resources, we move from the general swim area where help resources are available and swimmers are selecting from a variety of help resources to meet their needs, to the shallow end, limiting students to focus on specific skills. Supports provide help for learners to practice the whole task, scaffolds focus on a specific part of a task, and extensions push beyond the task (see Figure 6.3). Supports are like life-jackets or floats allowing the swimmer to complete the whole task. Scaffolds are like kickboards that focus the swimmer on just one part of a whole task, working on the kick. The scaffold is removed after sufficient practice; the swimmer will try swimming without the kickboard to measure how focused practice on just the kick improved the overall stroke. Extensions work like goggles and a snorkel, enabling swimmers to go beyond the expectations for the task. You can see from our swimming example that to develop mastery of a task, a learner will at times need a support to practice the whole task, a scaffold to focus developing skills for just one part of the task, and extensions to stretch beyond expectations.

Task Analysis. Before creating a specific type of help, you will need to identify the parts within the whole task so that you can predict where some students will need help (or will need some additional challenge). We use task analysis to break down tasks into parts and we break down skills into the smaller skills used in larger skills. For example, you have probably seen signs with pictures that break down the task of

Figure 6.3 Differences between Supports, Scaffolds, and Extensions.

washing your hands into seven steps starting with 1. realizing your hands are dirty, 2. turning on the water, 3. putting on soap, 4. scrubbing hands, 5. rinsing hands, 6. shutting off the water, and 7. finally drying hands. By breaking down the task into clear steps we can now build a scaffold to work just on the part of scrubbing the hands properly. Or we might build a scaffold check sheet just for the part of putting on soap without making a mess with soap on the floor. Most tasks we ask students to complete and learn at school are very complex and have many parts. We want to encourage students to say, "I can do step one and two, but I need help with _____ or I have a question with *step three*." We know task analysis is needed when we hear students saying, "I don't know where to start" or "I can't do it."

Let's look at an objective for small group discussions in Figure 6.4, *Task Analysis: Breaking Down Collaborative Conversations*. We have an initial list of a few of the communication skills that would show mastery of the larger task, collaborative conversations. We can take each of the smaller tasks and brainstorm criteria for quality so that students could monitor not only if they are able to do the skill, but also use the quality criteria to monitor how they are doing. For example, 1. Follow agreed upon rules for discussions; might have these criteria – *Must Haves*: Equitable turn-taking, speaking, and listening; and *Amazing*: Offers compliments, uses vocabulary. We might also assign a support to help students focus in on just one of these skills, such as 2. Meaningfully build on the responses of others by requiring students to use sentence frames that build on a previous response in small group discussions.

Task analysis has benefits for both students and teachers. For students, the list creates a visible pathway of small attainable tasks that they can work on to accomplish the broader goal. Students can also use the list to identify specific skills that they need to develop or bypass practice on skills they are able to do. Teachers in turn can use lists like these to listen and look for student struggles and mastery. They can then provide instruction and practice designed to close gaps and extend learning. Task analysis of objectives also enable teachers to identify when similar small tasks are across units throughout the year.

Interpreting data tables is another example of a complex objective that begins in elementary school with tasks, such as reading a weather chart, and continues all the way through high school in every subject, when students analyze data in reference tables. Students often struggle with making predictions based on a data table. Before we think about how to help students, let's identify the parts that students must be able to do to meet this objective. Let's start with the objective, "Students can make predictions using a table." In Figure 6.4, we break the objective down into skills

---

Objective: Students will be able to participate in collaborative conversations.

1.   Follow agreed upon rules for discussions.
2.   Meaningfully build on the responses of others.
3.   Ask questions to seek understanding.
4.   Sustain focus for multiple exchanges on a topic.
5.   Add explanation or elaboration to ideas being discussed.
6.   Explore more than one perspective through conversation.
7.   Consider and respect different cultural norms for conversations.

Figure 6.4 Task Analysis: Breaking Down Collaborative Conversations.

Variable	Monday	Tuesday	Wednesday	Thursday	Friday
	I	2	3	4	?
Humidity	94%	99%	60%	96%	?
Precipitation	Light Rain	Heavy Rain	None	?	Rain
Cloud Cover	Overcast	Overcast	Scattered	?	?

Figure 6.5 Ms. Ford's Data Table Problem

that students need to master this objective. Can you identify criteria for each of these steps? For step one, *Must Have* criteria might include naming the unit being represented, such as miles, hours, or relative humidity. Task analysis and identifying the criteria for high-quality work (*Must Haves* and *Amazing*) prepares teachers to offer help that is specific and that enables students to monitor their own progress promoting independence.

Ms. Ford assigns her students to examine a data table, Figure 6.5, with missing information marked with a question mark (?). She directs the students to complete the problem, "Based on the patterns you see in the data, predict the unknown information in the data table. The answers must include observations from the data table that support your prediction."

When Ms. Ford circulated around the room, she noticed that many students skipped this problem on their worksheet. A CARR Check suggested that students needed greater clarity of the question and access to writing a relationship statement to engage in the task. Instead of running to provide individual help, Ms. Ford analyzed the task and made a list of the steps on the board as a general resource for all students. Her task analysis from the chalk board is Figure 6.6.

Now, with clear steps displayed on the board, more students know how to begin the task. The quality criteria enable students to monitor their own work, so they are not asking Ms. Ford if their work is done or good enough. However, many students are struggling with writing a relationship statement. Ms. Ford decides to assign that group of students a support.

Supports. Ms. Ford wants to provide a support so that all students can complete the whole task of writing a relationship statement independently, since she sees that many students are struggling with this task. Before making supports, let's return to the community pool to review how supports work. In the pool, supports are like a float or a life jacket. Supports enable a learner to practice the whole task. When a float or life jacket is used, the swimmer is completing the entire task using the arms, legs, and breathing. Supports can be used during introductions to new content to allow students to get in and try something out—maybe to play and have fun with the topic or task before breaking it down and getting serious. Supports foster academic risk taking because students know that the support will keep them from drowning.

Supports provide help that enables students to complete the whole task without being hampered by learning challenges and enables learners to experience the whole task. Specific challenges and parts of the task that need practice are addressed in another lesson. When the content or material of the lesson is new to the student, providing supports to work around learning challenges enables the student to focus on acquiring the new information, skills, and understanding.

Ms. Ford realized that even though students knew the steps to complete the task, they were not clear on how to complete the last step of writing a relationship

Objective: I can make a prediction based on a data table.

1. Circle the names of the variables in the data table.
2. Explain how the data is changing: does it stay the same, increase, or decrease? Are there other changes?
3. Describe the pattern in the row for each variable.
4. Compare the patterns in the variables from two rows.
5. Predict what the data could be where there is a question mark.
6. Write a relationship statement to summarize your findings from steps one through five.
7. Annotate your statement identifying the Criteria for Quality (check *Must Haves*, underline *Amazing*).

Criteria

Must Haves

- States relationship.
- Provides example data.
- Uses the data to make an inference about the pattern.
- Predicts what this pattern might mean or explain.

Amazing

- Makes a connection to another variable, data from an experiment, a text, another lesson, or life experience in explanation of results.
- Uses key vocabulary terms to provide details in inference and explanation.
- Represents the data from the table in another graphic form that shows relationships.

Figure 6.6 Ms. Ford's Task Analysis.

statement. She used task analysis again, breaking down the relationship statement into visible parts and identifying the purpose of each part so that students understood both what to do and why they were doing each part. Ms. Ford offered this support for writing a relationship statement in the next lesson, as a response to her students' confusion.

With this support, more students are able to engage independently in the task of writing a relationship statement. However, some students need more practice identifying the variables in the word problem, others need help recognizing a pattern in a row of values on a data table, while other students need help with making an inference, and many students need practice explaining their inference using data from the table and facts from their text book. Ms. Ford decides to use scaffolds to focus students on the part that they most need to practice.

Scaffolds. Let's put the data table example on hold for a moment and return to our community pool to examine exactly how scaffolds work. Scaffolds are a form of help that focuses the learner on a specific part of a larger task. For example, a swimmer wants to swim faster. The coach determines that the swimmer needs to use a straighter leg motion in her kick. So, the swimmer uses a kickboard as a scaffold. The kickboard enables swimmers to focus on their kicks—straightening the legs— the scaffold or kickboard takes care of everything else (the arms and floating) so that all of a swimmer's energy is focused on developing the kick. Later, the swimmer may use a different scaffold, a pull-buoy, that prevents swimmers from using their legs to kick in order to strengthen their arm strokes. The kickboard and pull-boy are scaffolds because they enable swimmers to develop a specific skill. After focused practiced, the scaffold is removed as the swimmer uses both the stroke and the kick to practice the whole task of swimming.

Scaffolds are often used to help students focus on learning one aspect of new content without attending to all parts of a task at the same time. Students practice the task using the scaffold. To remove the scaffold, students alternate between prompts that provide the scaffold and tasks the student completes. This process continues until the student knows the components of the scaffold so well that the student can make the scaffold independently. There may be a time when the student first makes the scaffold independently and then uses the newly made scaffold to complete the task. Later, the student may have internalized the scaffold so that the task was completed without thinking about the scaffold.

Students are completing the whole task with support, but Ms. Ford can see from student work that when the support is removed, groups and individual students clearly lack different specific skills. Notice in our example displayed in Table 6.5,

Table 6.5 Example One of Relationship Statement Support

Purpose	Parts of a relationship statement
1. State relationship	*Model: As X increases, Y decreases.* *Try it: ____ _____ _____, _____ _____.*
2. Provide Data	*Model: For example, when _____ then _____* *Try it:*
3. Make an inference about the data pattern	*Model: From this pattern, we can infer that _____.* *Try it:*
4. Predict what the pattern might explain	*Model: When _____ happens, then we can predict that _____* * because _____.* *Try it:*

Reread and annotate answer noting Criteria used in statement

Criteria

Must Haves

- States relationship.
- Provides Example Data.
- Uses the data to make an inference about the pattern.
- Predicts what this pattern might mean or explain.

Amazing

- Makes a connection to another variable, lesson, or personal experience in explanation of results.
- Uses key vocabulary terms to provide details in inference and explanation.
- Represents the data from the table in another graphic form that shows relationships.

Rewrite the relationship statement below. You may use your own words to begin the sentences. Check to make sure the *Must Haves* are in your statement and include at least one *Amazing* criteria.

Table 6.6 Example Two of Relationship Statement Support

Purpose	Parts of a relationship statement
1. State relationship 2. _____	As X increases, Y _____. For example, when X is 94%, then Y is Light Rain, and when X is 99%, then Y is Heavy Rain. In addition, when X is 60%, then Y is Scattered.
3. Make an inference about the data pattern 4. Predict what the pattern might explain	*Model: From this pattern we can infer that when X is* _____ *y will be* _____.

Reread and annotate answer noting Criteria used in statement

Criteria

Must Haves

• States relationship.
• _____
• Uses the data to make an inference about the pattern.
• _____

Amazing

• Makes a connection to another variable, lesson, or personal experience in explanation of results.
• Uses key vocabulary terms to provide details in inference and explanation.
• Represents the data from the table in another graphic form that shows relationships.

Rewrite the relationship statement below. You may use your own words to begin the sentences. Check to make sure the *Must Haves* are in your statement and include at least one *Amazing* criteria.

Example One of Relationship Statement Support, that the data has been provided. This focuses student attention on interpreting the data. Scaffolds were made that focused on different parts of writing a relationship statement and then assigned based on student needs. In Table 6.6 *Example Two Relationship Statement*, some of the prompts have been removed for students to generate. The scaffold would be used alternating prompts and ultimately removing prompts for students to complete the task. The use of the scaffold continues until students can independently name all of the parts and purposes of each part as well as write a relationship statement without any prompts.

In addition to being able to write a relationship statement when directed, Ms. Ford ultimately wants her students to be able to recognize when a problem or question calls for the use of a relationship statement. So, the scaffold may be accompanied by sorting problems and questions into ones where a useful response would be a relationship statement. Scaffolds help students by focusing their time to work on the parts of a task that need practice.

Extensions. Finally, extensions help students reach beyond, like a snorkel or scuba gear that allows swimmers to go deeper and stay underwater longer. An extension stretches students' ability for the deep dive into learning a topic or skill. Too often our students are not challenged, do not see their current learning in the context of the next step, or see ways that the current task can be improved. Posting beyond or *Amazing* criteria prompts learners in the self-regulated learning cycle of setting goals, monitoring, reflecting, and revising, and then setting new goals. Students are

Table 6.7 Sample Supports and Extensions by Objective

Student Need	Objective	Supports	Extensions
Problem Solving (answering questions)	Identify known and unknown variables	Circle known values and information Restate question in own words (clarify)	Provide different types of problems that ramp up difficulty
Academic Vocabulary	Use a word bank to explain answer meaningfully through academic vocabulary	Provide words with images, cognates, or synonyms Use a word match or make connections from previous units	Use advanced vocabulary Explain Latin roots Provide multiple meanings Create a thesaurus
Concept Application	Solve a puzzling situation ("Why is a giraffe's neck long?")	Sample puzzle and solution Make clues available Bridge concept to present life	Find conflicting evidence Provide a counterintuitive example Bridge this concept to concept from other units
Reading	Find main idea	Chunk text Highlight text Embed vocabulary definitions	Higher level text Routine – connect/extend/ wonder Compare main ideas

not just finishing tasks, but are actually connecting their learning to the next steps as a continuous cycle. *Amazing* criteria help teachers build a classroom culture of rigor, challenging students to stretch and go beyond. Extensions are always provided in our *Amazing* criteria for every task, but whenever possible, should also be planned for each part of OSCAR.

Extensions stretch students who have mastered the objectives being taught in a lesson so the students receive activities that relate to current learning goals but go beyond the expectations of the required task. When you are planning supports to address likely student needs, it is always good to also plan extensions. In this way, you are not focused only on providing help for students who may struggle. See Table 6.7, *Sample Supports and Extensions by Objective*, for examples of student needs and possible supports and extensions.

Teaching Approach to Specific Help Resources

Specific Help resources are most effective when the teacher uses a systematic teaching approach. This is very different than the method for general help resources of teach, prompt, and provide. First, teachers must identify the goal of the systematic teaching. We identify two purposes for the design of instruction, Practice and Fade or Independent Use. These two purposes are not mutually exclusive, meaning at times teachers may implement first Independent Use and then Practice and Fade. However, the teaching is completely different based on the purpose of the teacher's approach to offering help.

In Practice and Fade the systematic teaching is designed for students to practice a specific skill and then the scaffold is explicitly and strategically removed or faded as the student develops mastery of the skill and no longer needs the scaffold. The student should be totally aware of the scaffold, the purpose, and how the scaffold is helping with a specific skill. Help should not be hidden because students will want to know how to scaffold tasks on their own, when they are not in school.

The second goal is Independent Use, where the student is taught how to ask for the scaffold or make the scaffold so that the student can independently acquire the help that is needed to accomplish a task. This approach is used when the teacher antici-pates that the student will require an extended period to develop the skill or that the student might not be able to complete tasks without this scaffold. So, the short-term instructional goal is not to remove the scaffold, but rather to teach the student how to independently notice the opportunity to use help and then get the help that they need. For example, a young child might use a number line to check her/his math. The num-ber line can be removed as the child develops stronger number sense and automaticity. However, an adolescent student may not have enough time to work solely on number sense. So, the teacher instructs the adolescent in how to draw a number line on scrap paper before beginning to solve problems with negative numbers.

The two different approaches are often used at different times for students. It is criti-cal that the teacher have a specific purpose and strategic teaching plan in mind for sup-ports, scaffolds, and extensions to be effective. Offering help is confusing for teachers because the same supports, scaffolds, and extensions may be used as tools in General Help and Individualized Help. The difference is not in the actual resource or material— the difference is in the teaching approach that accompanies the use of the help resource. When offering help, you must plan specifically the purpose and approach to teaching the lesson. You will probably offer more than one approach over time, so the only wrong choice is not to make a clear choice about the teaching approach. Now that the importance of the teaching approach is clarified, let's define individualized help, paying attention to how the approach differs from general and specific help.

Individualized Help

In addition to General Help Resources and Specific Resources: Scaffolds, Supports, and Extensions, teachers also provide individualized help. In learning to swim, indi-vidualized help is like the lap lanes where each swimmer is doing their own workout using a variety of help resources. Just like swimmers have focused workout or lap time, where they may use different scaffolds, supports, and extensions, students need individualized workouts geared to their specific learning needs.

Individualized workouts can be as simple as assigning a few different warm-up questions focused on particular skill practice. You may choose to repeat a routine warm-up assignment from the week before. For example, during "Mastery Monday" students repeat an assignment from the week before that they missed, need to increase fluency in, or that they misunderstood. Routine individualized help builds a culture where students expect to have to review and repeat, and work to achieve learning goals. It also provides a routine opportunity for students to close gaps and extend their learning. As we learned in the Introduction, spaced practice is much more effective than attempting to close gaps in a six-week review at the end of the year. Individualized help or practice is used to close gaps and extend learning on a regular basis.

We know that students come to our classrooms with a wide range of experi-ences, interests, and knowledge, so we expect starting positions for every learning objective to vary widely among students in our classrooms. In addition to differ-ent starting positions, students will learn at different rates and remember different information. Therefore there has to be room in each unit of study for individualized help and practice for *all* students. This individualized help should not be confused with individualized education programs (IEP) for students with disabilities. Special education services are different than, and additional to, differentiated instruction in the general education inclusive classroom that we are describing in this book.

Teacher Approach to Offering Individualized Help

The goal of the teacher's approach for individualized help is for students to use practice and help resources systematically to achieve their own goals. The role of the student is different in individualized help in that they should be participating along with teacher guidance in determining the "workout." You can picture the differences if you imagine how swimmers are using help resources in the general or free swim area and the lap lanes. You should make time for all tiers of help during every unit.

Teacher's Approach Makes the Difference

All help resources must be taught. Students need to know the purpose of the help resources, when and how to use the resource, including how to return or put away the resource, and the procedures for when and how to request help. This instruction includes alerting students to how they are expected to benefit from help strategies. Students need reminders of the help resources available for tasks in the directions. Consistently stating the help available for a task makes using help a normal part of learning for all students and enables the teacher to easily assign specific help to learners based on their needs. This type of introduction and teaching is done for all tiers of help resources. Figure 6.7 displays the relationship between the different tiers of help (General, Specific Resources, and Individualized), teacher approach (provide, teach, and assign), and the level of decision making for teachers and students. You will notice that all help is taught; however, general resources differ in that they are provided or are available for students to choose. For General Help, student decision making is high. When help is assigned, student decision making is limited. This is an important difference to remember as you assign help to address a specific student learning need and require use within a structured or systematic teaching process to reach a specific goal.

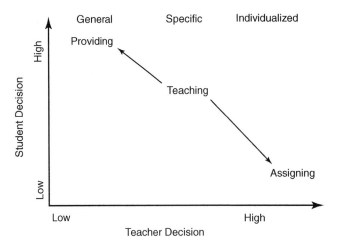

Figure 6.7 Type of Help and Approach by Teacher and Student Decision Level.

Teachers often use the word scaffold when they are referring to any help resource. However, scaffolds are significantly different than supports and extensions and very different than general help resources. For help resources to promote effective learning, you must make decisions in the approach to offering help. Remember it is not one single final decision, but when help is offered there should be a specific approach that is known to both the students and the teacher. The approach may change, but there is always a specific approach being used. Once a decision is made then students and teachers can measure the impact of help on student learning. Also, students can reflect on the kind of help used during different times in learning something new. This reflection enables your students to learn how to ask for specific help in other settings, such as in college, the workplace, and with friends or family.

Rooted in Research: Focus on Help Seeking

As any teacher would attest, getting students to seek help appropriately can be very challenging. Not only do students generally become more reluctant to seek help as they get older, students who often need to seek help the most never do, or they become so dependent on others that they never learn to take ownership of their own learning.

Researchers who study help-seeking make a distinction between different types of help-seeking. Students who seek help for adaptive and appropriate reasons, such as to become better at a task or to acquire new skills, are engaging in what researchers call *instrumental* help-seeking. Students also sometimes seek help because it is quicker to do so, or because they feel like they can off-load the work on someone else, engaging in *expedient* or *executive* help-seeking.[1] Still, others refuse to seek help altogether; such students are considered to be *avoidant* help seekers. The primary question driving most of the research on help-seeking is how to get students to seek instrumental help.

We have detailed several strategies in this chapter to promote help-seeking in general, but especially instrumental help-seeking that promotes self-regulated learning. Help-seeking is considered to be an important behavioral self-regulated learning strategy that students employ as they would cognitive and metacognitive strategies, such as rehearsal or planning (Karabenick, 2011; Zusho, Karabenick, Bonney, & Sims, 2007). What makes help-seeking somewhat different is that it involves other people. Given what it can imply about a student's abilities or lack thereof, help-seeking can be risky (Karabenick, 2011). Not surprisingly, studies have found that students, especially those who struggle with low self-esteem, become reluctant to seek help in public, particularly on tasks that they perceive to be diagnostic of highly-valued abilities (Karabenick & Knapp, 1991). Having readily available general help resources is crucial for these students.

What does the research say about ways to promote instrumental help-seeking? Theoretical models of help-seeking point to the importance of building awareness that there is a problem. Students will not seek help if they do not know that they need help. In order for students to detect that there is a problem, they must become dissatisfied in some way, with their level of comprehension, or performance, or they have failed in achieving some self-set goal. From an ALL-ED perspective, this is facilitated with frequent formative self-assessments, as well as through conversations with peers where students can compare their understanding with others.

Students must also come to realize that they *need* to seek help. In some cases, simply detecting that a problem exists is not enough to spur students to seek help, especially if they believe that they have the internal resources to solve the problem on their own. In order for students to realize that they need help, they must come to real-ize that their impasse cannot be overcome by things within their control (i.e., putting in greater effort). They must also *want* to seek help; they need to feel some sense of motivation to solve the problem. There is an inverse association between seeking help and motivation; students are less likely to seek help if they feel more competent to be able to solve the problem on their own *and* if they feel like seeking help is not likely to help them overcome very low levels of performance (Karabenick, 2011). In general, studies demonstrate that students with adaptive motivational profiles—academically competent students who value and have greater interest in coursework—are more likely to seek help when needed (Karabenick, 2011). As we have shown throughout this book, the ALL-ED routines are essentially meant to build motivation.

It is important to consider the sources from whom students decide to seek help. The amount, type, and quality of helping resources available to students can greatly impact whether or not students decide to seek help and what kind of help they seek (e.g., instrumental, expedient) (Karabenick, 2011). Researchers often classify sources of help-seeking in terms of whether they are formal or informal. Formal resources, including teachers, often have more expertise but are limited in number. In comparison, informal sources such as friends or other peers may have less exper-tise, but they may be more available and less critical.

Studies find that younger children are generally more likely to request help from teachers than other peers, especially if they perceive that their teachers like them. As children get older, however, they become more wary of asking for help, thinking that their teachers will think that they are "dumb" if they ask for help. This research also suggests that as students get older, they are more likely to ask for help from informal sources (i.e., peers) than from formal sources like teachers (Karabenick & Knapp, 1988; Newman & Goldin, 1990). Having general help resources readily available to students can solve some of the problems related to lack of help-seeking, especially among older students.

Finally, considering the focus ALL-ED places on group learning routines, we conclude this section with a summary of the research on help-seeking in groups. One of the reasons that ALL-ED promotes the use of group learning routines is to facilitate the use of peers as a resource. Assistance is readily available when students work in collaborative or cooperative learning groups. Nevertheless, research also suggests that the manner in which students work together in groups greatly affects help-seeking. Noreen Webb and her colleagues found that the nature of questions directly affects the level of help students receive when working in groups; students who ask specific questions are much more likely to receive help than students who ask general questions. The quality of group interactions also affects help-seeking; students are less likely to seek help when their group members insult one another, or when group members encourage others to copy their work (Webb, Ing, Kersting, & Nemer, 2006). As we mentioned in Chapter 4, the ALL-ED group learning routines are specifically designed to counteract negative and unproductive group interactions.

Fading Help Resources

When it comes to providing help-seeking resources, an important question to con-sider is when to take these resources away. For this, let's turn to the research on tutoring, scaffolding, and self-regulated learning. Research indicates that tutoring has a positive impact on learning (Graesser, D'Mello, & Person, 2009). Similarly, research on scaffolding suggests that providing scaffolds can help students engage in complex tasks that they otherwise wouldn't be able to complete on their own (Hmelo-Silver, Duncan, & Chinn, 2007; Puntambekar & Hübscher, 2005).

Implicit in the concept of scaffolding is the idea that, at some point, scaffolds and supports need to be taken away—a notion referred to as fading. Research on scaffolding is based in large part on the theoretical work of Vygotsky, who suggested that fading should occur when a process of internalization takes place. Internalization essentially occurs when learners (not tutors) are in control and taking responsibility for their learning. From an ALL-ED perspective, the process of internalization is enhanced when students build metacognitive awareness and self-regulatory skills. The research on fading suggests that scaffolds should be removed only when students can complete the task *and* when they understand how the strategies used to complete that task can be applied to other similar tasks. As Puntambekar and Hübscher (2005) note:

> Good scaffolding implies that a learner is provided with support that can enable him or her to function independently. The best scaffolding can be faded because it will eventually lead the learner to internalize the processes he or she is being helped to accomplish (Rogoff, 1990). Therefore, it is important to understand how students are using the tools and whether they are actually able to work independently when the tool is removed.
>
> (p. 8)

Help is an essential component in ensuring that all learners are learning in every lesson. Research on help-seeking focuses our attention on the importance of using specific resources with systematic approaches for offering help and the importance of continuously monitoring the impact of help on student learning.

Try Classroom Routines: Precise, Effective, Efficient Learning for All

Plan: Task Analysis

Review your curriculum and make a list of the most challenging concepts, strategies, and skills that are required for students to master. Reread the list and place a star next to items that come up for students frequently. Look for items used in several different units in your subject area, have strong connections to other subject areas, build on skills from previous learning, or establish skills needed for future learning. Identify one item that is challenging and used often.

Use task analysis to break down this concept, strategy, or skill into the smallest parts. Task analysis routines can be done with colleagues or students to identify the parts of this complex task. Task analysis can be used to build student independence by teaching the parts one at a time or by starting with the whole task and breaking it down with students.

Teach: Help Desk

Designate a place in the room for help resources specific to the assigned task. Help Desk resources can include: an answer sheet, a model of completed student work, an iPad with a video of how to complete the steps, a peer who has finished early to offer feedback and explanations, and the teacher to provide mini-lessons. Open the Help Desk during table talk and individual tasks so that students are not waiting for teacher assistance.

Adjust Instruction: Teach, Prompt, Provide, and Assign Help

Before circulating around the room to provide help, try prompting students to use general help resources that are available in the classroom. In addition, find time for a short routine individual workout in your daily or unit schedule. In the early childhood classroom, you might assign students to a specific center for ten minutes before allowing them to choose a second center, to provide a short targeted time to practice or extend a skill. With older students, the individual workout could be to repeat a worksheet from the previous week for practice or fluency, or a few assigned questions from previous units based on student needs. Routine *Individualized Help* is essential to closing gaps and extending learning, so looking for small routine ways to get started is an important first step.

Checklist to Try Routines in Your Teaching

See https://www.routledge.com/9780815370819 for additional resources: Templates – Group Learning Routines and Help Resources.

Plan	Teach	Adjust Instruction
❑ Plan to offer help in a unit or a lesson.	❑ Open a Help Desk during individual work time.	❑ Teach General Help. ❑ Adjust Help Resources available prior to circulating around the room to offer help. ❑ Plan a routine time for an individual workout, perhaps repeating a worksheet from the previous week on Mondays or assigning different review questions in each unit to practice or extend specific skills or knowledge.

Quality Criteria to Implement Classroom Routines

Must Haves	Amazing
• A variety of help resources are available. • Help resources are offered on a daily or weekly basis, or are tied to a specific activity. • Help resources are offered with a clear teacher approach.	• Teacher adjusts help offering prior to circulating to provide help to individuals. • Teacher reminds students of available help and the purpose of the resources in the teacher directions. • Teacher uses task analysis to increase student clarity of a task.

Chapter Reflection

Chapter Summary

In this chapter, we clarified the three tiers of help and the different approaches to offering help to students. All students need different types of help at times during learning. We identified the many help resources that are already available in most classrooms and examined three approaches to offering help. For *General Resources*, we discussed the Teach, Prompt, Provide approach. *Specific Resources* require an assigned and systematic teacher approach of Practice and Fade or Independent Use. *Individualized* workouts are essential for closing gaps and extending learning. The teacher approach to individualized help involves the student in managing a sustained systematic workout. We learned how task analysis is used to break down tasks to develop scaffolds and supports. Our approach to offering individualized help is not at all related to Individualized Education Programs or specialized instruction; students with disabilities would receive special education service in addition to this general help being offered to all learners in inclusive classrooms.

Learning Journal: Record Important Takeaways

Continue your *Learning Journal* to track your thinking about meeting the needs of diverse learners by recording answers to the following four questions:

1.   What was most interesting and useful for you in this chapter?
2.   Why was this interesting and useful?
3.   How does this connect to what you know about meeting the learning needs of all learners?
4.   What research from this chapter could you use to explain or support decisions to adjust instruction?

Save these responses for reflection after reading more of this book, and trying out ideas in your classroom. We will answer these same four questions at the end of every chapter.

Return to Your Starting Position

Return to your preliminary first draft answer to our chapter question, "How do teachers adjust instruction to meet the needs of all learners?" Add new ideas or revise in another way. Circle the most important part and save to return to after Chapter 7: Closing Gaps and Extending Learning.

Note

1   Incidentally, researchers refer to this as executive help-seeking because it mimics what executives do with their personal assistants—offload tasks to their assistants because it is easier and saves time.

Step 4

SHOp Adjustments—Options

Overview

Objective:

How do teachers adjust instruction to meet the needs of all learners?

   Think: Reread your list of ways that teachers adjust instruction from Chapter 6. Try the Criteria Checklist routine, with the criteria of <u>Plus Two</u>. Add two ideas— either two new ideas—or add one and annotate an idea that you had noted before but is more important now or that you have changed in some way.

Criteria

- Identify how to adjust instruction for including student choice, using Options, to increase the range of students able to engage in learning and to assess the possible adjustments for effectiveness and efficiency.
- Explain how the research on offering choice impacts learning.
- Try Classroom Routines

   - Plan—*Structured Student Choice.*
   - Teach—*Idea Carousel.*
   - Adjust Instruction—Assign to reflection, not completion or finishing work.

Starting Position: Before Reading This Chapter

Record Your Starting Position: Pluses, Minuses, Interesting

Think about when you offer students choice. Rank the three most important pluses or benefits of student choice and the three most relevant negative aspects or outcomes for you and your students. Add things that are interesting and/or questions that come up when you think about offering students choice in Table 7.1.

From the Classroom: Giving Students Choice

Ms. Ford felt perpetually pulled between offering students choice and giving assignments. When she offered students choice, often they would choose an assignment that was too easy or too hard, or would make a choice based on being with friends versus something they were truly interested in learning. Some students even had a hard time making a choice. She felt the answer must lie in balancing options, sometimes offering student choice and sometimes assigning tasks. So Ms. Ford decided to

Table 7.1 Choices: Pluses, Minuses, Interesting Chart

Pluses (+)	Minuses (–)	Interesting/Questions
Encourages autonomy	Grading	How can you give choice when
Increases motivation	Management	students all need to achieve
Captures interests	Planning time	same standards?
Provides differentiated tasks	Students choose wrong task	How often? When?
Requires thinking to make an	Finding materials	
informed choice	Students feel overwhelmed	
Builds on student strengths	by choices	

alternate between these options, sometimes giving students assignments and other times letting students choose what to do or what topic to explore. Despite these efforts, student choice remained a problem, and often resulted in a tremendous amount of additional grading with minimal student gains in learning.

When Ms. Ford reflected on the diverse strengths her students brought to class every day, she knew that tying in student strengths was essential to building meaning. She also knew that students progressed at very different speeds, so she needed ways to keep all learners engaged. She started to think about offering student choice in different ways. She stopped thinking of student choice as an on–off switch—either allowing a student choice or offering no student choice. Instead, she started thinking about student choice as a continuum of options from total teacher assignment to a middle ground of teacher-structured student choice to total student choice. Suddenly, there was new opportunity to provide options in every assignment. She could structure student choice, increase student thinking, and have all students working on a single assignment. For example, she could direct students to, "Complete one through five and then choose two additional questions to work on from questions six through nine. Write a note explaining why you chose the two questions to answer (for example, you knew the answer, or the questions challenged you)." This was the beginning of a new way to adjust instruction. She could adjust the options along the continuum from assignment to choice to increase student feelings of autonomy and to create room in every task for specific assignments geared toward individual or group learning needs.

Options

In the previous chapter we defined structures and help—two teacher responses that can be used to adjust instruction to meet learner needs. In this chapter, we define Options—the Op in SHOp adjustments. Together, SHOp—Structures, Help, and Options—enable teachers to ensure that all learners are learning. So, let's learn more about how to implement Ms. Ford's discovery of offering Options along a continuum ranging from total student choice to teacher-structured student choice to total teacher assignment. Options provide greater opportunities for students to complete a task successfully. If the objective is for students to remember what the previous day's lesson was about as the starting position, the students are offered total student choice: write a story, draw a picture, or make a list of important words and facts from yesterday's lesson. All three of those tasks accomplish the objective of remembering the previous lesson while giving students total choice for that task.

Another example of how options for success may be used to adjust instruction would be to assign students to either solve the problem, or circle and explain the part of the problem that is new. In this way, students are either solving the problem or identifying their questions so that all students can engage in the task. Often when all students are given a common text, many students will find the reading to be far above their independent reading level or below a challenging level. To solve this common problem, you could provide options for independent reading. You can, for example, give an option of doing a careful read from beginning to end, or an option of circling the familiar words and summarizing what the text might be about from those words. In this way, all students will be engaged in reading the text in an independent, accessible way. So Options are used to ensure all students are working toward the objective of the task. In addition, Options ensure student engagement—there is no reason for students not to engage in the task because there are options that both accomplish the objective and allow students with a range of skills to be successful.

Choice Continuum

Remember, Options always fall on a choice continuum extending from total student choice to teacher-structured student choice to total teacher assignment (see Figure 7.1). For example, when students choose a book from the library, they are typically participating in total student choice. If the teacher wants to ensure that students select a book matched to their independent reading level or a book on a specific topic, the teacher could organize different boxes of books by similar reading levels or topics. The teacher could then assign students to select a book from a specific box of books that matches their need. Students are still selecting a book and making a choice, but within the limits of the teacher's structure to ensure that a specific learning goal is accomplished. Finally, total teacher assignment is used to close gaps and extend learning. The teacher assigns different tasks to students based specifically on their learning needs (Figure 7.2). Let's discuss each of these options on the choice continuum a little further.

Total Student Choice: As we discussed above, total student choice involves providing several options for students and then allowing students to choose without restrictions. For example, you can ask students to jot down what they remembered from yesterday's lesson in words, numbers, or a drawing. Allowing students to make choices promotes a sense of autonomy and can send messages to your students that you care about them. Keep in mind that total student choice should only be offered when all options lead directly and efficiently to the learning objective, or you may run into problems related to students making inappropriate choices.

Teacher-Structured Student Choice. When you assign students to complete a required task, and then provide them with an opportunity to choose additional tasks to complete as part of the overall assignment, you are providing structured student choice. Directions as simple as "Complete five questions: the first two are required, then choose three additional questions," or "Choose a library book from the box of books gathered for your independent reading level," are great examples of teacher-structured student choice.

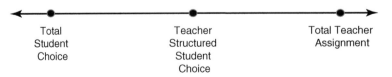

Figure 7.1 Options Fall along the Choice Continuum.

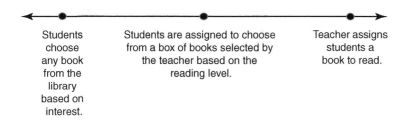

Students choose any book from the library based on interest.

Students are assigned to choose from a box of books selected by the teacher based on the reading level.

Teacher assigns students a book to read.

Figure 7.2 Example of Options for Choosing a Book from Total Choice, Teacher-Structured Student Choice to Total Teacher Assignment

Structuring choice aids differentiation of instruction by giving teachers an opportunity to provide supports and extensions within a common assignment. Supports and extensions can be assigned by the teacher to meet specific student needs and to support student autonomy by allowing students to make choices that are matched to their needs or strengths. The free choices available all lead to mastering a common curricular goal, and the structure, or the way the tasks are arranged and assigned, creates the opportunity for differentiated instruction.

To structure the choices more effectively, it is useful to lay out the options in visible paths showing a progression toward an objective, so that students can both monitor their progress and choose their next task. For example, Figure 7.3 might be a learning path to complete a project with each box representing one task or piece of the project. As you can see, all students have to complete a total of five tasks. All students need to complete the first three tasks, but then they are given an option of choosing one task from each side. This assignment can easily be differentiated by organizing the tasks on the two branches by level of difficulty; for example, "develops required skill," "applies required skill," and "exceeds required skill." You can then assign students one of the three choices from both branches and ask them to select one task from each branch. In this case, all students will complete the same first three tasks, the fourth task will be differentiated by teacher assignment, and the fifth task will be differentiated by student interest. You could even ask early finishers to select an additional task from either branch.

Structured Choice sends a message to the students that the teacher believes all students will accomplish the learning goals and that there are necessary different routes to that success. The assignment has not been reduced to a simple version and an advanced version, but rather large tasks or concepts are broken down into specific skills that are visible, along with an expected learning progression. The teacher and students share the responsibility for structuring learning and monitoring progress. This shared responsibility fosters a culture of respect and collaboration, as well as encourages intrinsic motivation (see *Rooted in Research*). *Structured Learning Choices* are:

- effective because both the learning goals and the process for achieving the goals are visible to both teachers and students.
- efficient because one assignment can hold choices that enable teachers to assign specific tasks to students that respond to many different learning needs.
- precise because the assignment ensure that students spend time on tasks that are matched to their learning needs.

Teacher-structured student choice supports student autonomy and increases access, rigor, and relevance by helping you to adjust instruction to accelerate or extend, review, and close gaps in student learning. Visual arrangement and directions for completion of the learning choices are keys to providing students with choices that emphasize learning to achieve specific goals. Examine Figures 7.4–7.7 to imagine how the options offered to students are guiding choices toward learning objectives. Consider tasks and assignments that you use with students and how a visual path might represent both teacher assignment and options for student choice.

- In Figure 7.4, there are core concepts, skills, or tasks that everyone must complete. The students branch off for in-depth learning, perhaps choosing a specific topic within a unit. Then students come back together, sharing their in-depth learning and connecting ideas back to the core tasks from the beginning.
- In Figure 7.5, we can see how five different paths lead to one common learning goal. This is an example of using multiple questions or multiple materials to answer one research question.

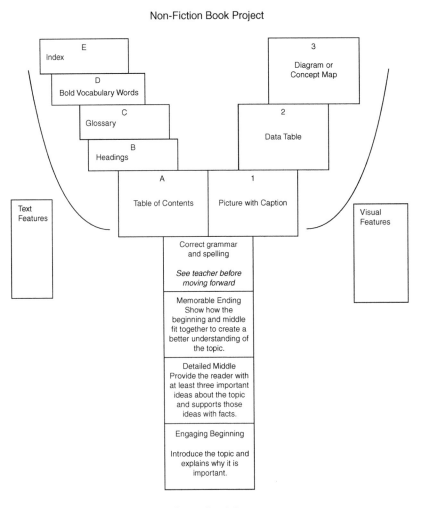

Figure 7.3 Structured Choice: Nonfiction Book Project

- In Figure 7.6, the initial tasks are broken down to offer skill development and practice or review of a needed concept.
- In Figure 7.7, we see a typical Tic-Tac-Toe formation, which you can use to both structure and assign specific tasks for students to complete. You can, for example, assign students to complete a Tic-Tac-Toe that crosses the middle square, putting an essential assignment in the middle. You might also assign the

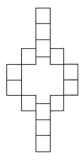

Figure 7.4 Core Concepts, Skills, and Tasks Pathway

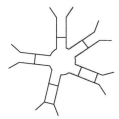

Figure 7.5 Five Paths, One Common Learning Goal

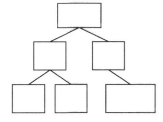

Figure 7.6 Breakdown of Initial Tasks for Skill Development

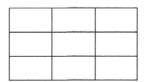

Figure 7.7 Tic-Tac-Toe Formation

four corners, if there are four required tasks, and then allow your students to choose one other task to create a Tic-Tac-Toe.

During every unit teachers need to adjust instruction to extend, review and practice, close gaps, and promote student interests. Teacher-structured student choice provides opportunities for these different instructional goals in daily instruction. Note that you are not creating something new here. Rather, you are tweaking ways to assign a practice sheet, a book to read, or an art project by considering how the option continuum can be used within that assignment. Table 7.2 offers some examples of small changes to normal tasks and assignments that can enable you to adjust instruction to meet diverse learner needs.

Options along the choice continuum ranging from total student choice to teacher-structured student choice to total teacher assignment provide many opportunities to promote student autonomy and durable learning while making adjusting instruction to fit learner needs easier for teachers. Most importantly, these options stretch the curriculum to engage students who vary widely across many dimensions. Although providing options is an important part of building motivation, it is also necessary to think about how you can routinely use your expertise to assign precise tasks to advance student learning. For this, total teacher assignment may be necessary.

Total Teacher Assignment (Targeted Practice): Total teacher assignment or targeted practice can be routinely incorporated into the class schedule. To ensure effective learning for learners with diverse needs, targeted practice should be included as a regular (meaning daily or weekly) routine in every unit. During targeted practice, teachers provide time for students to repeat assignments for fluency, review material, acquire missing skills, and extend skills on a regular basis.

In Chapter 6, we described "Mastery Monday" where students re-use handouts from the previous week to complete missing assignments, practice challenging assignments, repeat an assignment to increase automaticity, and/or complete an extension assignment during the opening activity. You might consider a routine time of the day for targeted practice, or a place in every unit where practice is planned. You might place learning targets on a chart on the wall and place student names on the chart next to objectives that they have demonstrated mastery of and indicated to you that they are interested in sharing their expertise. Then, on a regular basis students can make appointments with "Experts" for a specific learning objective they would like to learn more about and see a demonstration. You might consider adding learning objectives such as, "I can draw without looking at the paper," or "I can keep my body and brain fit with perfect push-ups" to make sure that all students are experts in at least one objective and would have an interest in learning an expertise, too. This targeted practice is individualized and may use the individualized help discussed earlier.

Given the student diversity we described in the Introduction, it would be impossible for all students to achieve standards within a set amount of time. Some students will need less time, whereas others will need more practice time to achieve durable learning. Therefore, precise teacher assignment is just as essential as student choice to meet the wide range of learner needs. Whether offering total student choice, teacher-structured student choice, or total teacher assignment, placing these options within classroom routines that are designed to facilitate management and offering feedback is essential for sustainability. We give another example of targeted practice in Chapter 9, when we discuss our research on *Flag Time*.

Table 7.2 Options to Adjust Instruction in Daily Assignments and Tasks

Extend: Stretch students to reach beyond expectations Examples 1. Use task analysis to divide the assignment into parts and add challenging parts that stretch beyond the expectations, assign students who need extension to skip parts they do not need to practice and complete the more challenging parts. 2. Add a column to a standard rubric that identifies criteria for beyond the top score. 3. Assign two Amazing Criteria instead of two of the Must Have criteria for a task. 4. Include a write-in challenge question or create a problem in daily assignments. Assign students a skill or topic that the create a problem or questions must address. **Close Gaps:** Provide opportunities to learn missing information/skills. Examples 1. Use the same task analysis done to create extensions to identify prerequisite skills and knowledge. Assign different starting places based on student needs. Some students will begin by working on missing skills, while others start on the task and move toward extension tasks; all students will complete required common assignments. 2. Assign projects that are intended to require different amounts of time to complete. For example, create one project that will take students a significantly shorter amount of time to complete, but that will assess the same content knowledge. Pull students for a lesson to provide background knowledge or missing skills who have been assigned the shorter project. 3. Include both common (for all students) and specialty tasks or games in daily assignments. Assign students the "specialty" sets of questions, problems, or games that develop needed skills as part daily assignments. Specialty assignments should use a familiar routine so that no new instruction is required to provide additional practice. If instruction is needed then it may be provided at a Help Desk during individual work time.	**Review and Practice:** Offer an opportunity to repeat previous instruction and skill practice Examples 1. Pull small group by assigned choices for instruction and correction. 2. Reduce the amount of new content knowledge on some homework assignments and add review material as homework. 3. Review material as part of a project in an upcoming unit. 4. Include one night of homework or class activity once a week as Design Your Own (DYO). Require choices to be based on results from a review of student work or an assessment. 5. Plan for review in every unit as a routine. This avoids stopping instruction to review skills and knowledge for exams and other assessments and spaces practice time for better memory. **Promote Student Interests:** Recruit student interests to build meaning and motivation so the teacher can learn more about students and students can begin to appreciate each other. Examples 1. Ask students what they find interesting about each topic and task. Invite students to begin at an interesting question or topic point and then progress in their learning from there. 2. Draw students into the required topics by providing sample images or words representing the topic that will be studied. Ask students to select an image that connects to their experiences, relates to things they know about, or leaves them with questions. Show students how these images also connect to the topic, bringing student interest along with the image or word to the topic under study. 3. Ask students how they learned something that they can do well. For example, a student might say they practiced 100 times a game, a song, or a skill in sports. Align the practice required for an academic skill to the process that the student has already used to successfully learn. Students may mentor other students on how to motivate yourself to practice something 100 times.

Rooted in Research: Autonomy and Choice

As we mentioned previously, research on motivation is largely predicated on the notion that intrinsic motivation flourishes when individuals feel a sense of autonomy, which by definition means to self-govern, indicating regulation by the self. Autonomy is therefore associated with an internal locus of control—or a feeling that you (and not others) are in control.

Ryan and Deci (2017) further note that autonomy can be defined in terms of actions that are endorsed and chosen by the self. In other words, one primary way to increase autonomy is to provide choice options (Patall, Cooper, & Wynn, 2010). Research generally confirms that providing choices to students can be beneficial (Patall, Cooper, & Robinson, 2008). For example, provision of choice has been associated with greater liking and interest in tasks as well as enhanced effort and achievement of learning outcomes (Cordova & Lepper, 1996; Iyengar & Lepper, 1999). Patall et al. (2010) randomly assigned students within classrooms to receive either a choice of homework options or to be assigned an option for all homework across two units. They found that students performed better on the unit test, and also reported higher intrinsic motivation and perceptions of competence to do the homework when they had homework choice options than when they did not have a choice.

There is a caveat to the research on choice and options that is important to keep in mind. Although providing choices to students may be the most concrete way for teachers to convey a sense of autonomy to students (Patall et al., 2010), simply giving students total choice is not always effective. There is research to suggest that too much choice can be debilitating since it can lead to choice overload and decision fatigue (Hattie, 2009; Schwartz, 2004). For this reason, we generally advocate for structured rather than free choice.

Motivational theorists also claim that choice may only be effective when it actually satisfies the fundamental psychological needs of autonomy, competence, and relatedness (Katz & Assor, 2007; Patall, 2013) and gives students an internal sense of control. Merely giving students options may not be enough to support their motivation; it is equally if not more important to consider whether the choices are relevant to students' interests and goals, in sync with their abilities, and in line with their family and cultural values.

Research also demonstrates that when it comes to providing choices, teachers typically only offer a narrow range of options, such as choice of partner, task format, or input on due dates (Rogat, Witham, & Chinn, 2014; Stefanou, Perencevich, DiCintio, & Turner, 2004). Although such options may initially provide students with a sense of control over their environment or over the form of the task, some have argued that they do little to engage students cognitively and are therefore not likely to have long-term effects on learning. Some researchers also advocate for choices that promote cognitive autonomy or student ownership of their learning (Stefanou et al., 2004). Examples of teacher behaviors that provide cognitive autonomy support include asking students to substantiate their point, or to generate their own solution paths, or to self-assess their learning, or provide evaluative feedback on their peers' solutions. In this regard, OSCAR and the CARR Check discussed earlier in this book promote cognitive autonomy, as do the structured learning paths discussed in this chapter.

Finally, it is important to note that promoting choice is not the only way to enhance students' sense of autonomy in the classroom. Researchers commonly describe teachers who are rated as high in autonomy support as teachers who not only provide choice, but who also listen to students and allow them to manipulate instructional materials and ideas. These teachers consider student preferences and interests in selecting and designing tasks, provide rationales for those activities, and give students opportunities to ask questions (Patall et al., 2017; Reeve, Bolt, & Cai, 1999; Rogat et al., 2014). Autonomy-supportive teachers are not controlling—they embrace student perspectives and do not pressure students to think, act, or feel in particular ways (Patall et al., 2017).

Return to Ms. Ford and the Blinking Red Light

Let's return to Ms. Ford from Chapter 5: CARR Check to solve her dilemma of students not engaged in the science reading on genetic diseases, even after she has offered two different choices. To increase clarity and relevance, Ms. Ford asked students to brainstorm questions that they hoped to answer to ensure all students knew about the topic that they were about to read. This brainstorm encouraged them to use what they knew about genetics to generate questions so Ms. Ford could correct misunderstandings just from the question generating routine. Then Ms. Ford offered a total student choice for students to select the article written in the style that most interested them—either a narrative biography or a logical scientific research report. The information needed to answer the same five questions was present in both texts, so truly students could select either text and accomplish the goal. This seems so right—high marks for Ms. Ford on clarity and relevance. But, things fall apart when the students can't independently read the text or they find the level of the text too easy. Now, Ms. Ford is faced with a problem of access and rigor. Can you think of a few ways that she might address this problem? If she could go back in time, perhaps she should have assigned the different texts based on student reading level. But, it is too late—the students have chosen and are not reading independently. Her first approach might be to change the structure for the task, moving from independent reading to partner reading. She could assign students to a partner who has chosen the same reading and use a group learning routine called *Read and Summarize*. In this routine, she would assign the student who is able to read the text to go first, reading out loud for two or three minutes. While listening, the summarizer follows along and circles the most important word or fact that was read. The partner then shares the most important word or fact and they discuss why it is important and how it connects with their life. They repeat this exercise until the end of the article. Ms. Ford can assign students to switch roles if everyone is able to read the text independently or the roles can remain the same until the end of the exercise. Shifting structures from independent to a structured group learning routine ensure engagement of all learners. Now, students can reorganize into small groups with representatives who read both articles to discuss the same and different information in the articles and preliminary answers to the five questions. All students are likely to be able to answer the five questions independently. You can learn with Ms. Ford that these decisions are continuous, and one decision leads to the next. You may never solve all of the problems, but you can make an adjustment to increase CARR and then assess CARR again and make new adjustments continuously as you move through each part of the lesson.

Try Classroom Routines: Precise, Effective, Efficient Learning for All

Plan: Teacher-Structured Student Choice

The easiest way to begin structured choice is to offer a structured choice in every assignment. For example, instead of completing questions one through ten, assign one through eight and choose one between nine and ten. Or ask students to complete one through ten and then go back and circle the problem and response of which they are most proud. This is offering a choice, but still requiring all students to complete the entire assignment.

To build your own structured choice, go back to your planning routine, Task Analysis. Plan a structured choice activity using the parts that you analyzed for this task. Another approach is to use these reflection questions to consider a unit that you are about to teach:

1 Can you think of a way that structured learning choice would lead to efficient and effective learning in the unit?
2 What is the toughest unit for students? How could structured student choice be used to support the hardest parts of a unit?
3 What are the interests and talents of my students and how can structured student choice make those interests and talents assets in learning the established curriculum?

When designing structured choice activities, always anticipate possible problems and capitalize on the positive outcomes. For example, require the choice that all students must complete or add a stop to check in with the teacher or peer for feedback as a required choice.

Every activity usually begins with some form of review to activate prior knowledge and engage learners in remembering what they already know or can do. This is a great moment to routinely offer total student choice. Because the goal is for students to remember, how the students communicate their memory can be varied so that all students efficiently accomplish the goal. The individual routine *List, Write, Draw* that you completed as your starting position in Chapter 1 can be used with any question asking students to recall something. Simply ask students to answer your question using a list, story, or quick drawing or sketch to capture what they remember, and then go back and add two details. Encourage students to review their writing, list, or drawing another time and circle the most important part. Students can share their answer to your question with a partner in an *Elbow Exchange* or at a table with a *Show and Share* and then return to their answer to add two more details. This routine provides options for communication while activating background knowledge and providing teachers with a dashboard of student readiness for the next task.

Another option for you to try out is to provide teacher-structured student choice within assignments that are repeated daily, weekly, or in every unit. Figure 7.8 provides an example of a repetitive assignment, vocabulary practice. In this

---

Vocabulary Practice Learning Choices

Name _____ Words that I am studying _____

Complete two Tic-Tac-Toes to learn your words.

---

1. If your words were colors then what colors would they be and why?	2. Compare each of your words to another word using this format. (your word) is like _____ because _____. Repeat this pattern for each word.	3. Find your words in a textbook. Make a list of your word, the page # where it can be found, and copy the sentence where the word is used. If you can't find the word in your textbook then try other books, newspapers, magazines, and the Internet.
4. Draw an image or symbol that represents your word.	5. Write the definitions of each of your words.	6. Write a question where the answer would be one of your words. Create a question for each of your words.
7. Explain why this word is important to know. Offer examples of how people can use the word.	8. Find an image that represents each of your words.	9. Create a group of five words that one of your words would fit into. Give the group a title. Create a group of words with a title for each of your words.

Figure 7.8 Example of Teacher-Structured Student Choice for Vocabulary Practice.

way, the teacher can require all students to complete the center box and write a definition.

Consider providing students with choices in daily tasks and assignments:

- Assign students to use one row of a rubric to improve their work based on their need, and require students to choose one additional row based on their interest.
- Ongoing homework assignments, such as vocabulary development and spelling practice.
- Multiple projects on a single topic to deepen understanding (possibly using different communication methods or focusing on different perspectives).
- Large projects, broken down into smaller tasks with choices within the smaller tasks.
- Review problems or vocabulary for a unit.
- Do Now or warm-up activities that include one option.

Teach: Idea Carousel (Group Routine)

See how students use their knowledge to explain answers and share ideas with peers.

ALL-ED Classroom Routine Directions: Idea Carousel

Idea Carousel is used to allow students to generate responses collaboratively in small groups while documenting the ideas. This is used when a topic is new, and it might be hard for students to activate their background knowledge to respond to a question. The small group conversation supports students in remembering information, practicing using academic vocabulary, and developing their knowledge. The disadvantage is that the teacher is not able to gather individual response during the activity. So, gathering responses in this way furthers student learning but does not lead to information that can be used for grouping individual students. Young children can do this routine by annotating pictures, drawing pictures, or building ideas with manipulatives. Older students usually do this routine by writing their ideas.

Strengths of this routine:

- encourages collaboration
- provides written feedback to each small group
- gathers responses into patterns for easier understanding of responses from the class
- gets students up and moving
- enables teachers and students to track their responses from the beginning to the end of the activity, enabling them to reflect on how their thinking grew and stayed the same.

Implementation Directions

Objective: To collaboratively brainstorm and evaluate a brainstorm of ideas.

Starting Positions: Ask individuals to gather by the topic or prompt that they have a response for.

Criteria

- *Must Haves*: Responds to each chart as groups circulate around the room, ensures each person in the group contributes to the response, answers the question or prompt.
- *Amazing*: Connects to a previous lesson or text, uses vocabulary from unit, unusual ideas.

Action Pattern

The teacher identifies in the directions:

- **Roles**: Recorder (rotates so that each student serves as a recorder; start by assigning the student with the best handwriting as the recorder; in this way, the initial responses will be easy for the other groups to read when students rotate).
- **Turns**: Students are assigned to first go to a chart where they have an idea to contribute to the response. Then groups discuss and record their ideas

for a set amount of time. The teacher directs the student to move to the next chart. All groups move one chart in the same direction around the room as the teacher directs.

- **Rules**: Use only one color marker assigned to group, all group members must contribute ideas at each station, all group members must be the recorder
- **Time**: 15 to 30 minutes

1 Post topics or questions and chart paper around the room (one topic per chart paper). Divide chart paper if more than one task is given, such as "things you think that you know" and questions.

2 Ask learners to stand by a topic that interests them most (guideline: limit group size to four or fewer).

3 Direct groups to brainstorm answers to the question or information about the topic on the chart paper.

4 Instruct groups to rotate systematically, completing the routine for each round. Require groups to take their marker with them so that students as well as the teacher can assess the thinking of a group by looking at the color of the writing on the chart. Assign the student with the best handwriting or spelling to be the recorder first and then students change who is the recorder each time they rotate. Add rounds if time permits for students to view charts.

  - Round One: **Read** the chart, check ideas that resonate with you as well
    - **Add** new ideas to the chart
  - Round Two: **Read** the chart, check ideas that resonate with you as well
    - **Add** new ideas to the chart
    - **Star three** ideas or questions that you would like to discuss or the three most important ideas
  - Round Three: **Read** the chart, check ideas that resonate with you as well
    - **Add** new ideas to the chart
    - **Circle one**—the most important idea.
  - Round Four: **Invite** students to continue around the room, just viewing the remaining charts until the students arrive back at their starting place.

Reflections

1 Ask students to return to their first chart to notice the changes. Students may place an exclamation point next to things that surprise them.

2 Ask students to return to their normal seats to discuss the charts. Direct students to discuss what patterns and differences they observed in the charts and what they think about the circles and underlines. Invite students to generate questions or plan next steps.

3 Ask students as individuals to write down their own learning or takeaway from the *Idea Carousel* and/or answer one of the initial questions or topic prompts.

Adjust Instruction: Assign to Reflection, Not Completion

Daily assignments and tasks should routinely end in reflection instead of finishing or completing the task. This teacher habit shifts students from completing work for you to reflecting on their learning in every assignment simply by changing the end goal from completion to reflection. For example, rather than assigning students to complete problems one through ten, ask students to complete one through eight and read nine and ten, then choose either nine or ten to complete, and write a note why you selected that problem. Or students might complete one through ten and go back to reflect on their work by being instructed, "Read your work, circle two vocabulary words that were used that a reader should notice," or "Read your work, put a star next to the most interesting answer." Students might, "Read their work and put a number next to evidence of a quality criteria that they see in their work." Assigning to reflect rather than to finish helps students see evidence of their abilities and growth in every assignment. A habit for giving directions is to assign to reflection, not completion.

Planning options into tasks including the full continuum from total teacher assignment to total student choice increases the possible ways to successfully engage students to complete tasks. During lessons, try agile thinking (see Chapter 8) by increasing options for successful responses when students are hesitant to engage in a task. Monitor which options lead to more detailed and better student responses. Consider adding help resources such as supports and extensions into the options offered in assignments. In this way, supports and extensions can be assigned to students, as appropriate, without having to create new or additional materials.

Checklist to Try Routines in Your Teaching

See https://www.routledge.com/9780815370819 for additional resources: Examples of Structured Choice.

Plan	Teach	Adjust Instruction
❏ Plan to offer options along the choice continuum. ❏ Put supports and extensions into structured choice assignments.	❏ Implement structured choice in repetitive or daily assignments. ❏ Provide Options for student responses using routines such as *List, Write, Draw.* ❏ Increase options through agile thinking during lessons to increase all students being able to produce a successful response.	❏ Add the direction, "When you are finished, go back and (look for a specific criteria)." For example, *"Reread and (underline or circle <u>criteria</u> in your work)."* Assign students specific criteria based on their next steps in learning. For example, assign those who need further challenge *Amazing* criteria.

Quality Criteria to Implement Classroom Routines	
Must Haves	*Amazing*
• Classroom routine is implemented on a daily or weekly basis, or is tied to a specific type of instruction, such as a mini-lesson, independent practice, or review.	• Assignments routinely provide a range for engagement and success.

Chapter Reflection

Chapter Summary

We explored how adjusting the Options for success provides increased opportunities for all learners. We thought of options along a choice continuum with one end being total student choice; in the middle, teacher-structured student choice; and at the opposite end, total student assignment. Teachers use options to increase student engagement and the abilities needed to complete the task. We examined the research roots in offering students choice. We practiced our agile thinking, considering how to provide needed guidance and promote student autonomy through teacher-structured student choice.

Learning Journal: Record Important Takeaways

Continue your *Learning Journal* to track your thinking about meeting the needs of diverse learners by recording answers to the following four questions:

1 What was most interesting and useful for you in this chapter?
2 Why was this interesting and useful?
3 How does this connect to what you know about meeting the learning needs of all learners?
4 What research from this chapter could you use to explain or support decisions to adjust instruction?

Save these responses for reflection after reading more of this book and for trying out ideas in your classroom. We will answer these same four questions at the end of every chapter.

Return to Your Starting Position

Return to your preliminary first draft answer to our chapter question, "How do teachers adjust instruction to meet the needs of all learners?" Add new ideas or revise in another way. Circle the most important part and save to return to after Chapter 9: Closing Gaps and Extending Learning.

Chapter 8

Agile Teacher Thinking

Deciding to Adjust Instruction

Overview

Objective:

What does the four-step teacher decision-making framework look like in practice?
Think: Underline the word that is most <u>important</u> in this Objective.

Criteria:

- Identify opportunities to use the teacher-thinking framework: "*At* OSCAR, *look and listen; if* (all, some, or individual) *students* need/have CARR, *then adjust* SHOp" to perceive student learning needs, and use agile thinking to adjust instruction.
- Explain how decisions to use ALL-ED classroom routines are supported by research.
- Try Classroom Routines

  - Plan—Agile Teacher Decisions: *At-If-Then Statements.*
  - Teach—*Question, Answers, Practice, Switch (QAPS-Peer Tutoring).*
  - Adjust Instruction—Record Agile Teacher Decisions.

Starting Position: Note, Rank, Reflect (Individual Routine)

Student diversity is an abundant natural resource in every classroom. Adjusting instruction requires agile thinking to change directions quickly and to turn potential problems into opportunities. When teachers differentiate instruction they are working like an environmentally conscious developer who surveys the resources in the community and plans ways to leverage those resources when building new structures. Adjusting instruction challenges teachers to continuously mine the community of students for assets that can be used for learning. Classroom routines will help you notice and build on what students bring as valued starting places for learning. So let's warm up your agile thinking by placing student skills in situations where the need can be used productively.

Notice:	Read the skills in the first column of Table 8.1.
Add:	Skills of your students in blank rows.
Note:	Think of different situations when these skills and habits might be a strength to be leveraged or a challenge to be eliminated by adjusting instruction. Consider different units of study and times of the year.

Table 8.1 Leveraging Student Strengths

	When is this a strength that could be used or built upon?	When is this a challenge to minimize or eliminate?
Copying other students		
Being confident to take risks		
Needing basic or foundational skills		
Missing class or instruction		
Talking with friends		
Texting and using cell phones and technology		

Rank: Place a star next to the skill you notice in students most.

Return: Go back to your starting position from Chapter 2: Changing Extremes. Consider how this list of student characteristics is similar or different.

Reflect: Think about and jot down questions this activity raised for you. Have you observed patterns in the things that you notice about students? Ask colleagues if they can think of other situations when these skills might be strengths.

Plan: Consider your next steps for learning from your students. Plan an activity where you can learn from students in every lesson. Make plans to use student strengths to leverage learning.

From the Classroom: Five Minutes until the Bell

There are ten minutes before the lunch bell. Ms. Ford is circulating offering help to students. The noise in the classroom rises as students who are finished with the independent practice look for other things to do. The noise makes it even harder for students who have not gotten started to focus. Ms. Ford literally cannot get around fast enough to help all students. She pauses and takes a moment to think about the problem using a CARR Check.

Students who have not started need greater clarity and better access to understand what actions to take. Students who are finished need a more rigorous task or clarity on what to do next. The teacher decides to adjust the structure of the action pattern, switching from independent work to a group learning routine. She decides to form triad stations using the peer tutoring routine, *Question, Answer, Practice, Switch (QAPS)*.

To form groups, Ms. Ford asks for students who are finished to stand up with their notebook and *Show and Share*. She quickly scans the work that each standing student is showing to make sure that those standing have completed the problems correctly. In seconds, Ms. Ford assigns two students who are struggling to each standing student. She is glad that she has practiced the routine *QAPS, Questions, Answers, Practice, Switch* when she led mini-lessons last week. During this routine, Ms. Ford played the role of the tutor or the student who is helping peers and the whole class played the role of learners with questions. So, now she can simply say,

"Our objective is for everyone to be clear on the steps to solving these problems. Let's do *QAPS—Question, Answers, Practice, Switch*. I will time the rounds.

Two students in the role of *Questions*—raise your hands and get ready to ask questions (ten seconds to think) and go."

The discussion begins with the two students who have not finished the assignment in the role of *Questions*, sharing and brainstorming as many questions about the assignment as possible. In round two, the students who have completed the assignment are in the role of *Answers*, answering only the questions that students need most to understand. Then there is a practice period for about two minutes. During the practice period, the students work through one problem or question together. They focus in on a hard part to practice or clarify confusing words. Students are not allowed to copy answers as they are learning the thinking they need to solve the problems for themselves. In this case, the only student with a notebook is the student who had the completed assignment to use as a model for explanations.

Finally, the students switch roles. Now, the student who had the answers poses questions that our new experts must answer. The students who were struggling answer the most important question and explain their approach to solving the problems. When the triad is convinced that each person can independently work on the questions then they all sit back down. In about six minutes of time, 100% of the students are clear on how to get started with the questions. Note that not all instructional problems have been solved by this one routine. For example, not all students will complete the questions correctly, the students who are finished need an extension activity, and some students may need an additional mini-lesson from the teacher. However, this use of a group learning routine decreased the extremes of students unable to start individual practice and provided early finishers an opportunity to consolidate their thinking while giving the teacher six minutes of thinking, listening, and observing time to plan the next steps of instruction. Ms. Ford's next move will be to offer an extension to those who are already finished. She has time to do this because everyone else is now completing the activity independently.

Classroom routines enabled Ms. Ford to complete a CARR Check and then adjust instruction using structures (using *TTO*) to ensure that no student left class confused. Let's visualize this lesson and the teacher's decision making (see Figure 8.1).

Figure 8.1 is an example of what differentiated instruction looks like in practice and reflects how Ms. Ford used *Show and Share* to conduct a CARR Check. She determined that clarity needed to be increased, so she adjusted instruction by changing from individual practice to a group learning routine, *QAPS*, for peer support. Then she returned to individual practice. Finally, she checked the impact of her adjustment to instruction by collecting their independent practice as the exit card.

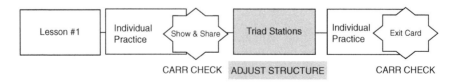

Figure 8.1 Teacher Decision Making in Practice

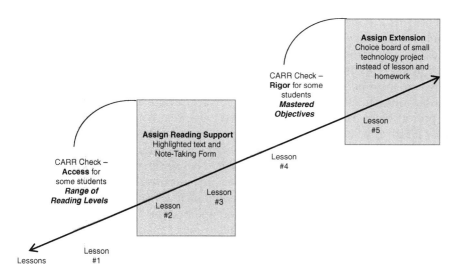

Figure 8.2 Teacher Decision Making in Planning a Series of Lessons by Adjusting Help

This method of visualizing teacher decisions as a series of connected steps and adjustments can also be used in planning. See Figure 8.2 where a series of lessons focused on students' understanding a reading is represented. Here, Ms. Ford preemptively plans times for a CARR Check to perceive differences in student clarity, access, rigor, and relevance that may impact learning. From the beginning of her lesson plan, she plans classroom routines that will enable her to look for differences among the students that may pose a challenge or offer an opportunity for learning. In addition, she prepares responses to anticipated differences in independent reading levels or ability to access a required text used in the lessons by adding help in the form of supports in lessons two and three. In lesson four, a CARR Check will be used to determine if some students have mastered the objectives that Ms. Ford plans to reteach and practice in lesson five. She anticipates a problem with rigor for students who do not need the reteach and practice lesson. Ms. Ford adds a Help resource in the form of an extension and will assign the extension to those students who do not need the reteach and practice lesson.

The support in lessons two and three is something that will enable students to acquire new content without the challenge getting in the way. In this case, Ms. Ford knew from lesson one that some students were reading below the grade level of the text required in lesson two. So she used differentiated instruction to meet three instructional goals:

1 All students need to be familiar with this text;
2 Logistically, the students need to finish reading at about the same time so that the class can have a discussion; and
3 The students need to comprehend the most important content from the text to participate in the discussion.

Therefore, the teacher assigned the students who are struggling with the reading a highlighted text along with a guided summary note-taking form. This support will enable the students to learn the new content without struggling as much with independent reading and comprehension. Ms. Ford will focus on developing independent reading skills and comprehension strategies at another time, most likely in a lesson where the topic is a review.

In lesson four, there was an assessment, or a CARR Check again, perhaps a quiz or project that enabled Ms. Ford to determine that some students had mastered the objectives being taught in lesson five. She assigns a choice board of small assignments—a help extension that includes Options—to groups of students who have mastered the objectives rather than having them sit through a lesson that they have already learned. The choice board includes assignments that review and extend the learning goals of lesson five. The choice board includes only options that can be completed individually without teacher support and that further the skills learned in these lessons. For example, options can include students making a review game for the class to play, on the topic of the lesson, or an animation or drawing that explains an important and complex concept or that shows how this topic connects to previous topics studied. Students who do not need lesson five continue their learning through the choice board while the rest of the class completes lesson five. There is a bonus if the products students create from the choice board can be used by the rest of the class as review or practice materials.

These examples from practice and planning illustrate how differentiated instruction is the outcome of a continuous decision-making process where teachers search for academic diversity that will either strengthen or impede effective and efficient learning, and then respond to their perceptions with precise adjustments to instruction that ensure clarity, access, rigor, and relevance (CARR) for all learners. We believe that the decisions to adjust or differentiate instruction to meet learner needs reflect teacher agility in thinking and decision making both on their feet in the classroom and in planning lessons.

Agile thinking enables teachers to effectively consider a broad range of ways that students might vary that could either impede or facilitate student learning. When teachers are in the moment with students during lessons, alert for reasons why students are not engaged in learning, they demonstrate the disposition needed for agile thinking. Teachers use agile thinking to maintain their focus on a specific objective; analyze a situation for evidence of clarity, access, rigor, or relevance (CARR Check); and then brainstorm possible choices for adjusting or differentiating instruction. Agile thinking helps teachers evaluate SHOp adjustments to make instructional decisions that respond to the perceived learning needs in a precise, efficient, and effective manner. Table 8.2 displays the components of agile teacher thinking in terms of dispositions, skills, and actions. Try our sentence to understand how agile thinking works in the classroom, "When teachers are (*disposition*), they (*skills*) in order to (*action*)." As you can see from this table, agile thinking is complex and something that teachers continually work to develop. These dispositions, skills, and actions build on a lifetime of experiences, interactions with others, and reflections on learning from students. Agile thinking provides a constant challenge as well as inspiration for teachers throughout their career.

Table 8.2 Agile Teacher Thinking: When Teachers Are (Disposition), They (Skills) in Order to (Action).

Dispositions	Skills	Actions
Aware	Check for understanding	Recognize patterns and differences
Alert	Observe and listen	Learn from data
Open-Minded	Suspend judgment	Seek understanding
Intentional	Plan with task analysis (breaking down steps)	Keep objective and criteria in focus
Creative	Make unusual connections	Leverage strengths to meet needs
Empathic	Shift perspective	Respond to student need from student perspective
Flexible	Are nimble, yet deliberate, with change	Adjust rather than totally change
Problem-Solvers	Think logically (specifically cause and effect)	Use routines responsively
Potential Believers	Seek strengths and possibilities	Start with something students can do
Reflective	Think with care	Use teaching mistakes as opportunities

Agile Thinking and Instructional Decisions

The best way to become efficient at differentiating instruction is to practice agile thinking and decision making using our agile teacher thinking routine, *At-If-Then* (see Figure 8.3).

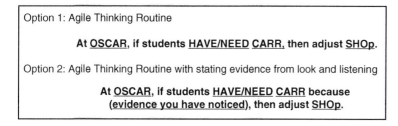

Option 1: Agile Thinking Routine

At <u>OSCAR</u>, if students <u>HAVE/NEED</u> <u>CARR</u>, then adjust <u>SHOp</u>.

Option 2: Agile Thinking Routine with stating evidence from look and listening

At <u>OSCAR</u>, if students <u>HAVE/NEED</u> <u>CARR</u> because (<u>evidence you have noticed</u>), then adjust <u>SHOp</u>.

Figure 8.3 Agile Teacher Thinking Routines (At-If-Then).

For example, "At the *Objective*, if *all* students *need greater clarity*, then the teacher will adjust the *structure* by including table discussion and gathering answers from each table before moving on in the mini-lesson." Later, "*At the Starting Position* if *some* students *need* greater *access* because a required text is above the independent reading level of some students, then the teacher will provide options during independent reading time. Options include assigning students who are struggling with the reading to circle familiar words in the text and write a few sentences about what they understand while other students complete reading the text." In the classroom, teacher attention is focused on responding to the problems that students are experiencing.

However, at least in planning, it is helpful to plan *At-If-Then* statements considering assets that students have. "At *starting position*, if *some* students *have* mastery of the lesson's objective *because* they demonstrated these skills on the previous week's unit test and *need* greater *rigor*, then adjust *structures*, using a peer tutoring

Table 8.3 At OSCAR, Look and Listen. If CARR Then SHOp Adjustments

At OSCAR	If students HAVE/NEED (CARR)	Adjustments to Instruction Choices (SHOp)		
		Structures	**H**elp	**Op**tions
Objective	Clarity	1 Explicit	1 All	1 Total Student Choice
Starting Position	Access	2 Table Talk	2 Some	
Criteria	Rigor	3 Individual	3 Individual	2 Teacher-Structured Student Choice
Action	Relevance	4 Group		
Reflections	because …			3 Assignment
Look and Listen	then			

routine or adjust *options* by assigning an extension activity to be completed in a small group while other students complete a mini-lesson with the teacher."

The *At-If-Then* statements are based on perceived student learning needs within a particular lesson or context. Choosing a SHOp adjustment requires agile thinking to form possible *At-If-Then* statements and determine the adjustments that will likely be most effective and efficient. Effective adjustments move all learners toward the objective and efficient adjustments ensure that the lesson objective is reached within the given amount of time. It is helpful to write *At-If-Then* statements into lesson plans in the area designated for differentiated instruction plans. We have listed the possible instructional choices to adjust instruction in Table 8.3. Agile thinking helps a teacher make decisions about what combination of SHOp adjustments will likely increase CARR for all students.

To launch your use of agile thinking and SHOp adjustments, we have brainstormed example SHOp adjustments for each part of a lesson or OSCAR. These ideas are meant to start your thinking about possibilities for your own setting. Adjustments should be made based on your own perceptions of your students in relation to the requirements of your curriculum and available time. *These ideas are meant to spark your creativity about adjustments for your setting and should not be considered a list of solutions.* Get ready to think about possible SHOp adjustments for each part of a lesson or OSCAR.

Objective

Teachers can use a CARR Check to determine why the objective may need adjustments or why the objective should remain consistent for all learners. Generally, it makes sense to use **task analysis** to break down objectives into manageable parts enabling learners to measure progress of one part at a time, while keeping the whole objective the same for all learners. In this way, all students are working toward a common objective and individual or groups of students are working on the part of the objective that is most relevant given their current skills. In addition to breaking down common objectives, teachers plan time within every unit where students work toward different objectives, including objectives from previous units and in some cases the previous year's curriculum. This is important because students do not start at the same place nor do they progress at standard speeds, so it is effective to routinely plan specific time within each unit for students to work on different objectives assigned by the teacher based on need. Typically, there are objectives in every unit that all students must learn. Table 8.4 displays possible ways that a common objective for all students may be adjusted to increase CARR for students with diverse abilities.

Table 8.4 At Objective, Possible SHOp Adjustments

Structures	Help	Options
Explicit—Objective is read out loud to the class and a story is told to demonstrate importance of this objective in the world today or why the teacher is passionate about this objective. *Table*—Free discussion of what students know about the objective. *Individual*—Students underline familiar words in the objective and circle one surprising or challenging word. *Group*—Students take turns in small groups sharing why this objective is important to learn.	*All* Important vocabulary words are illustrated with an image bolded or boxed so students know the importance. *Some* Definitions are provided for unknown terms and concepts. *Individual* A sample student work model of what mastery of the objective looks like is provided.	*Total Student Choice or Total Assignment* Objective is broken down into smaller achievable parts, so that students can recognize partial mastery and choose the needed next step. The teacher can also assign objective parts for each student. *Structured Choice* Options are offered within the objective, such as speaking, building, drawing, moving, and writing to demonstrate understanding. All students must complete two: one option is assigned by the teacher and the student chooses a second option.

Starting Position

The starting position is an essential means for teachers to assess the necessary adjustments needed in the next part of instruction and starting positions provide students with a record of their thinking to measure learning from the lesson. Therefore it is important that all learners complete the starting position. Teachers use adjustments like those listed in Table 8.5 to ensure every student is engaged.

Table 8.5 At Starting Position, Possible SHOp Adjustments

Structures	Help	Options
Explicit—Teacher provides an introduction, possibly a video *Table*—Free discussion of answer to a question. *Individual*—Students take a pre-assessment or answer a question using *List, Draw, Write.* *Group*—*Show and Share* Students show their work in silence all at the same time to the students in their group and then return to revise or add at least one idea to their own work.	*All* Hints, an answer key, or a sample answer for annotating can be provided to encourage all students to think about an answer to the question. *Some* Groups of students can be given problems or questions to review or launch a new investigation based on their skill level, interests, or another quality. *Individual* Students may use a resource, such as a word bank or tool, such as a calculator to help in completing the starting position.	*Total Student Choice*—Pen then Pencil assessment. Complete as many problems as you can using a pen in a given amount of time (five minutes). Then switch to a pencil and finish the problems. Examine your work from the first five minutes to the last five minutes. *Structured Choice* Assign first three questions and students choose between answering question four or five. *Total Assignment* Students complete a practice worksheet selected by the teacher.

Criteria

In addition to *Must Have* criteria, we recommend that there always be *Amazing* criteria to stretch students beyond the task as an adjustable part. The *Must Have* criteria are usually the same for all learners. However, some or individual students may be assigned to prioritize or focus on one *Must Have* criteria in an assignment or task. It is important to include both *Must Have* or required criteria and *Amazing* criteria to ensure every student is challenged. Engaging the students in establishing the criteria is a productive idea. Example adjustments to Criteria are listed in Table 8.6.

Table 8.6 At Criteria, Possible SHOp Adjustments

Structures	Help	Options
Explicit—Teacher models a think aloud annotating work for criteria and revision work. *Table*—Students discuss criteria with peers. *Individual*—Students use stamps, stickers, or annotations to identify specific qualities seen in their work. *Group*—Students use a *Think Talk Open Exchange* (*TTO*) to reflect by sharing how they have used criteria in their work or to discuss their plans to use criteria.	*All* Ask students to complete a performance summary tracking their progress toward objectives and use of criteria in their work. *All/Some* Post models of criteria with qualities identified. *Individual* Students complete a tracker to monitor their goals and work quality.	*Total Choice* Choose or create *Amazing* criteria *Structured Choice* Teacher assigns criteria by student need or by table to provide focus point and then students choose a criteria or two for a total of three. *Teacher Assignment* Rubric or formal checklist

Action Pattern

Only the Options and Help adjustments are typically made to the Action Pattern. Because more than one structure is used to create an action pattern, the agile thinking decision is not about what structures to use, rather the decision is about the order of the structures. For example, if a teacher assigns an individual task and students are not capable of starting the task independently then the teacher may need to change the structure to group learning first by asking students to discuss at their table how to begin the task, then return to completing the task as individuals. Teachers do not expect all students to complete every task correctly; however, changing the structure for tasks enables all students to feel capable in at least beginning a task. Additional examples of adjustments to Action Patterns are listed in Table 8.7.

Reflection

Students make learning meaningful when they think through why and how their thinking or skills have stayed the same, been challenged, or maybe have changed as a result of their learning. Reflection may include an evaluation of their work using quality criteria. Reflection may include feedback on the learning process for the teacher and/or their small group. Starting Position provides documentation that students need to remember where they thought they were prior to a learning experience.

Table 8.7 At Action Pattern, Possible SHOp Adjustments

Structures	Help	Options
Explicit Teacher explains a concept or strategy and then asks students a question to activate to check for understanding. *Individual* Students are instructed to think individually and then jot down their answer in their notebook. *Group—(Small)* Students share their thinking with a partner or at their table to create an answer incorporating the ideas of others. *Group—(Whole Class)* Table reporters share out the group's answer one at a time while the teacher records responses on the board to reflect on the answers. *Individual* Students return to their initial thinking and make revisions and reflect on how talking in their group and listening to the reporters has changed or confirmed their thinking.	*All* Wall charts display the actions. *All/Some* Supports, such as an answer that the student who was absent annotates, a truncated text, or a routine for circling known words and writing short summary sentences, may be offered for students who need reading supports. Students may be given a scaffold to work on a specific skill or part of a task, such as identifying supporting evidence or explaining reasoning. *Individual* Individuals may complete a behavior chart to track their participation. Individuals may be assigned to use a calculator, dictionary, bilingual glossary, timeline, manipulatives, or other help resources.	*Total Choice* Students choose the process for learning, such as *List, Write, Draw*. Students could choose between different questions to answer or completely different activities for learning. *Structured Choice* Options for assignments are offered to students within a structure controlled by the teacher. In this way all students complete assigned actions or tasks and students choose additional actions or tasks. *Teacher Assignment* Rubric or formal checklist generated by teacher. Teacher offers feedback and assigns students to apply teacher feedback to next task or a revision.

Reflection routines are often adjusted based on time constraints and shifted to ensure that all learners are able to engage in reflection (for example, adjustments are made for students who were absent to reflect at a different time). See Table 8.8.

Rooted in Research: Problem-Solving

The notion of thinking in terms of *At-If-Then* statements comes from the cognitive research on problem-solving (Anderson, 1983; Anderson, Corbett, Koedinger, & Pelletier, 1995). From a purely cognitive standpoint, skill acquisition can be considered to involve the formulation of thousands of rules relating task goals to specific actions and consequences—*At-If-Then* statements (Anderson et al., 1995). The cognitive scientist John Anderson has written extensively on the architecture of human cognition. His theory of learning, ACT-R (Adaptive Control of Thought-Rational), is based on the following three tenets.

First, ACT-R makes a distinction between declarative and procedural knowledge. Declarative knowledge is essentially topical or content knowledge—like knowing the side-angle-side theorem in geometry (i.e., if two sides and the included angles of two triangles are congruent, then the triangles are congruent). Procedural knowledge is just what you think it is—knowledge of procedures; in the case of the geometry

Table 8.8 At Reflection, Possible SHOp Adjustments

Structures	Help	Options
Explicit—Teacher leads whole class through a reflection. Might be facilitated with class sitting in a circle. *Table*—Free discussion about goals and progress. Some students may offer help to others. *Individual*—Students complete a *learning journal* or other structured routine reflection prompt that they can refer back to over time to review their reflections. *Group*—Structured feedback and reflection may be part of group learning routines where students listen and offer feedback to peers based on criteria. For example, students may examine the recorded responses from a *Domino Discover* to offer compliments for responses that meet *Amazing* criteria.	*All*—Quality criteria are posted to launch reflection. Sentence frames or starters are posted. Students annotate work prior to writing or discussing their reflection so that they can easily refer to examples and evidence in their work to support their ideas. Students may complete a performance summary analyzing the correct and incorrect items to determine next steps using the results of an assessment. *Some* Teacher may provide a scaffold by giving students a model of student work with evidence of qualities highlighted. The student only explains the qualities that the evidence shows and how the student might have achieved that quality. *Individual* Teacher, peer, or family member may conference with student and assist student in writing notes from the conversation.	*Total Choice*—Students choose or create their own reflection prompts. Students may add quality criteria or select one row in a rubric to use in their reflection. *Structured Choice* The teacher may prompt student awareness of particular criteria by circling examples in student work and requiring students to reflect on and explain those examples. Students would choose additional examples from the work to explain as well. *Assignment* The teacher may limit students to reflecting on specific evidence from their work using specific criteria.

example above, it is knowing how to actually use the theorem. ACT-R assumes that the acquisition of skills lies in the ability of translating declarative knowledge into procedural knowledge, specifically the ability of turning declarative knowledge into production rules (i.e., *At-If-Then* statements). Anderson's theory is suggesting that it is not enough for you to *know* about OSCAR, CARR, or SHOp; in order to become competent at differentiating instruction, you must also learn how to turn your knowledge about ALL-ED into specific *At-If-Then* statements. This is why we give multiple examples of *At-If-Then* statements in this chapter.

The second and third principles of ACT-R go together. The second tenet is that *At-If-Then* statements can only be learned by using declarative knowledge to solve problems. The third is that in order to develop competence and acquire skills, you simply have to practice. To become more competent at differentiating instruction, you have to actively use your knowledge of ALL-ED, to solve all different kinds of problems related to student diversity, repeatedly and over time. We understand that you will not become proficient at differentiating instruction as soon as you finish reading this chapter or even this book. To aid you on your journey toward skill acquisition, we have provided numerous dilemmas for you to solve so that you can put your knowledge of ALL-ED and differentiated instruction to use. We also offer (at the end of every chapter) some suggestions for classroom routines you can try with your own students so that you can become more proficient in developing these *At-If-Then* statements yourself.

Agility Thinking in Planning

Agile thinking is developed by thinking through ways to apply your answers to the *Traction Planner* in daily lessons and anticipating the results of CARR Checks to prepare SHOp adjustments prior to teaching lessons. Start practicing your agile thinking by thinking through a few challenging examples that often occur in units: Review, a Required Common Task, Teaching Skills from Previous Units, and Daily Individualized Practice.

Review

A typical "whole class" review or "going over" problems or homework with the entire class together often results in many students sitting unengaged. Often during a review, time does not permit the teacher to go over every problem so students end up taking the problems that they do not understand home to study. One way to avoid this problem is to do a CARR Check and then adjust Help by assigning the order that students tackle the review problems in class. Problems are assigned so that students work on things that require help during the review lesson. In this example (see Figure 8.4), all students receive the same review assignment, but students will be grouped by the objective that they need help to review. The teacher will call each group to a Help Desk during the review lesson to share a mini-lesson on the needed objective and review tasks related to that objective so that students can now practice independently. Students continue to work on the parts of the review assignment that they can do independently until the teacher calls their group.

Figure 8.4 Teacher Decisions for Planning a Review

The *Agile Thinking* routine is: *If at the Action Pattern, some students need access because their work in the unit shows reteaching is necessary, then Help will be adjusted during the review lesson to include a mini-lesson on specific objectives.*

When teachers think about trying out a Help Desk or different structures to facilitate student learning, they often ask, "What if my room is too small for students to move into groups or go to a Help Desk?" Perhaps physically moving students will take too much time and focus away from students who are working.

Possible Options:

1 *Teacher circulates*: Teachers write different independent practice assignments related to specific objectives on the board. Students are assigned the assignment that they need to complete and begin while staying in their seats. There will be students working on different assignments in each group. The teacher circulates among the students to assist and offer feedback.

2 *Students enter room and look for special assigned seats*. The teacher can post a desk configuration with assigned seats on the board. Students move the desks into the configuration that the teacher has drawn and sit in their assigned seat for Review day. In this way the groups are not even, but reflect the number of students who share a priority objective for review. Each group can have different warm-up activities related to their group's objective.

There are ways to work within space and time constraints. Teachers should first decide how students will learn most efficiently and effectively and then create classroom routines that are sustainable given the space and time constraints. For example, once students are taught the expectations of completing independent practice while mini-lessons are being conducted at a Help Desk, this Help routine can be used at any time when some students need review, reteaching, and/or extensions during a lesson.

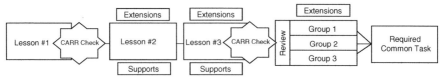

Figure 8.5 Teacher Decisions for Planning a Required Common Task

Required Common Task

Figure 8.5 shows a teacher using a CARR Check of a pre-assessment to adjust Help by assigning supports and extensions for lessons two and three, then a CARR Check is used to group students for Review (like the previous example), and then everyone completes a Required Common Task. The pre-assessment could be an exit card checking understanding of lesson one, a homework assignment from lesson one or an introduction activity at the beginning of lesson two.

The *Agile Thinking* routine is: If at *Objective some* students *have* mastery and *need rigor and relevance,* then adjust *Help by assigning extensions.* If at *Objective, some* students *need access.* then adjust *Help by assigning supports.* If at *Objective, some* students *need* access or *need rigor,* then assign use of the *Help Desk* and order of problems for independent practice.

The supports and extensions use specific resources such as different types and levels of reading material on a given topic, problems or materials that review a previous unit as supports, and problems or materials that provide a different perspective or application of the topic under study as extensions. The teacher is using the same type of supports and extensions for two consecutive lessons. This enables the learners to practice using the supports or extensions and save time in teaching a new routine for the next lesson. The supports and extensions in this example stay focused on accomplishing a common goal for all students that will be measured through a required common task. Therefore, it is likely that the expected homework or product for lessons two and three will be the same for all students. For example, students may read different texts but they will answer the same five questions with written responses or students may use different graphic organizers to complete a set of problems, but the set of problems would be the same for all students. The lessons prepare all students for a required common task.

Teaching Skills from Previous Units

In this example, an assessment from the previous unit serves as a starting position for lesson one of a new unit. Here it appears that the assessment revealed that some students need reteaching or a review of the previous unit while going forward with the next unit. In this case, the teacher divides the students into two groups for three lessons (see Figure 8.6). Group one might be both reviewing the previous unit and

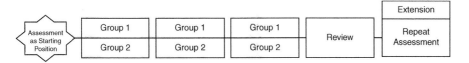

Figure 8.6 Teacher Decisions to Teach Skills from Previous Units

practicing missing skills while learning the next unit. Group two may be moving on to the next unit and completing a related project. The teacher has common objectives for both groups leading to the common assessment and different objectives to ensure instruction is rigorous for all students.

The teacher may have a co-teacher who is working with one group or the teacher may organize the structures so that Group one is doing independent practice or partner feedback/activities while he/she is teaching Group two, and then the teacher switches his/her focus to the other group. The teachers will need to plan SHOp adjustments for both groups of students because students will still differ, even within a group made by a common learning need. The teacher and students will know this differentiation was effective if all students succeed on the assessment. In this format, the homework assignments for lessons one, two, and three are often different.

Daily Individualized Practice

Differentiated instruction can be part of the everyday flow of teaching and learning. In this example, after lesson one, a CARR Check shows that students vary in a way that is important to address through lesson two. Perhaps students have different interests in the topic and they will be grouped by interest for lesson two. Some students may have misunderstandings of concepts or missing skills that will be needed for lesson two. Or students may have different previous learning experiences with the topic that if reviewed in lesson two will make acquiring new information in lesson three easier (see Figure 8.7). There are many different reasons why a teacher may group students in this way following a CARR Check.

In *Social Studies*, the groups could be studying the people, places, events, or daily life related to a topic and then regrouping students for lesson three to share that background information as everyone learns more about the topic together.

In *Math*, students might be grouped by ability for lesson two reviewing basic skills with one group related to the topic under study, exploring the topic with another group, and extending the topic with a more complex application or comparing the topic to another topic for students who have already mastered the skills and don't need an additional lesson.

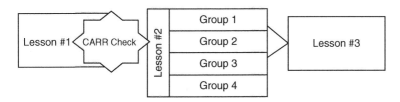

Figure 8.7 Teacher Decisions to Individualize Daily Practice

In *Science* class, each group may have a different research question for the same experiment.

In an *English Language Arts* class, the groups may be reading texts on different reading levels related to a common theme.

The key here is that differentiation in lesson two enables everyone to engage in lesson three. The importance of assessment is highlighted in this example. After lesson two, the teacher checks to make sure that the differentiated instruction was successful with a CARR Check before starting lesson three. Then, before the project, there is another CARR Check. This assessment may determine interest. The ongoing nature of perceiving student differences through assessment and then responding to learning needs through adjusting instruction is a routine part of each unit.

These four examples explore using the agile thinking routine *At-If-Then* to plan differentiated instruction across a series of lessons. Perhaps even more useful is implementing the *At-If-Then* to problem solve on your feet during lessons with the *At-If-Then* routine.

Agility Thinking in Practice: On Your Feet Instructional Choices and Outcomes

In this section we present six dilemmas from real classrooms. We provide four different instructional choices and identify one likely outcome of each choice. The purpose of these dilemmas is to help you practice your agile thinking and anticipate how different decisions play out with students. Always consider time, curriculum, and space constraints. There are no right answers. As we have demonstrated, these are dilemmas that are addressed through continuous decision making, not problems with single one-time solutions. *Think of the outcomes as moments leading to another decision versus endings to an activity or lesson.* Following each choice, we rate the efficiency and effectiveness of this decision to adjust instruction. You might imagine different outcomes that could take place in your setting. Thinking through choices and rating possible outcomes practices the agile thinking that you will use with split-second decisions as learning unfolds during lessons.

Dilemma #1: Absent Students

Five students came in late from a field trip to class. The teacher is halfway through a mini-lesson. How can the teacher ensure that all students meet the day's objectives?

Without Agile Thinking—Decision to place differences on hold until later
The teacher might welcome the late students and finish the mini-lesson. The teacher will meet with the students who were late at another time to catch them up. The problem with this approach is that the late students aren't learning during the mini-lesson and could distract other students.

Agile Thinking Choice 1: At Action Pattern, if Clarity is the challenge, then adjust Structure.
If students need greater Clarity then change the structure from Explicit Direct Instruction to Group Learning Routine. For example, the teacher might ask students to form "Sum-It-Up" groups and to summarize main points until now in the mini-lesson by taking turns saying one important point using the *Think, Talk, Open-Exchange* routine. The teacher states two rules:

1   *Plus One*—Students can repeat what was previously said by other students but then must also add a question or a second idea.
2   *Absent Reporter*—The reporter will be someone who joined the class late or who was most recently absent.

During *Open Exchange*, the groups prepare the reporter with their most important point or question. Allow five minutes total for the triad stations and then reporters type their most important point or question into a digital document or write on a chart paper.

Rate Choice 1: Precise, Effective, and Efficient? Changing the task structure would engage all of the students. For students who came in late, the small group summary would provide the information that they need while offering students who were there an opportunity to retrieve new vocabulary and concepts and practice summarizing their learning.

Agile Thinking Choice 2: *At Action Pattern, if Clarity or Access is the challenge, then* Help.

Provide students with a video of the teacher or student teaching the mini-lesson. This can easily be made during the first period when the lesson is given by a student with an iPad or cell phone recording the teacher, or videos from the Internet on the same topic may also be used. Latecomers are directed to watch the video version of the lesson on a computer, iPad, or phone with headphones while the live lesson with the teacher continues in class.

Rate Choice 2: Precise, Effective, and Efficient? Having options, such as a video of the mini-lesson or a video of the related concepts, ready for latecomers is a great strategy. Students who need longer for auditory processing or who need to hear and see lessons multiple times may also benefit. In addition, students who need practice with note-taking can watch the videos. Teachers sometimes have students videotape their mini-lessons on an iPad or cell phone and save the recording on a computer drive for this purpose.

Agile Thinking Choice 3: *If Access or Rigor is the challenge, then* Help. Give students a printout of the digital slide show and tell them to mark the slide that is up now so they remember when they entered the lesson and that they can go back to review what they missed after the lesson is over.

Rate Choice 3: Precise, Effective, and Efficient? The digital slide show printout is a good help resource because students can mark when they entered the lesson and literally see the topics that came before that were missed. In addition to the printout, you may consider an *Elbow Exchange* with the purpose of Connect and Question where students have to connect what they just heard to a previous idea or raise a question about how a previous slide connects to what they are currently discussing. Connect and Question engages all students in a purposeful review.

Dilemma #2: Wide Range of Student Learning Needs

Some students are bored because they have mastered the skills and concepts being reviewed. Other students need more practice. All students will be required to pass a common test, so how can everyone be challenged without a lot of extra planning or totally different activities?

Without Agile Thinking—*Decision to rely on teacher as the sole source of* Help.

Students have ample time to complete review activities at their own pace. The teacher should circulate to provide help and feedback to all students. The problem with this approach is that even though the teacher is circulating to support all students, many students are spending a lot of time waiting for help and find themselves off task. At the end of the review time, many students have only reviewed a few concepts.

Agile Thinking Choice 1: *At Action Pattern, if Access and Rigor is the challenge, then adjust* Structure.

Ask students to complete a short quiz based on the topics and/or skills that will be tested. Require students to complete a performance summary so that they know what topics and skills they have mastered and which they need to review. Have students number the sections of the review from number 1 being what they should do in class because they need the most help with this topic/skill to the highest number being the topic/skill that they need the least amount of practice. Students should structure their time during review and practice to work on their top priority. Help Desks focused on specific topics can be opened at designated times during the review lesson and manned by students who have mastered the topic or by the teacher.

Rate Choice 1: Precise, Effective, and Efficient? Using an independent check for understanding is a great idea to help students be more independent in their pursuit of reviewing a topic to develop mastery. You can vary the review practice time with independent practice for five minutes and then work collaboratively. At times students can meet with others who share their top priorities to review their progress and raise questions, or they can meet with a partner who can help with a top priority. The teacher might call groups of students with similar priorities for a short mini-lesson at a help station or table in the room.

Agile Thinking Choice 2: *At Action Pattern, if Access and Rigor is the challenge, then adjust* Options.

The teacher provides students with a structured choice activity as they complete the review. Students are required to complete certain problems/questions in the review activity and then are invited to make GIF animations for key vocabulary words or a card game for keywords that would extend a learner's thinking. Students might make definitions that show key vocabulary meanings in different subject areas. Students use criteria for what makes words memorable to create the animations and games. As students finish the review, they are invited to play the games that the early finishers made.

Rate Choice 2: Precise, Effective, and Efficient? Providing structure (assigned problems) and then offering student choice (GIF animations or word card game) provides student who need additional challenge with a meaningful and fun project. The completed animations and word games can be played by students who need additional review, so there will be a real audience for the extension projects.

Agile Thinking Choice 3: *At Action Pattern, if Access and Rigor is the challenge, then adjust* Help.

The teacher lists on the board the four main topics covered by this review and test with a corresponding 15-minute time period. During the 15-minute time period, the teacher opens up a Help Desk, and provides instruction on the designated topic. Students join the Help Desk for the topics where they need help.

Rate Choice 3: Precise, Effective, and Efficient? Opening a Help Desk is a great idea because students can literally practice asking for and receiving help.

Dilemma # 3: Engaging in a Mini-Lesson

The teacher is moving the students through a well-planned lesson. The pace is quick and engaging for most students. However, some students got lost early on and have "checked out." How can the teacher re-engage those who are lost, keep the others moving forward, and finish before the end of the period?

Without Agile Thinking—Decision to place differences on hold until later
    With most students engaged, it makes sense to finish the direct instruction. The teacher can circulate after the lesson to re-engage students who are lost. Continuing the lesson without specifically engaging students who are confused will leave students further behind in their learning. While saving time in the lesson, going on with the lesson may increase learning gaps among students in the class costing much more time on another day.

Agile Thinking Choice 1: At Action Pattern, if Clarity is the challenge, then adjust Structure.
    The teacher stops the lesson and asks students to write their names and the most important ideas from the lesson or a question that they have about the topic on a sticky note or a piece of paper. When students are ready, the teacher tells them that they should investigate if the most important ideas and questions are the same or different. To find out, they will exchange information using a routine called *Rumors*. Students will read their sticky notes to a partner, listen to the partners read their note, and then exchange notes. Each person will try to read, listen, swap, or exchange notes with at least four people looking for patterns. After three minutes, they will stop to find the patterns. Then the students swap ideas and questions, and the teacher stops them and gathers the ideas into groups on similar topics. *Rumors* enables students to gain feedback on their ideas while allowing the teacher to listen to and see student ideas and questions organized into groups.
    Rate Choice 1: Precise, Effective, and Efficient? While *Rumors* may take five to ten minutes, students will increase the clarity with the lesson topic through the inter-action. At the same time, *Rumors* offers the teacher a check for understanding that provides patterns of student understanding, enabling the teacher to tailor the next part of the lesson specifically to student learning needs. In the end, *Rumors* is much faster than re-teaching or reviewing the whole lesson.

Agile Thinking Choice 2: At Action Pattern, if Relevance is the challenge, then adjust Options and Structure.
    The teacher stops the lesson for a thinking pause. She invites students to answer one of the questions:

- If this topic were a color then what color would it be and why?
- How can we use only numbers to represent the ideas that we are talking about?
- If you were to interview someone about this topic, what would your two most interesting questions be?
- What are three reasons why students should care about this topic?

After students jot down their ideas to one of the questions, students may be invited to share their answers at the table or using *Think, Talk, Open Exchange (TTO)*. Students could also group by the question that they answered to gain feedback on their ideas.
    Rate Choice 2: Precise, Effective, and Efficient? After students jot down their ideas to one of the four questions, students may be invited to share their answers at

the table or using Triad Stations. Student could also group by the question that they answered to gain feedback on their ideas.

Agile Thinking Choice 3: At Action Pattern, if Relevance is the challenge, then *adjust* Structure and Help.

The teacher writes on the board buzzwords or key ideas that students should be listening for in the lesson. Students copy these words onto a paper in the middle of their table or a paper that is shared with an elbow partner. Students make a word map of every idea that they just heard that connects to this idea. Then as the teacher goes through the lesson, students connect more ideas to the key words. On the teacher's count of three, all students *Show and Share* their word map to the other groups by lifting up and showing their paper. Students look at the maps of nearby groups for words to steal and add to their own map. Every *Show and Share* should lead to a "Plus One" where students add to their map and circle the new idea. Students can use these maps as a help resource to answer questions after the mini-lesson and to clarify what was said during the mini-lesson at their table or with a partner.

Rate Choice 3: Precise, Effective, and Efficient? The word map shared by the table is a good way to create a help resource during the lesson that is concrete and accessible for use by all students. This helps students who have difficulty copying from the board in the front of the room to the paper on their desk. Also, students can work together enabling them to benefit from the spelling and writing skills of others at their table.

Dilemma #4: Instruction without Engagement

The teacher is modeling how to complete a complex task one piece at a time. While the support is helpful, most students are just mindlessly copying and waiting for the teacher to model the next part. How can the teacher provide support and foster student independence and thinking?

Without Agile Thinking—*Decision to place focus on completing a task instead of thinking*

At least when students are copying, they are engaged and they have a correct model that they can study. So, maybe if they copy this time, then the next time they will be able to do more independently and will copy less. Unfortunately, because students have copied without really thinking about what they are doing and why, they are not able to recall this information or use these skills in a similar task later in the unit.

Agile Thinking Choice 1: At Action Pattern, if Rigor is the challenge, then *adjust* Structure.

Instead of the teacher serving as the only model, students are paired with an Expert partner who is able to model completing the task for a partner called the Learner using the *Question, Answer, Practice, Switch* routine *(QAPS)*. The Learner begins by posing Questions that come to mind. The Expert listens to the questions and Answers only the most interesting and useful question needed to know how to complete the task. Then the Expert practices with the Learner until the Learner is able to complete the task. Then the actions are switched. The Expert now poses questions that come to mind and the Learner answers only the most interesting and useful. Then the Expert demonstrates completing the task and the Learner checks to make sure each part is done correctly. When both partners are able to complete the task, they go on to independent practice.

Rate Choice 1: Precise, Effective, and Efficient? Leveraging the expertise of students in the class is a great idea. Students will be able to get more questions answered and practice done with a partner than waiting for the whole class to learn each part. The teacher might model for the experts if they need support before or she may pull a small group of students and play the role of the Expert.

Agile Thinking Choice 2: *At Action Pattern, if Rigor is the challenge, then adjust* Structure.

Instead of modeling the whole task, the teacher breaks down the task into parts. The parts in the recommended order of completion are clearly displayed on a chart as a support for all students who may use this list of the steps to completion as a support to monitor and assess their progress. Then the teacher creates a scaffold for one specific part to focus learners who are struggling on one important part. Once students have mastered that part, they may go on to complete more steps. In addition, the scaffold can be adjusted to provide early finishers with an extension challenge.

Rate Choice 2: Precise, Effective, and Efficient? Breaking down the task and providing a list of the steps before demonstrating or modeling is an effective way to encourage students to try their thinking instead of relying on the teacher to model when they are unsure. While the list of steps provides a support for all students, the scaffold and the extension are specifically targeted to students who are on the extremes of struggling and excelling to ensure that all students are engaged and stretched.

Agile Thinking Choice 3: *At Action Pattern, if Rigor is the challenge, then adjust* Help

The teacher decides to stop modeling and instead provides a help resource of a completed task for students to grade. Asking students to grade a completed example requires students to do more than just see an example; they have to find evidence of quality criteria in the example to grade the sample student work. The teacher asks students to explain to a partner their grade for the sample work and the evidence they see in the work that justifies the grade. The students use the quality criteria to set goals of what criteria will be easier and more challenging to complete in their own work. The teacher offers specific help lessons based on the criteria that most students believe to be challenging.

Rate Choice 3: Precise, Effective, and Efficient? Example student work can be a great help resource, but only when students are required to think about the work, which they do when grading. With an answer key, the teacher might have students rank the problems hardest to easiest, asking students to think about the answers, not just notice the answers.

Dilemma #5: Group Learning Dependent on Teacher Management

The students enjoy working in small groups. Some students are working independently, some students are talking, and many students are waiting for the teacher to come around and give directions. The teacher is repeating the same directions for each small group. How can the teacher make the group learning more student-driven? The teacher could post the directions for the group learning on a digital slide show and display the directions on an interactive display board or he could write the directions on chart paper to display for students. The teacher could also circulate to remind students of the directions.

Without Agile Thinking—*Decision to allow students to avoid collaborating with peers*

The posted list of directions is a great start. The poster offers clarity for students about what they are supposed to be doing in the small groups and serves as a help resource or reminder that students can refer to as they complete each action. Unfortunately, some students are still dominating the discussions and a few students are continuing to work independently instead of collaborating with peers even when they know the process that the group should be following.

Agile Thinking Choice 1: *At Action Pattern, if Rigor is the challenge, then adjust* Structure.

The teacher decides that group learning will be more productive if students first prepare completely independently. Before getting into groups, the teacher asks students to complete an answer to a question and to reread their answer and start the most important part or circle a vocabulary word. Then the teacher reviews the purpose, roles, and rules for the group learning. Once students are in their groups the teacher establishes who will go first and the order for taking turns. The teacher makes sure that students are listening for quality criteria and are prepared to report out or record their learning from the small group learning.

Rate Choice 1: Precise, Effective, and Efficient? With the starting position prior to group learning and the clear directions with roles, turns, rules, and time, the teacher participates only as a listener and observer during the group learning routines.

Agile Thinking Choice 2: *At Action Pattern, if Rigor is the challenge, then adjust* Structure.

The teacher feels the group discussions are not engaging because students lack interest in the discussion prompt. To increase interest, the teacher provides one required prompt and asks students to brainstorm a second prompt for discussion. After completing the first required discussion, each group can choose a prompt from the brainstormed list for the second discussion. The teacher will ask students to summarize their learning from the discussion following the group work so students know that they need to listen and engage in the conversation because they will have to summarize the conversation individually after the group discussion.

Rate Choice 2: Precise, Effective, and Efficient? Providing structure ensures that students complete the required tasks while providing a second prompt of the students' choosing increases the discussion's meaning and relevance for students.

Agile Thinking Choice 3: *At Action Pattern, if Rigor is the challenge, then adjust* Structure.

Group discussion may be supported by sentence starters and a graphic organizer for students to record what other group members have said. The listening tracker can be used to record and compliment speakers during the discussion and can also be used to increase individual accountability.

Rate Choice 3: Precise, Effective, and Efficient? Increasing individual recording of what they hear is valuable for listening and engagement, but also allows students to reflect on the disciplinary vocabulary being used during discussions. Students can use a *buzzwords* vocabulary tracker to determine the most and least frequently used vocabulary words in the group's discussions. Based on this tracker the students might set goals for using targeted academic vocabulary words (*buzzwords*) in future conversations.

Dilemma #6: Inclusion of More Students with Diverse Needs

Recently arrived students who are learning English as a New Language are now included in your fifth-period class. Although students are responding to your directions and are interacting with peers, the students are often silent during lessons because the academic vocabulary is new and they cannot independently read most of the books and materials that you are providing during lessons. You teach this same subject during three other periods where there are no ENLs so you would like to keep fifth period on the same pace with lessons as the other periods. All periods will take the same standardized test on this subject.

Without Agile Thinking—Decision to expect students to learn in another lesson

English as a New Language learners will pick up a lot of vocabulary and understand the concepts by participating in small groups with their peers. Being in the groups is probably more important than the actual readings because even a simplified text would be challenging and other students might tease them because the text looks babyish. Eventually they will be able to read the materials, so it is just a matter of waiting for them to learn more English. However, after moving from class to class day after day where all of the materials are incomprehensible, the students begin to play around in class distracting the other students. In addition to the off-task behaviors, some students simply shut down because they are tired of trying to make sense of the texts that are given to them.

Agile Thinking Choice 1: At Action Pattern, if Access is the challenge, then adjust Structure.

The teacher decided that when the text is not comprehensible for all students then structures provide alternate ways to read the text. For example, a small group can be reading the text out loud in unison or the teacher can read the text out loud to a group at a table somewhere in the classroom. The students may be assigned to circle words that are familiar before the text is read aloud. After the text is read then students can discuss through an *Elbow Exchange* what the text meant. The teacher might use the routine *Fact, Question, Answer (FQA)* to foster comprehension. Alternating between a group reading and discussion and independent reading will support students in their understanding of the text.

Rate Choice 1: Precise, Effective, and Efficient? Shifting the task structure from completing the task independently to listening to the text and discussing the meaning using a group learning routine increases the accessibility of the task for all students. In addition, you might consider asking students to write or draw a summary or to say the key word to check for comprehension of the meaning of the text.

Agile Thinking Choice 2: At Action Pattern, if Access is the challenge, then adjust Help.

With preparation time, the teacher can cut a text down into fewer sentences making the text more comprehensible for all students. The teacher can easily adjust the Lexile level of nonfiction texts by using websites, such as Newsela (https://newsela.

com/) independently because the text is within their current reading ability. You can also change the style of the text to increase the relevance and access.

Agile Thinking Choice 3: *At Action Pattern, if Access is the challenge, then adjust* Options.

The teacher can offer options of independent reading routines making any text more accessible to all students in the class. The teacher might invite students to read in one of three ways:

1   A careful read, reading all of the words;
2   Circle and draw: Skimming the text and circling the keywords identified by the teacher, then only reading the sentences with the keywords in them and drawing a quick sketch or line graphic in the margin of what is happening in the text; or
3   Listen: Have the text read out loud at least twice by different students, the teacher, or a recording, and circle the key words on the second read.

Rate Choice 3: Precise, Effective, and Efficient? Routine options of independent reading ensure that all students will be able to make some sense out of every text that is distributed in class. Sometimes it will be possible to offer students text specifically on their independent reading level. However, much of the time, strategies such as Options routines are needed when the text cannot be differentiated or changed and students need to comprehend the text.

Try Classroom Routines: Precise, Effective, Efficient Learning for All

Plan: At-If-Then Thinking Routine

Plan classroom routines in every lesson to conduct a CARR Check. Refer to our Example OSCAR adjustments in the tables from this chapter to support your planning of lessons. You can use the box for differentiated instruction normally at the bottom of lesson plan templates to list *At-If-Then* statements.

Teach: Questions, Answers, Practice, Switch (QAPS)

Group learning routines are used for three different purposes: to gather student responses, provide help, and collaborate. Try a group learning routine, such as peer tutoring, to provide help. For example, *Question, Answer, Practice, Switch (QAPS)* is a routine that enables students to learn how to offer help that teaches a peer to use a new skill independently. Without a routine, students often just copy the work to complete an assignment, although the peer is "caught up" in terms of completion, the gap in understanding remains. This routine can be first taught through explicit whole class instruction. You can be in the role of peer or the tutor and the whole class can be in the role of the student. Once students understand the routine, peers can effectively tutor each other.

ALL-ED Classroom Routine Directions: Questions, Answers, Practice, Switch (QAPS)

Peer-to-peer tutoring usually refers to students working in pairs or groups of three to help one another learn material or practice an academic task. Typically, teachers group students who are currently working at different levels of fluency or confidence with a given task for tutoring. Students switch roles partway through the tutoring routine so that the tutor becomes the one being tutored and the learner becomes the teacher. Having a structured routine for tutoring sessions helps students move through the process effectively. For example, the roles are Teacher and Learner. Round one: Learner poses questions about topic or skill to be learned while the teacher notes important questions to answer first. Round two: Teacher answers questions and models the skill or task to be learned. Round three: Learner practices and Teacher offers feedback. Round four: Learner teaches the Teacher the skill or task. The teacher follows the Learner's directions and offers feedback on any missed steps. Tutoring should happen routinely in each unit, providing a vehicle where students know how to ask for help. The skills for making an appointment for tutoring should be diverse to ensure that all students are both tutors and learners at different times.

Strengths of this routine:

- promotes critical thinking
- encourages collaboration
- requires students to use and develop language skills
- develops appreciation of the talents and strengths of others
- students can efficiently clarify confusions and build confidence.

Implementation Directions

Objective: Teach an expertise to another person.

Starting Positions (individually and then in small groups)

Individually: Use the individual routine, *Criteria Checklist*—check and circle. Ask students to review their work in progress. Place a check next to something you are confident about or something that is going well. Circle one thing that raises questions or is confusing.

Groups: The teacher assigns students into groups of three with a range of student skill and background knowledge levels in each group. The teacher designates where in the room each group of three will meet, with the students sitting or standing knee-to-knee and eye-to-eye so that it is easier to hear each student in the group.

Criteria

- *Must Haves:* All learners leave the group able to work independently on the task.
- *Amazing:* Each group member, including the tutor, shares how the discussion furthered their learning.

Action Pattern

The teacher identifies in the directions:

- **Roles:** One Teacher or Tutor, Two Learners
- *Note: Whenever a participant's task is to listen then the participant cannot talk.*
- **Turns:** The teacher assigns one student in each group to "Go first" stating a fact from the text and then the student who will go second and third.
- **Rules:** "Add or Repeat" Students can repeat an answer from a previous student or add a new response. Students cannot copy finished problems or questions from other students.
- **Time:** The teacher times each round so that all groups move through the routine at the same pace.

Actions: Questions, Answers, Practice, Switch

1 **Round One Questions:** Learner asks questions and Teacher notes important questions to answer first. *(Two to three minutes)*
2 **Round Two Answers:** Teacher answers questions and models the skill or task to be learned. Learner listens and follows directions. *(Three to five minutes)*
3 **Round Three Practice:** Learner practices and Teacher offers feedback. *(Five to ten minutes)*
4 **Round Four Switch Roles:** Learner teaches the expert the skill or task. Teacher follows Learner's directions and offers feedback of any missed steps. *(Five to ten minutes)*
5 Repeat rounds with another problem or question until learner feels ready to try task independently.

Reflections

6 An *Open Exchange* can be added before group members return to their seats to discuss the task and process writing down plans to make *QAPS* even more effective for next time and turning those suggestions into the teacher (five minutes). Individually, students might write down what they learned from *QAPS* on their assignment before beginning so that they can remember and refer to their notes later when completing the assignment.

Adjust Instruction: Record Agile Teacher Decisions

Choose one type of adjustment to focus on in your practice for a month or even a quarter. Try to respond to student differences by adjusting instruction using either Structures, Help, or Options. Notice times when your directions are particularly successful fostering student engagement. Write down successful directions in your *Learning Journal*. Keep a list of the *At-If-Then* decisions that you make in one lesson each week. Reflect on these questions:

1   Are there patterns in student needs/haves that require SHOp adjustments?
2   Do you find yourself responding most to perceptions of Clarity, Access, Rigor, or Relevance?
3   Are your responses relying on Structure, Help, or Options, or are your adjustments to instruction varied?

Checklist to Try Routines in Your Teaching

See https://www.routledge.com/9780815370819 for additional resources: *Agile Thinking* by Shifting Structures.

Plan	Teach	Adjust Instruction
❑ Plan *At-If-Then* statements for OSCAR in every lesson.	❑ Focus on implementing just one type of adjustment, structures, help, or options.	❑ Practice using agile thinking within the context of the project and in daily instruction. Record your agile teacher decisions. Annotate decisions for choices that were most precise (specifically addressing CARR), effective, and efficient.

Quality Criteria to Implement Classroom Routines	
Must Haves	Amazing
• Classroom routine is implemented on a daily or weekly basis or is tied to a specific type of instruction, such as a mini-lesson, independent practice, or review.	• Assignments routinely provide a range for engagement and success.

Chapter Reflection

Chapter Summary

In this chapter we put our agile thinking to work determining instructional responses to classroom dilemmas of student differences.

Learning Journal: Record Important Takeaways

Continue your *Learning Journal* to track your thinking about meeting the needs of diverse learners by recording answers to the following four questions:

1   What was most interesting and useful for you in this chapter?
2   Why was this interesting and useful?
3   How does this connect to what you know about meeting the learning needs of all learners?
4   What research from this chapter could you use to explain or support decisions to adjust instruction?

Save these responses for reflection after reading more of this book and trying out ideas in your classroom. We will answer these same four questions at the end of every chapter.

Return to Your Starting Position

Return to your preliminary first draft answer to our chapter question, "What does the four-step decision making method look like in practice?" Add new ideas or revise in another way. Circle the most important part and save to return to after Chapter 8: Closing Gaps and Extending Learning Stories from the Classroom.

Chapter 9

Closing Gaps and Extending Learning

Stories from the Classroom

Overview

Objective:

How can we examine the impact of adjustments to instruction on student learning?

Think: Go back to your Starting Position from Chapter 2: Perceptions of the Extremes. Consider the extremes that would be important to measure how adjusting instruction impacted student learning. Identify an extreme and how you might measure change.

Criteria

- Identify a story from the classroom that you might replicate or that inspires you to implement ALL-ED.
- Explain how early research is exploring how the ALL-ED four-step decision-making framework may support teacher efforts to close gaps and extend learning.
- Try Impact Project

  - Plan—*Choose an impact project to modify for your setting.*
  - Teach—*Routine implementation for impact project.*
  - Adjust Instruction—*Collect student work to examine the impact of routines on student learning.*

Starting Position: Review Your Starting Positions

Go back and review your starting positions from each chapter:

1 Best and Worst Times of Motivation
2 Perceptions of the Extremes in Networks
3 Moment of Successful Learning
4 Thinking Minutes: Measure Teacher's Time to Think in Lesson Plans
5 Challenges to Engaging All Learners
6 Classroom as a Resource for Learning: Help Resource
7 Student Choice: Pluses, Minuses, and Interesting Ideas/Questions
8 Strengths to Leverage and Challenges to Reduce, Work Around, or Eliminate

Notice when you went back and made adjustments to your starting position after reading the chapter. Make a bulleted list with the ideas that come to mind regarding yourself as a teacher, book reader, and implementer who shares ideas from the book with colleagues and your students or thinks of sharing ideas from this book with others. Place a check next to ideas that you have seen before and circle one item that is new. Share with a colleague one old and new idea that you have learned about yourself from reading this book.

From the Classroom: Our Own Research and Observations of ALL-ED

At the time of writing this book, we have shared our framework and routines with Pre–K–12 educators in many states across the United States and in six other countries (the Netherlands, Brazil, Chile, China, Singapore, Switzerland). Sharing the classroom routines and practicing decision making with educators has helped us develop the framework. We have also learned a great deal by watching students enjoy our classroom routines at many different grade levels and in a variety of cultural contexts.

In addition to supporting school communities, one of our major goals is to better understand how the classroom routines and decision-making framework actually impact student learning and teaching practices. When we work with teachers, we often invite them to participate in our research, which focuses on understanding how teachers learn agile thinking and the impact of ALL-ED classroom routines on student learning outcomes. In line with our goal of addressing the extremes, we highlight here two case studies that are representative of some of the work we do with schools: one is focused on a secondary, public school in New York City that serves students who are new to the United States and are often helping to support their families after school; the other case study is focused on young children who live with many resources and attend a private school in São Paulo, Brazil.

ALL-ED in the Bronx

The story of Oscar is based on a true story, like all of the stories from classrooms in this book. We got to know Oscar when we started to collaborate with students and teachers in a Bronx high school that serves students learning English as a New Language. This experience has been truly rewarding and has resulted in many of the insights that we have shared in our writing and teaching (Bondie & Zusho, 2016, 2017).

When collaborating with this school, one focus area related to the challenges of engaging every student during ALL-ED group learning routines. We wondered what kinds of adjustments teachers could make when giving directions, and how students developing language skills would respond to daily group learning routines. One problem an experienced teacher at the school expressed was uneven student partici- pation in small group discussions. She found that the more talkative students and those with greater English skills were consistently volunteering to report the group's findings to the class. In addition, the principal noticed that boys were volunteering to be the reporter more often than girls. So, the teacher described how she changed the routine to address this problem:

This time I said I will choose the reporters and everyone got tense. I saw the seriousness they put into it. I picked the students who do not speak often and they did fabulous. Sometimes I let them pick and sometimes I say, I will choose or I let a student from another group choose a reporter in a different group … they like it, you can see the pride in their eyes.

Students confirmed the success of this solution saying, "If we don't know who the group's reporter will be, then everyone has to be prepared." We watched teachers use agile thinking and the group learning routines to solve problems that occurred during lessons. The teacher summarized her reasoning for using group learning routines on a daily basis, often two or three times in a 60-minute period. She reflected that she uses group learning routines to "let students be in charge of their own learning. They are hands-on and participating. I am feeding them and transmitting knowledge but they are in charge of their own learning. I learned everything from them. We learn from each other."

As we mentioned above, this school primarily serves students who are new to the United States. With only a few years before aging out, many of the students who attend this school must race to acquire a new language while learning academic skills to pursue career and college goals. This race is particularly daunting for students who receive special education services and who are learning English as a New Language, considering that they may begin their junior or senior year reading in English at a first-grade level. We reasoned that ALL-ED, with its emphasis on promoting an environment supportive of autonomy, belonging, competence, and meaningfulness (ABC+M), could positively impact these students' motivation to learn. We therefore examined the impact of ALL-ED classroom routines with these students as we developed our framework.

The results of this study generally supported our claim: the students reported that ALL-ED group learning routines helped them become more confident learners. The routines not only encouraged them to speak more in English, but the built-in structures, like peer-to-peer conferencing, made them less wary of taking academic risks. For example, one student noted, "Sometimes it is simpler and talk is slower when you work together." Speed and repetition were important; students agreed with one boy's comment, "So, you have the feeling of being comfortable to ask for someone to explain again." Another student chimed in, "And also if you do something wrong, your group members can help you fix it."

The students also commented on how clarity and access in goals and quality criteria helped them to improve and to feel "happy, proud, liked, and challenged." For example, they noted the importance of rubrics in providing clear and focused feedback. In response to many different questions throughout the interviews, students offered remarks similar to "The rubrics give you feedback. It shows competent, outstanding, and needs improvement. Then you know how to do better—where you can improve. It motivates you to do better because you can see it right there." Whether the interview question was about preparing for or taking a standardized test or simply participating in class, students returned to this theme of feedback and opportunities to improve as keys to their learning and motivation.

ALL-ED in Brazil

In Chapter 7, we mentioned the importance of including targeted practice in regular instruction. Our work in a private school in Brazil helped us to better understand how to implement interest-driven targeted practice for individual students on a daily basis. In this case, we were fortunate to collaborate with teachers and children in the early years program. The teachers were working on how to provide students instruction tailored to their specific needs in a sustainable manner. Children were often unmotivated to receive individual support, noticing that they had been singled out from their peers. Teachers focused on providing additional help to struggling students, leaving them little time to provide extended learning opportunities for those with higher abilities. There was not enough time to both focus on student strengths and to make sure students were working on skills that needed development.

To address this common problem of practice, the teachers developed a routine called *Flag Time* (Baldisseri et al., n.d.), a daily 20-minute academic intervention designed to provide opportunities for remediation as well as extension of literacy, math, visual–motor, artistic, and social skills. During *Flag Time*, teachers place a flag with each child's name and picture at a learning center where a specially chosen task is waiting. Kindergarteners use the target language, English, to complete specifically assigned activities where their academic needs and strengths are paired with their interests. Each day, children are strategically placed into new groups with others who share an interest, need to develop the same skill, or provide a model or challenge.

Since the tasks used in *Flag Time* are personalized to students' strengths, interests, and/or needs, not all students encounter the same tasks. Teachers may leverage students' love of adventure to develop their math skills by having them use tiny magnifying glasses to find and solve math fact problems that are hidden in tiny font on pictures of adventure locations before the timer rings. To develop reading skills, a teacher might hide many cards with sight words around the room and ask students who enjoy playing games (and who need further support in reading) to find a small list of the hidden words. Once a word is found, the children look through their list to determine if the sight word they found matches the words on their personalized list. To finish their practice, students write the words using sidewalk chalk on large paper on the floor. They reach out to a peer from another group to check their spelling.

It is important to note how our four-step thinking routine supports teachers in sustaining this practice. Teachers use *Inclusive Directions* reminding students of the *Flag Time* rules each day. A chart of routine behaviors and expectations of quality work promotes student autonomy. Many *Flag Time* activities use the same routines children know from previous lessons, such as rules for a game or an individual practice activity. Consequently, teachers do not need to provide directions for each activity during *Flag Time*. In addition, management is easier because, rather than waiting for teacher help, the activities include help resources, such as an answer key, checklist, and model student work. Also, students receive immediate feedback from peers as a step in the routine. Planning time is also saved by teachers collecting observational assessment data during *Flag Time* to organize the next day's activity for each child. Daily, teachers develop their understanding of everyone's learning, so writing progress reports to families is easier and less time consuming. Most importantly, students are not wasting precious class time by practicing skills that have already been mastered, waiting for help on a task that is too difficult, or filling time because they have finished early; instead all time is used for learning.

Although a key component, it is important to note that the development of interest was not the main goal of *Flag Time*. As indicated earlier, it was to close achievement gaps in reading, writing, and arithmetic. We contributed to this initiative by helping teachers promote self-regulated learning (SRL) skills as part of the intervention. We encouraged teachers to incorporate in *Flag Time* self-regulatory prompts that were designed to encourage student planning, monitoring, and reflection. In the math case above, students self-assessed their mastery of addition facts and used numeracy learning progressions to determine which skill they needed to practice next. In the literacy example above, students were asked to consult with another peer who checked their work, to identify words that were most challenging for them, and to report patterns that they saw in their list of challenging words to the teacher. In line with research suggesting that SRL can be further developed through the maintenance of learning diaries (Glogger, Schwonke, Holzäpel, Nückles, & Renkl, 2012), students' SRL skills were further developed by reflecting in learning journals on the week's *Flag Time* activities, and considering next steps to learning.

Flag Time was an excellent means to improve student motivation. Students would routinely comment on how much they enjoyed *Flag Time*; for many, it was their favorite time of day. In terms of impact on achievement, we found that *Flag Time* was especially beneficial for closing achievement gaps in reading. We attributed these findings in part to the fact that the majority of *Flag Time* activities were literacy-based. We also noticed that the effects of *Flag Time* were not always uniform—the first round of research findings indicated that they were especially beneficial for boys and for non-native speakers of English.

Flag Time is a wonderful example of sustainable individualized targeted practice. We worked with the teachers on sustaining the routine by developing systems for sharing the individualized activities digitally, using task analysis to break down objectives into parts that could be practiced and developed through individualized practice, using activities such as "skill stamps" where students place a stamp on their work to indicate the skill that they feel they developed through the practice, and using *Learning Journals* to increase student awareness of their own growth as learners. Over the past five years, we served as thought partners, cheerleaders, and problem-solvers in this effort led by the educators committed to personalizing learning in general education classrooms. We have taken lessons from this experience to support high school teachers in replicating the idea with "Mastery Monday" (see Chapter 6). We hope that our continued work in sharing individualized instruction and help routines will ensure that differentiated instruction will become a common essential part of school for all students.

Both of these case studies provide emerging evidence for the potential of ALL-ED routines to promote students' motivation and achievement. As we continue to do research on ALL-ED, we plan to examine how ALL-ED classroom routines can promote culturally-relevant pedagogy and facilitate co-teaching in inclusive classrooms. We are interested in how classroom routines support learners across different cultures in different countries as well as within classroom and school cultures.

Ultimately, we hope to understand how teachers develop agile thinking and adjustable instruction to help all students learn every day in inclusive classrooms. We believe digital platforms may be used to personalize and differentiate teacher preparation both modeling and furthering agile teacher decision-making skills as a habit. Much research has focused on the student as the learner in the classroom. We would like to expand that focus to examining the teacher as a learner and thinker during lessons. In order to adjust instruction, teachers must learn from the students, think about possible instructional choices, and make decisions based on an evaluation of the most effective and efficient choice for the given context of curricular objective, time, and student needs. Clearly, the thinking and learning that teachers do while teaching in order to differentiate instruction is complex and needs to be better understood both by researchers and by teachers themselves.

Rooted in Research: Review Each Chapter

Throughout the book, we have embedded numerous discussions of research to substantiate our ALL-ED framework. In this concluding chapter, we highlight the main points by revisiting the research on effective classrooms (Patrick, Mantzicopoulos, & Sears, 2012). Patrick and her colleagues describe effective classrooms as having specific characteristics that help students to develop skills for navigating a rapidly changing world. We briefly summarize those characteristics in relation to the ALL-ED framework below.

Students and teachers share responsibility for student learning. In the ALL-ED classroom, both students and teachers share the responsibility for student learning. Teachers are responsible for structuring clear, accessible, rigorous, and relevant learning activities. Students, in turn, are responsible for being engaged behaviorally, emotionally, and cognitively, and for fully attending to and participating (alone and with others) in the deep and effortful work needed for durable learning.

Students view learning and personal improvement as realistic and their primary goal. In the ALL-ED classroom, one of the primary goals is competence for *all*. It is important for all students to feel like learning and improving is not only a possibility but actually attainable. To that end, we have discussed the importance of adjusting instruction so that tasks are not too easy but not too hard. We have also discussed the importance of maintaining high expectations for all students, and for fostering an environment where learning *is* the goal—an environment where all students feel like they want to develop (and not demonstrate) their competence.

All students learn and improve relative to what they know and could do previously. Bandura suggests that one of the key ways to build students' competence and self-efficacy is for students to experience academic success (what he calls mastery experiences). Mastery experiences largely depend on designing tasks that are in students' zones of proximal development, meaning that the task requires the learner to stretch, but the task is not totally out of the learner's current range of difficulty. As teachers know, finding the right level of challenge for each learner is very difficult. This is why ALL-ED emphasizes continuous formative assessments using OSCAR to make the starting position and quality criteria clear to all so students know where they are and where they need to go. In addition, we routinely provide help resources, specifically supports, scaffolds, and extensions, that adjust the range of a good fit for learners with diverse abilities.

The focus is on understanding, not memorizing or following procedures. Although memorizing information is sometimes a necessary part of learning, ALL-ED assumes that durable learning will not result when students simply cram information. Rather, the research on WERMS suggests that effective learning entails overcoming the limits of working memory, and engaging deep-processing cognitive and metacognitive strategies, which facilitate proper encoding and retrieval of information from long-term memory. We further suggest that understanding entails the development of detailed conceptual frameworks, which can be aided by the use of appropriate scaffolds, supports, and extensions and by the CARR Check.

Talking during lessons is valued and encouraged. A big part of the ALL-ED framework is encouraging students to talk to each other in productive ways, and giving teachers the time to be able to listen to students' thinking to give System 2 a chance to check in with System 1. We have shared numerous group learning routines, specifically designed to promote students' behavioral, affective, and cognitive engagement. During ALL-ED group learning routines, students are provided equal opportunities to listen and contribute through roles and rounds, as they work toward a common goal. Group learning routines are designed to provide students more opportunities to consolidate information, thereby facilitating knowledge building.

Ability comparisons and competition among students are low. ALL-ED rests on the fundamental assumption that getting students to talk and listen to each other builds a sense of community and belonging. Belonging is another important goal of ALL-ED, which research on motivation suggests can only flourish when members in the learning community value and respect one another. ALL-ED routines typically minimize ability comparisons and competition. ALL-ED is designed to promote what motivational researchers would call a mastery-oriented learning environment where the focus is on the development rather than the demonstration of competence. Mastery-oriented environments are much more likely to facilitate the development of learning than competitive environments.

Students receive informational feedback and recognition for their progress and effort. Throughout the book, we have reviewed research that underscores the importance of feedback. Without proper and clear feedback, students cannot judge their progress, which ultimately impedes learning. The ALL-ED framework provides students with multiple ways of receiving feedback. Through OSCAR, teachers are encouraged to engage in frequent formative assessments, and to make the results of those assessments visible to students. Students also receive feedback from their peers when they engage in ALL-ED group learning routines and through the quality criteria and various help options. Above all, ALL-ED emphasizes informational feedback that facilitates the development of a growth mindset. In the ALL-ED classroom, mistakes are viewed not as deficiencies that need to be corrected, but as opportunities to understand student thinking.

Students develop sound learning and work habits. A major goal of ALL-ED is to develop self-regulated learners—strategic learners who are metacognitively aware of how they think; who set appropriate goals and plans for learning; monitor progress toward goals; adjust or regulate their thinking, motivation, and study habits. Throughout the book, we have demonstrated how the four steps of the framework: OSCAR, Look and Listen, CARR, and SHOp, can facilitate the development of self-regulated learners. The individual self-regulatory routines have also been designed to combat illusions of knowing, one of the major obstacles of learning.

Students apply what they have learned to new situations. When discussing the research foundation of *At-If-Then* statements introduced in Chapter 8, we briefly touched upon the notion that in order to acquire skills, individuals must learn to act upon their declarative knowledge. They need to learn how to turn inert, factual knowledge into production rules (i.e., *At-If-Then* statements). We further emphasized the importance of using those *At-If-Then* statements in a variety of problem-solving scenarios repeatedly and over time. The underlying reason for those suggestions is transfer. Transfer is when students are able to use what they have learned in one task or context in a totally different task or context. For example, students who participate in the routine *Think, Talk, Open Exchange (TTO)* in science can usually use the routine in math without additional instruction. They transfer their understanding of *TTO* from one class to a different class. The overall research on transfer of learning suggests that it happens infrequently at best, and that it is more likely to occur when learners apply what they have learned to a variety of situations and when students engage in practices associated with durable learning. Getting students to think in terms of *At-If-Then* statements will not only promote self-regulated learning, but it should also promote transfer.

Students value learning and are motivated to learn. Apart from the focus on self-regulated learning, a recurring theme of ALL-ED is student motivation. Ultimately the goal of ALL-ED is to ensure that all members of the learning community experience the ABC+M of learning. As an integral and valued member of the learning community, a student should feel competent and in control of their learning and find learning to be personally meaningful. The CARR Check is designed to promote these outcomes.

Students have positive relationships with their teachers. Research consistently shows that when students believe that their teacher is supportive and cares about them, they engage in a range of adaptive behaviors (e.g., expending effort, help seeking, self-regulation) that lead to positive learning outcomes. To that end, we have discussed the importance of maintaining high expectations for *all* students, and in providing ways to support students' autonomy. We have also discussed how the ALL-ED group learning routines can provide teachers the time to look and listen, which will also help them to get to know their students better.

Classmates are emotionally, socially, and academically supportive of one another. We have also reviewed research findings related to the role of peers in the learning process, and how insensitive peers can derail learning and help seeking. The ALL-ED routines have been designed in ways to ensure that vulnerable students feel like they have a chance to succeed. As mentioned previously, the group learning routines stress collaboration over competition, and provide students multiple opportunities for academic engagement. We also stress the importance of *Inclusive Directions* as a means of promoting motivation.

Learning environments are well-structured, emotionally secure, and predictable. Research suggests that when students perceive their classroom environment to be respectful and well-managed, they are more likely to engage in academic risk-taking and problem-solving, facilitating durable learning. In the ALL-ED classroom, students engage in predictable yet powerful thinking routines, which aid working memory and promote multiple opportunities to learn. Students are not fearful of what others might think or say when they make mistakes; rather, students are encouraged to explain and share ideas, even if they are tentative. As the students from one school told us, ALL-ED makes them feel "happy, proud, liked, and challenged."

Try Classroom Routines: Precise, Effective, Efficient Learning for All

Start your own exploration of agile thinking and adjustable instruction to meet diverse learner needs by trying out an impact project. We describe five possible projects that you may adapt and implement with your students to begin to measure how adjustable instruction impacts student learning. These projects are useful when they are implemented by a team to provide support for regularly implementing the classroom routines and feedback on observations of student learning.

Option 1: Buzzwords: Assessing Use of Group Learning to Increase Use of Academic Vocabulary in Speaking and Writing

Monitor student use of targeted academic vocabulary words measuring both the quality and frequency of use by students. Ask students to tally their peers' use of targeted vocabulary words, *Buzzwords*, during *Think Talk Open Exchange (TTO)* or *Elbow Exchange* group learning routines, using a vocabulary tracking form. Ask students to reflect on the words that were used during small group discussions, considering both frequently and infrequently used words. Monitor student growth by administering a pre- and post-vocabulary test and monitoring unprompted use of vocabulary words in other assignments.

Option 2: Self-Regulated Learning Journals for Student Achievement

Implement a weekly self-regulation learning reflection task with students. Analyze student responses to monitor student use of self-regulated learning skills. Implement a pre-post self-regulated learning survey with students.

Option 3: Mastery Monday: Target Practice to Close Achievement Gaps

Measure the impact of regular individualized targeted practice within the general education classroom on student learning as seen in student work and unit assessments.

Option 4: Scaffolding for Access and Rigor for Student Independence and Achievement

Measure the impact of scaffolds on student learning and independence level at completing the targeted task through student work and performance on unit assessments. Develop a method with students to monitor student persistence.

Option 5: Student Engagement in Inclusive Classrooms

Measure the level of student engagement in lessons through classroom observation data and lesson video analysis. Test how changes in *Inclusive Directions* (Roles, Turns, Rules, and Time) impact students' on-task behavior, positive feelings about their interactions with peers, and learning from the discussions.

Adjust Instruction: Practice Using the Four-Part Decision-Making Framework

Record your planned decisions to differentiate instruction and your agile thinking adjustments to practice using the *At-If-Then* (see Chapter 8) routine. Do you find yourself responding most to perceptions of clarity, access, rigor, or relevance? Are your responses relying on structure, help, or options, or are your adjustments to instruction varied? Which part of the lesson (OSCAR) receives the most and the least adjustments? Based on your responses, plan next steps for furthering your use of agile thinking to meet the needs of all learners every day.

Checklist to Try Routines in Your Teaching

See https://www.routledge.com/9780815370819 for additional resources: Agile Teacher Thinking—Impact Project Resource.

Plan	Teach	Adjust Instruction
❏ Select an Impact Project and organize a colleague or small team for implementation support and feedback.	❏ Teach the routine and then regularly implement, saving student work from the starting position and throughout the study.	❏ Practice using agile thinking within the context of the project and in daily instruction.

Quality Criteria to Implement Classroom Routines	
Must Haves	Amazing
Classroom routine is implemented on a daily or weekly basis, or is tied to a specific type of instruction, such as a mini-lesson, independent practice, or review.	Assignments routinely provide a range for engagement and success.

Return and Reflect on Your Learning in This Chapter

Chapter Summary

In this chapter, we explored how to measure the impact of ALL-ED on student learning. We examined two case students, one high school and one early childhood, as models of how we are working with teachers to ensure all students are learning every day in several countries. We reviewed research from previous chapters. We proposed different impact projects for you to try out with students to determine the impact of your interventions on student learning.

Learning Journal: Record Important Takeaways

Continue your *Learning Journal* to track your thinking about meeting the needs of diverse learners by recording answers to the following four questions:

1 What was most interesting and useful for you in this chapter?
2 Why was this interesting and useful?

3   How does this connect to what you know about meeting the learning needs of all learners?
4   What research from this chapter could you use to explain or support decisions to adjust instruction?

Reread your responses from the beginning of this book, notice how your ideas both stayed the same and changed. Reflect on what you have made routine in your practice and note what you find challenging in implementing our four-step framework. Save your *Learning Journal* the way Ms. Ford saves the video of her students from the first day of school. Return to your reflections in a few months or at the end of next year and reflect once again on what has remained interesting and useful to you over time. When planning instruction complete a quick CARR Check, asking yourself if each part of the lesson OSCAR will be clear, accessible, rigorous, and relevant for *all* students. When the answer is "no" for any part of the lesson, then adjust SHOp structures, help, or options to ensure all learners will learn every day.

Return to Your Starting Position

Return to your preliminary first draft answer to our book, "Why do we differentiate instruction?" Review your *Learning Journal* from each chapter. Now go back to your answer to the question, "Why do we differentiate instruction?" Circle the most important part. Consider how your answer has both stayed the same and changed through reading this book. Plan your next step to learn more by considering what questions have emerged or remain from the start of your reading. Determine one next step that you can take to move toward answering that question. We look forward to hearing about your learning and next steps through our website, all-ed.org. We also have a course to learn more about differentiated instruction and adjustable instruction rooted in motivation and self-regulated learning, *Differentiated Instruction Made Practical*, through the online Programs in Professional Education at the Harvard Graduate School of Education.

Differentiated Instruction Made Practical

Offered jointly by Harvard Teacher Fellows and the Programs in Professional Education at the Harvard Graduate School of Education, Differentiated Instruction Made Practical, is an online course designed to build educator abilities to differentiate instruction as a part of their daily classroom routines. By using the ALL-ED four-step teacher-decision making framework and implementing structured classroom routines rooted in research on cognition and motivation, you will increase equity, access, rigor, and engagement for all students. This program will prepare you with the agile thinking required to analyze problems of student learning and then make decisions to adjust and differentiate instruction within given time and curriculum constraints. The course provides a professional development experience that models differentiated instruction in practical ways for immediate classroom use to ensure that all learners are learning every day.

To register and learn more, please visit
https://www.gse.harvard.edu/ppe/program/differentiated-instruction-made-practical

Glossary of Terms

ABC+M of Motivation Students are more likely to put forth effort, persist, take academic risks, and achieve when they feel **A**utonomous, a sense of **B**elonging with others, and **C**ompetent, and when they perceive that what they are learning is personally **M**eaningful.

Academic press Academic press refers to the extent to which students are pressed to explain their thinking or justify their arguments.

Agile thinking Agile thinking refers to adjusting or differentiating instruction to meet learner needs, both on their feet in the middle of instruction and in planning lessons. Teachers use agile thinking to maintain their focus on a specific objective; analyze a situation for evidence of clarity, access, rigor, or relevance (CARR Check); and then brainstorm possible choices for adjusting or differentiating instruction.

ALL-ED ALL-ED is the acronym for All Learners Learning Every Day. The ALL-Ed Framework has four steps:

- Step 1: Identify OSCAR.
- Step 2: Look and Listen.
- Step 3: CARR Check.
- Step 4: SHOp Adjustments.

At-If-Then Agile thinking routine to guide teacher decisions to differentiate instruction.

Buzzwords Targeted academic vocabulary words

CARR Check: Step 3 of the ALL-Ed Framework CARR Check stands for "Check for Clarity, Access, Rigor, and Relevance."

- Clarity—clear goals give direction and purpose to behavior, while clear and immediate feedback informs the individual how well she or he is progressing and whether to adjust or maintain the present course of action. Students learn more when teachers are clear and easy to understand.
- Access—the importance of tasks being designed at an appropriate level of challenge. Students must perceive a match between their skills and opportunities to use those skills (or perceived level of challenge). Lessons must not be too hard or too easy.
- Rigor equals effort multiplied by complexity. Effort equals required time of sustained focus for students. Complexity equals the number or parts of the

topic, the number of ways the parts can fit together, and the type of think-ing required to manipulate the parts

- Relevance is where the student perceives the task and/or subject domain to be important (what researchers refer to as attainment value), interesting (also referred to as intrinsic interest value), and/or useful (or utility value).

Conceptual change   If students know very little or believe something that con-tradicts the information to be learned, then they must transform or revise their schema in some way, which typically taxes working memory.

Conceptual growth   If students know something about a topic and the new information to be learned is in line with their prior knowledge, then students can simply add the new knowledge into their existing schema.

Connective instruction   Connective instruction refers to teaching practices that promote emotional connection to the content being taught, the teacher, and the instruction of the class.

Co-regulation or shared regulation   Effective groups utilize high-level cog-nitive strategies, such as helping each other summarize, elaborate, and refine each other's thoughts and ideas, or helping each other plan or revise their work rather than simply telling each other the answers with little to no explanations.

Differentiated instruction   Differentiated instruction is the outcome of a con-tinuous decision-making process where teachers look and listen for academic diversity that will either strengthen or impede effective and efficient learning.

- *Adjustable common instruction* is where students are learning with the same goals, resources, and assessments.
- *Specific resources instruction* is where some students (groups or individuals) are using different resources accompanied with a specific teaching approach to *achieve the objective*.
- *Individualized instruction* refers to individual workouts to review, practice, extend, or pursue an interest.

Do Now   Opening activity at the start of the lesson; usually produces a starting position for the lesson.

Durable learning   Durable learning is learning that gets consolidated in long-term memory.

Elaborate schema   Elaborate schema is a mental model of extensive prior knowledge.

English as a New Language   Replaces the previously used English Language Learners, English for Speakers of Other Languages, and English as a Second Language.

Flag Time   A daily 20-minute academic intervention designed to provide oppor-tunities for remediation as well as extension of literacy, math, visual–motor, artistic, and social skills. Individualized practice for all students during regular instruction. Developed by teachers in Brazil (Baldisseri et al., n.d.).

Growth mindset   Growth mindset is the understanding that abilities and intel-ligence can be developed (Dweck, 2006).

Illusions of knowing   Illusions of knowing refers to the perception that we know more than we actually do, or overconfidence.

Inclusive Directions   There are four parts to *Inclusive Directions*. Each of these parts are identified because being specific with students increases clarity of the outcome and behaviors expected.

- *Roles*. During group learning routines the roles should be essential to furthering discussion. A recorder and/or a reporter or group representative may be added to share, materials gatherer or clean-up (before or after a group learning routine but not during).
- *Turns*. Identify who is going first as the speaker in each group. This resolves problems with social loafing and problems associated with wasted time. The turns should always be assigned by the teacher to reach an instructional goal.
- *Rules*. Rules ensure rigor and access for all students.

    ○ "Add or Repeat"
    ○ "Point, Repeat"—later in the year—"Point, Repeat, Repeat and Add"
    ○ Each Person Will Share
    ○ Exchange Ideas with People Who Do Not Sit at Your Table.

- *Time*. Time is always designated to ensure equity in opportunities to share ideas in the class as well as to protect time to think about responses before being required to reply. Time may be kept by the teacher using a watch, or a timer may be used.

Jot Notes   Individual activity for generating, organizing, and making sense of ideas. Individual brainstorming activity to make patterns of thinking about a topic visible.

Look & Listen: Step 2 of the ALL-Ed Framework   Look & listen to examine problems occurring as learning unfolds. Look under the surface to understand the roots of student responses and how students are making connections. Listening to students as a check for understanding. Use two structures—individual and group learning routines—as dashboards and shoulders along the road to free the teacher to observe student learning.

Mastery experiences   Mastery experiences are experiences of academic success. Mastery experiences are one source of academic efficacy.

Memory

- *Working memory* is the "memory system that allows us to 'keep things in mind' when performing complex tasks" (Baddeley, Eysenck, & Anderson, 2014, p. 13).
- *Long-term memory* is the memory system that holds all of our knowledge.

Metacognitive awareness   Metacognitive awareness refers to awareness of your own thinking. Metacognitive awareness is the hallmark of a self-regulated learner—a learner who, upon given an assignment, thinks about what she knows about the topic, what she did in the past to succeed on similar assignments, and her goals for the assignment.

Monitoring chart   A monitoring chart is a chart that monitors student progress toward completing a large task or mastery of learning objectives, or special skills students are willing to share with others. Students move a sticky note with their name to match their movement in learning through the unit.

Motivation   Motivation is something that influences or explains why a person will start a task, whether a person will approach or avoid a task, how much effort a person will put into a task, and whether a person will continue to work on the task once they start. *Motivation is NOT a personality trait. Altering the task or the general learning environment can change it.*

OSCAR: Step 1 of the ALL-Ed Framework

- *Objective* sets a focus for your learning.
- *Starting position* is a short routine designed to activate your background knowledge and to record your initial thoughts.
- *Criteria* is a means for you to gauge the quality of your understanding.

  - *Must Haves* are usually the same for all learners.
  - *Amazing* is an extension of the required knowledge.

- Action Pattern, for example:

  - a mini-lesson that includes a group learning routine, *Elbow Exchange*, prior to the mini-lesson;
  - an individual routine during the mini-lesson, *Note and Question*; and
  - a return to the *Elbow Exchange* to review, retrieve, and measure learning from the mini-lesson.

- Reflection: Returning to the starting position to describe how one's thinking has stayed the same or been challenged, changed, or added to during the lesson.

Response to intervention (RTI) model   The RTI model is a multi-tiered approach to the early identification and support of students with learning and behavioral needs. The RTI process begins with high-quality instruction and universal screening of all children in the general education classroom (Gorski).

Roles   Group work can only be successfully completed when each group member carries out their role.

Rounds   Everyone in the group takes turns completing the same task in a circle, helping to ensure even participation by all group members.

SHOp: Step 4 of the ALL-Ed Framework   SHOp refers to the three ways teachers adjust instruction to respond to perceived learner needs. Teachers can adjust instruction by planning to use more than one structure for tasks or shifting between at least two task structures for an activity. This gets students in the habit of shifting from one task structure to another; individual learning to table talk to group learning to explicit instruction.

- *Structures*:

  a   explicit instruction,
  b   table talk,
  c   individual learning routines, and
  d   group learning routines.

- *Help* (three different tiers, aligned to the different types of differentiated instruction).

a *General Help Resources*

- Wall information such as charts with learning strategy steps, directions for routines, or goal monitoring, student work, criteria charts, and word walls.
- Tools such as calculators, rulers, timers, and bookmarks that help students accomplish tasks.
- References such as libraries, dictionaries, and textbooks.
- Materials such as graphic organizers, note-taking guides, rubrics, checklists, paper, pencils, and markers.
- People, including the students themselves, peers, experts, and the teacher.

b *Specific Resources*: The objectives and assessments are the same, however, some students (groups or individuals) are using different resources accompanied with a specific teaching approach to achieve the objective These include supports, scaffolds, and extensions that help learners with a specific task. A learner will at times need:

- a support to practice the whole task,
- a scaffold to focus developing skills for just one part of the task, and
- extensions to stretch beyond expectations.

Specific Help resources are most effective when the teacher uses a systematic teaching approach.

c *Practice and Fade*: the systematic teaching is designed for students to practice a specific skill and then the scaffold is explicitly and strategically removed or faded as the student develops mastery of the skill and no longer needs the scaffold.

d *Independent Use:* where the student is taught how to ask for the scaffold or make the scaffold so that the students can independently acquire the help that is needed to accomplish a task.

e *Individualized* help: assignments aimed at remediation, review, preview, and beyond. Individualized help may include specially designed instruction, accommodations, modifications, and remediation as designated on students' individualized education programs.

- *Options*. Options always fall on a choice continuum extending from total student choice to teacher structured student choice to total teacher assignment

Self-Regulated Learning (SRL) SRL is the acronym for self-regulated learning (or learner), which is the awareness one's knowledge and limitations and what one needs to successfully learn a concept. SLR is a teachable skill.

Task analysis Task analysis identifies the parts within the whole task. We use task analysis to break down tasks into parts, and we break down skills into the smaller skills used in larger skills.

Testing (or retrieval–practice) effect Testing (or retrieval–practice) effect refers to increasing the frequency of retrieving knowledge from memory; to be most effective, retrieval must be repeated over and over again, spaced out over time, and effortful.

Transfer   Transfer is not just acquiring new information, but also being able to apply it later—when students are able to use what they have learned in one task or context in a totally different task or context.

Triad Stations   Teacher assigned groups of three students.

Universal design for learning (UDL)   UDL is a scientifically valid framework for guiding educational practice that

- provides flexibility in the ways information is presented, in the ways students respond or demonstrate knowledge and skills, and in the ways students are engaged; and
- reduces barriers in instruction, provides appropriate accommodations, and supports, challenges, and maintains high achievement expectations for all students, including students with disabilities and students with limited English proficiency (UDL Center).

WERMS   WERMS refers to overcoming the limits of **W**orking memory by engaging in **E**laborative and **R**etrieval-based strategies to interrupt the process of forgetting, to consolidate learning, and to overcome **illusions of knowing**. Research also demonstrates that **S**elf-regulated learners—students who are **M**etacognitively aware of how they think, who set appropriate goals and plan for learning, monitor progress toward goals, and adjust or regulate their thinking, motivation, and study habits—are more likely to achieve academic success than those who do not.

References

Adams, G. Engelmann, S (1996). *Research on direct instruction: 20 years beyond DISTAR*. Seattle, WA: Educational Achievement Systems.

American Psychological Association, Coalition for Psychology in Schools and Education. (2015). *Top 20 principles from psychology for pre-K–12 teaching and learning*. Retrieved from http://www.apa.org/ed/schools/cpse/top-twenty-principles.pdf

Anderson, J. R. (1983). *The architecture of cognition*. Cambridge, MA: Harvard University Press.

Anderson, J. R., Corbett, A. T., Koedinger, K. R., & Pelletier, R. (1995). Cognitive tutors: Lessons learned. *Journal of Learning Sciences*, 4, 167–207. doi:10.1207/s15327809jls0402_2

Baddeley, A. (2004). *Your memory: A user's guide*. Buffalo, NY: Firefly Books.

Baddeley, A., Eysenck, M., & Anderson, M. (2014). *Memory*. New York, NY: Psychology Press.

Baldisseri, A., Boschi, M., Gallagher, M., & Processo, M. (n.d.). The challenge of applying differentiated instructions in the classroom. Retrieved August 30, 2017, from https://www.flagtime.org/english

Bandura, A. (1997). *Self-efficacy: The exercise of control*. New York, NY: Freeman.

Bondie, R., Gaughran, L., & Zusho, A. (2014). Fostering English learners' confidence. *Educational Leadership*, 72(3), 42–46. Retrieved from http://www.ascd.org

Bondie, R., & Zusho, A. (2016). Out of the book and into the classroom: Applying motivational and self-regulated learning theories to daily instruction with English language learners. In J. DeCuir-Gunby & P. Schutz (Eds.), *Race and ethnicity in the study of motivation in education* (pp. 82–98). New York, NY: Routledge.

Bondie, R., & Zusho, A. (2017). Racing against yourself: High-stakes for adolescent English language learners with disabilities. *Teachers College Record*, 119(9), 1–42. Retrieved from http://www.tcrecord.org

Brophy, J., & Good, T. L. (1984). Teacher Behavior and Student Achievement. Occasional Paper No. 73.

Brophy, J. E. (1985). Teacher–student interaction. In J. B. Dusek (Ed.), *Teacher expectancies* (pp. 303–328). Hillsdale, NJ: Lawrence Erlbaum.

Brophy, J. E. (1986). Teacher influences on student achievement. *American Psychologist*, 41, 1069–1077.

Brown, P. C., Roedinger, H. L., & McDaniel, M. A. (2014). *Make it stick: The science of successful learning*. Cambridge, MA: Harvard University Press.

Christenson, S., Reschly, A., & Wylie, C. (Eds.) (2011). *Handbook of research on student engagement*. New York, NY: Springer.

Cooper, K. S. (2014). Eliciting engagement in the high school classroom: A mixed methods examination of teaching practices. *American Educational Research Journal*, 51, 363–402. doi:10.3102/0002831213507973

Cordova, D., & Lepper, M. (1996). Intrinsic motivation and the process of learning: Beneficial effects of contextualization, personalization, and choice. *Journal of Educational Psychology*, 88, 715–730. doi:10.1037/0022-0663.88.4.715

Csikszentmihalyi, M. (2014). *Flow and the foundations of positive psychology*. Dordrecht, Netherlands: Springer.

Dweck, C. S. (2006). *Mindset: The new psychology of success*. New York, NY: Ballantine Books.

Eccles, J. S., & Wang, M. (2016). What motivates females and males to pursue careers in mathematics and science? *International Journal of Behavioral Development*, 40, 100–106. doi: 10.1177/0165025415616201

Elliot, A. J., Dweck, C. S., & Yaeger, D. S. (2017). *Handbook of competence and motivation* (2nd ed.). New York, NY: Guilford.

Fredricks, J. A., Blumenfeld, P. C., & Paris, A. (2004). School engagement: Potential of the concept, state of the evidence. *Review of Educational Research*, 74, 59–119. doi:10.3102/00346543074001059

Fuchs, D. (2006). Cognitive profiling of children with genetic disorders and the search for a scientific basis of differentiated education. In P. Alexander & P. Winne (Eds.), *Handbook of educational psychology* (pp. 187–208). Mahwah, NJ: Erlbaum.

Gardner, H. (1999). *Intelligence reframed*. New York, NY: Basic Books.

Gay, G. (2010). *Culturally responsive teaching: Theory, research, and practice*. New York, NY: Teachers College Press.

Glogger, I., Schwonke, R., Holzäpfel, L., Nückles, M., & Renkl, A. (2012). Learning strategies assessed by journal writing: Prediction of learning outcomes by quantity, quality, and combinations of learning strategies. *Journal of Educational Psychology*, 104, 454–468.

Graesser, A. C., D'Mello, S., & Person, N. (2009). Meta-knowledge in tutoring. In D. Hacker, J. Dunlosky, & A. Graesser (Eds.), *Handbook of metacognition in education* (pp. 361–381). New York, NY: Routledge.

Hadwin, A. F., Jarvela, S., & Miller, M. (2011). Self-regulated, co-regulated, and socially shared regulation of learning. In B. Zimmerman & D. Schunk (Eds.), *Handbook of self-regulation of learning and performance* (pp. 65–86). New York, NY: Routledge.

Hall, T. E., Meyer, A., & Rose, D. H. (2012). *Universal design for learning in the classroom: Practical applications*. New York, NY: Guilford.

Harackiewicz, J. M., Tibbetts, Y., Canning, E. A., & Hyde, J. S. (2014). Harnessing values to promote motivation in education. In S. Karabenick & T. Urdan (Eds.), *Motivational interventions: Advances in motivation and achievement* (Vol. 18, pp. 71–105). Bingley, England: Emerald Group Publishing.

Hattie, J. (2009). *Visible learning: A synthesis of over 800 meta-analyses relating to achievement*. New York, NY: Routledge.

Hiebert, J., & Stigler, J. W. (2017). Teaching versus teachers as a lever for change: Comparing a Japanese and U.S. perspective on improving instruction. *Educational Researcher*, 46, 169–176. doi:10.3102/0013189X17711899

Hmelo-Silver, C., & Chinn, C. A. (2016). Collaborative learning. In L. Corno & E. Anderman (Eds.), *Handbook of educational psychology* (3rd ed.) (pp. 349–363). New York, NY: Routledge.

Hmelo-Silver, C. E., Duncan, R. G., & Chinn, C. A. (2007). Scaffolding and achievement in problem-based and inquiry learning: A response to Kirschner, Sweller, and Clark (2006). *Educational Psychologist*, 42, 99–107. doi:10.1080/00461520701263368

Iyengar, S. S., & Lepper, M. R. (1999). Rethinking the value of choice: A cultural perspective on intrinsic motivation. *Journal of Personality and Social Psychology*, 76, 349–366. doi:10.1037/0022-3514.76.3.349

Kahneman, D. (2011). *Thinking fast and slow*. New York, NY: Farrar, Straus, and Giroux.

Kaplan, A., Sinai, M., & Flum, H. (2014). Design-based interventions for promoting students' identity exploration within the school curriculum. In S. Karabenick & T. Urdan

(Eds.), *Motivational interventions: Advances in motivation and achievement* (Vol. 18, pp. 243–291). Bingley, England: Emerald Group Publishing.

Karabenick, S. A. (2011). Methodological and assessment issues in research on help seeking. In B. Zimmerman & D. Schunk (Eds.), *Handbook of self-regulation of learning and performance* (pp. 267–281). New York, NY: Routledge.

Karabenick, S. A., & Knapp, J. R. (1988). Help-seeking and the need for academic assistance. *Journal of Educational Psychology*, 83, 221–230. doi:10.1037/0022-0663.80.3.406

Karabenick, S. A., & Knapp, J. R. (1991). Relationship of academic help seeking to the use of learning strategies and other instrumental achievement behavior in college students. *Journal of Educational Psychology*, 83(2), 221–230. doi:http://dx.doi.org/10.1037/0022-0663.83.2.221

Katz, I., & Assor, A. (2007). When choice motivates and when it does not. *Educational Psychology Review*, 19, 429–442. doi:10.1007/s10648-006-9027-y

Kuhn, D. (2015). Thinking together and alone. *Educational Researcher*, 44, 46–53.

Ladson-Billings, G. (1995). Toward a theory of culturally relevant pedagogy. *American Educational Research Journal*, 32(3), 465–491.

Lapinski, S., Gravel, J. W. Rose, D. H. (2012). Toolers for practice: The universal design for learning guidelines. In T. E. Hall, A. Meyer, & D. H. Rose (Eds.), *Universal design for learning in the classroom: Practical applications* (pp. 9–24). New York, NY: Guilford Press.

Lazowski, R., & Hulleman, C. (2016). Motivational interventions in education: A meta-analytic review. *Review of Educational Research*, 86, 602–640. doi:10.3102/0034654315617832

Linnenbrink-Garcia, L., & Patall, E. A. (2016). Motivation. In L. Corno & E. Anderman (Eds.), *Handbook of educational psychology* (3rd ed.) (pp. 91–103). New York, NY: Routledge.

Maehr, M. L., & Zusho, A. (2009). Achievement goal theory: The past, present, and future. In K. Wentzel & A. Wigfield (Eds.), *Handbook of motivation in school* (pp. 76–104). New York, NY: Routledge.

Mandinach, E., & Lash, A. A. (2016). Assessment illuminating pathways to learning. In L. Corno & E. Anderman (Eds.), *Handbook of educational psychology* (3rd ed.) (pp. 390–401). New York, NY: Routledge.

Mayer, R. E. (2011). *Applying the science of learning*. New York, NY: Pearson.

Measures of Effective Teaching Project. (2010). *Learning about teaching: Initial findings from the measures of effective teaching project*. Seattle, WA: Bill & Melinda Gates Foundation.

Middleton, M. J, & Midgley, C. (2002). Beyond motivation: Middle school students' perceptions of press for understanding in math. *Contemporary Educational Psychology*, 27, 373–391. doi:10.1006/ceps.2001.1101

Musu-Gillette, L., Robinson, J., McFarland, J., KewalRamani, A., Zhang, A., & Wilkinson-Flicker, S. (2016). *Status and trends in the education of racial and ethnic groups 2016* (NCES Report No. 2016-007). Washington, DC: U.S. Department of Education, National Center for Education Statistics. Retrieved from http://nces.ed.gov/pubsearch

NAEP (2015). U.S. Department of Education, Institute of Education Sciences, National Center for Education Statistics, National Assessment of Educational Progress (NAEP), various years, 1992–2015 Mathematics Assessments. https://www.nationsreportcard.gov/reading_math_2015/#reading?grade=4; https://www.nationsreportcard.gov/reading_math_2015/#mathematics?grade=4

Newman, R. S., & Goldin, L. (1990). Children's reluctance to seek help with schoolwork. *Journal of Educational Psychology*, 82, 92–100. doi:10.1037/0022-0663.82.1.92

OECD (2016). *PISA 2015 Results (Volume 1): Excellence and Equity in Education*. Paris, France, OECD Publishing. http://dx.doi.org/10.1787/9789264266490-en

Patall, E. A. (2013). Constructing motivation through choice, interest, and interestingness. *Journal of Educational Psychology*, 105, 522–534.

Patall, E. A., Cooper, H., & Robinson, J. C. (2008). The effects of choice on intrinsic motivation and related outcomes: A meta-analysis of research findings. *Psychological Bulletin*, 134, 270–300. doi:10.1037/0033-2909.134.2.270

Patall, E. A., Cooper, H., & Wynn, S. R. (2010). The effectiveness and relative importance of providing choices in the classroom. *Journal of Educational Psychology*, 102, 896–915. doi:10.1037/a0019545

Patall, E. A., Steingut, R. R., Vasquez, A. C., Trimble, S. S., Pituch, K.A., & Freeman, J. L. (2017). Daily autonomy supporting or thwarting and students' motivation and engagement in the high school science classroom. *Journal of Educational Psychology*. doi:10.1037/edu0000214

Patrick, H., Mantzicopoulos, P., & Sears, D. (2012). Effective classrooms. In K. Harris, S. Graham, & T. Urdan (Eds.), *APA educational psychology handbook: Individual differences and cultural and contextual factors* (Vol. 2, pp. 443–469). doi:10.1037/13274-018

Pickering, S. J. (2006). *Working memory and education*. Burlington, MA: Academic Press.

Pintrich, P. R., & Zusho, A. (2002). The development of academic self-regulation: The role of cognitive and motivational factors. In A. Wigfield & J. Eccles (Eds.), *The development of achievement motivation* (pp. 249–284). San Diego, CA: Academic Press.

Pintrich, P. R., & Zusho, A. (2007). Student motivation and self-regulated learning in the college classroom. In R. Perry & J. Smart (Eds.), *The scholarship of teaching and learning in higher education* (pp. 731–810). Dordrecht, The Netherlands: Springer.

Puntambekar, S., & Hübscher, R. H. (2005). Tools for scaffolding students in a complex learning environment: What have we gained and what have we missed? *Educational Psychologist*, 40, 1–12.

Reeve, J., Bolt, E., & Cai, Y. (1999). Autonomy supportive teachers: How they teach and motivate students. *Journal of Educational Psychology*, 91, 537–548. doi:10.1037/0022-0663.91.3.537

Renninger, K. A., Nieswandt, M., & Hidi, S. (2015). *Interest in mathematics and science learning*. Washington, DC: American Educational Research Association.

Roderick, M., & Stoker, G. (2010). Bringing rigor to the study of rigor: Are advanced placement courses a useful approach to increasing college access and success for urban and minority youths? In J. Eccles & J. Eccles (Eds.), *Handbook of research on schools, schooling, and human development* (pp. 216–234). New York, NY, Routledge: Springer.

Roedinger, H. L. (2013). Applying cognitive psychology to education: Translational educational science. *Psychological Science in the Public Interest*, 14, 1–3. doi:10.1177/1529100612454415

Rogat, T. K., Witham, S. A., & Chinn, C. A. (2014). Teachers' autonomy relevant practices within an inquiry-based science curricular context: Extending the range of academically significant autonomy supportive practices. *Teachers College Record*, 116, 1–46.

Rogoff, B. (1990). Apprenticeship in thinking: Cognitive development in social context. New York, NY: Oxford University Press.

Rosenthal, R., & Jacobson, L. (1968). Pygmalion in the classroom. *The Urban Review*, 3(1), 16–20. doi:10.1007/BF02322211

Roseth, C. J., Fang, F., Johnson, D. W., & Johnson, R T. (2006). *Effects of cooperative learning on middle school students: A meta-analysis*. Paper presented at the Annual Meeting of the American Educational Research Association, San Francisco, CA.

Roseth, C.J., Johnson, D.W., & Johnson, R.T. (2008). Promoting early adolescents' achievement and peer relationships: The effects of cooperative, competitive, and individualistic goal structures. *Psychological Bulletin*, 134, 223–246. doi:10.1037/0033-2909.134.2.223

Rubie-Davies, C. M., Peterson, E. R., Sibley, C. G., & Rosenthal, R. (2015). A teacher expectation intervention: Modeling the practices of high expectation teachers. *Contemporary Educational Psychology*, 40, 72–85. doi:10.1016/j.cedpsych.2014.03.303

Ryan, R., & Deci, E. (2017). *Self-determination theory: Basic psychological needs in motivation, development, and wellness*. New York, NY: Guilford.

Schunk, D. H., & Pajares, F. P. (2005). Competence perceptions and academic functioning. In A. J. Elliot &C. S. Dweck (Eds.) *Handbook of competence and motivation* (pp. 85–104). New York, NY: Guilford.

Schwartz, B. (2004). *The paradox of choice*. New York, NY: HarperCollins.

Snyder, T. D., & Dillow, S. A. (2015). *Digest of Education Statistics 2013* (NCES Report No. 2015-011). Washington, DC: U.S. Department of Education, Institute of Education Sciences, National Center for Education Statistics.

Stefanou, C. R., Perencevich, K., DiCintio, M., & Turner, J. C. (2004). Supporting autonomy in the classroom: Ways teachers encourage student decision-making and ownership. *Educational Psychologist*, 39, 97–100. doi:10.1207/s15326985ep3902_2

Titsworth, S., Mazer, J. P., Goodboy, A. K., Bolkan, S., & Myers, S. A. (2015). Two meta-analyses exploring the relationship between teacher clarity and student learning. *Communication Education*, 64, 385–418 doi:10.1080/03634523.2015.1041998

Tomlinson, C. A. (1999). *The differentiated classroom: Responding to the needs of all learners*. Alexandria, VA: Association of Supervision and Curriculum Development.

Tomlinson, C. A., Brimijoin, K., & Narvaez, L. (2008). *The differentiated school: Making revolutionary changes in teaching and learning*. Alexandria, VA Association of Supervision and Curriculum Development.

Turner, J. C. (2014). Theory-based interventions with middle-school teachers to support student motivation and engagement. In S. Karabenick & T. Urdan (Eds.), *Advances in motivation and achievement: Motivational interventions* (pp. 341–378). Bingley, UK: Emerald http://dx.doi.org/10.1108/S0749-742320140000018009

Webb, N. M., (2013). Information processing approaches to collaborative learning. In C. Hmelo-Silver, Chinn, C., Chan, C., & O'Donnell, A. (Eds.), *The international handbook of collaborative learning* (pp. 19–40). New York, NY: Routledge/Taylor & Francis Group.

Webb, N. M., Ing, M., Kersting, N., & Nemer, K. (2006). Help seeking in cooperative learning groups. In S. Karabenick & R. Newman (Eds.), *Help seeking in academic settings: Goals, groups, and contexts* (pp. 45–88). Mahwah, NJ: Erlbaum.

Wentzel, K. R. (2010). Students' relationships with teachers. In J. Meece & J. Eccles (Eds.), *Handbook of research on schools, schooling, and human development* (pp. 75–91). New York, NY: Routledge.

White, M. C., & DiBenedetto, M. K. (2015). *Self-regulation and the common core: Application to ELA standards*. New York, NY: Routledge.

Wigfield, A., & Eccles, J. S. (2000). Expectancy-value theory of achievement motivation. *Contemporary Educational Psychology*, 25, 68–81.

Wolf, M. K., Crosson, A. C., & Resnick, L. B. (2005). Classroom talk for rigorous reading comprehension instruction. *Reading Psychology*, 26, 27–53. doi:10.1080/02702710490897518

Zimmerman, B. J., (1990). Self-regulated learning and academic achievement: An overview. *Educational Psychologist*, 25, 3–17.

Zimmerman, B. J. (2008). Investigating self-regulation and motivation: Historical background, methodological developments, and future prospects. *American Educational Research Journal*, 45, 166–183. doi:10.3102/0002831207312909

Zimmerman, B. J., & Schunk, D. H. (2011). *Handbook of self-regulation of learning and performance*. New York, NY: Routledge.

Zusho, A., Karabenick, S., Bonney, C. K., & Sims, B. C. (2007). Contextual determinants of help-seeking and motivation in the college classroom. In R. Perry & J. Smart (Eds.), *Handbook on teaching and learning in higher education* (pp. 611–659). Dordrecht, The Netherlands: Springer.

Taylor & Francis eBooks

Helping you to choose the right eBooks for your Library

Add Routledge titles to your library's digital collection today. Taylor and Francis ebooks contains over 50,000 titles in the Humanities, Social Sciences, Behavioural Sciences, Built Environment and Law.

Choose from a range of subject packages or create your own!

Benefits for you

>> Free MARC records
>> COUNTER-compliant usage statistics
>> Flexible purchase and pricing options
>> All titles DRM-free.

Benefits for your user

>> Off-site, anytime access via Athens or referring URL
>> Print or copy pages or chapters
>> Full content search
>> Bookmark, highlight and annotate text
>> Access to thousands of pages of quality research at the click of a button.

REQUEST YOUR **FREE** INSTITUTIONAL TRIAL TODAY

Free Trials Available
We offer free trials to qualifying academic, corporate and government customers.

eCollections – Choose from over 30 subject eCollections, including:

Archaeology	Language Learning
Architecture	Law
Asian Studies	Literature
Business & Management	Media & Communication
Classical Studies	Middle East Studies
Construction	Music
Creative & Media Arts	Philosophy
Criminology & Criminal Justice	Planning
Economics	Politics
Education	Psychology & Mental Health
Energy	Religion
Engineering	Security
English Language & Linguistics	Social Work
Environment & Sustainability	Sociology
Geography	Sport
Health Studies	Theatre & Performance
History	Tourism, Hospitality & Events

For more information, pricing enquiries or to order a free trial, please contact your local sales team:
www.tandfebooks.com/page/sales

Routledge
Taylor & Francis Group

The home of
Routledge books

www.tandfebooks.com